SCM STUDYGUIDE TO   TICS

SCM STUDYGUIDE TO BIBLICAL HERMENEUTICS

2nd Edition

David A. Holgate
and
Rachel Starr

scm press

© David A. Holgate and Rachel Starr 2019

Published in 2019 by SCM Press
Editorial office
3rd Floor, Invicta House,
108–114 Golden Lane,
London EC1Y 0TG, UK
www.scmpress.co.uk

SCM Press is an imprint of Hymns Ancient & Modern Ltd (a registered charity)

Hymns Ancient & Modern

Hymns Ancient & Modern® is a registered trademark of Hymns Ancient & Modern Ltd
13A Hellesdon Park Road, Norwich,
Norfolk NR6 5DR, UK

All rights reserved. No part of this publication may be reproduced,
stored in a retrieval system, or transmitted,
in any form or by any means, electronic, mechanical,
photocopying or otherwise, without the prior permission of
the publisher, SCM Press.

The Authors have asserted their right under the Copyright, Designs and Patents Act 1988
to be identified as the Authors of this Work

Scripture quotations are from the New Revised Standard Version of the Bible, Anglicized
Edition, copyright © 1989, 1995 by the Division of Christian Education of the National
Council of the Churches of Christ in the USA. Used by permission. All rights reserved.

British Library Cataloguing in Publication data

A catalogue record for this book is available
from the British Library

978 0 334 05731 4

Typeset by Regent Typesetting
Printed and bound by
Ashford Colour Press

For our parents

Contents

Acknowledgements ix

Introduction xi

1　Where Do We Want to Go?　1
2　Past Experience and Present Expectations　7
3　Tools for Exegesis　45
4　Our Reality　82
5　Committed Readings　125
6　Enabling Dialogue with the Text　154
7　Our Goal: Life-Affirming Interpretations　186

Summary of the Interpretative Process　196
References and Further Reading　200
Index of Biblical References　217
Index of Names　221
Index of Subjects　226

Acknowledgements

We prepared the first edition of this book while working with teaching colleagues and students of the Southern Theological Education and Training Scheme. Though the approach is our own, we are thankful to all those who helped us develop it. Since then, the book has been widely used in theological education, and we are grateful for the invitation from SCM to revise it for a second edition. This process has shown us how much the discipline of Biblical Studies, we and the world have changed since 2006.

For this second edition, we would like to thank all those who have continued to encourage us to be better biblical interpreters. David would like to thank friends and colleagues at Manchester Cathedral, the Department of Religions and Theology at the University of Manchester, participants in the Scriptural Reasoning and Scriptural Encounter groups, and John Vincent of the Urban Theology Union. Rachel offers her thanks to friends and colleagues at the Queen's Foundation for Ecumenical Theological Education, Birmingham, especially David Allen, Dulcie Dixon McKenzie, Paul Nzacahayo and Carlton Turner for offering comments and resources for different sections of the book. Thanks also to Bob Bartindale for his helpful comments and other colleagues from the Methodist Church in Britain for their support and use of the book in the Worship Leaders and Local Preachers course.

Working together on this project has reminded us that biblical interpretation is a collaborative activity. We hope that you will find opportunities to interact with others each time you seek to work out what the Bible is saying to you today.

Introduction

Purpose

This book offers a framework for interpreting the Bible. It goes beyond showing you how to do exegesis and enables you to relate the Bible to your experience of everyday life. While we have tried to provide a clear approach to biblical interpretation, we do not intend to be prescriptive. We offer this Studyguide to you as a practical tool to help you to develop good interpretative strategies of your own. There should come a time when you feel confident enough to be able to set this book aside. By then, we hope that you will have proven to yourself that, while there is no single, agreed method for interpreting the Bible, there is a great deal of agreement on the resources that need to be used by responsible interpreters.

Practicalities

You can use this Studyguide in a number of ways. Initially, you may find it helpful just to review the Contents page and the Summary at the back. As you need to learn more about each of the steps in this process, we hope that you will read through each chapter more fully. Please enter into dialogue with the book.

Where you disagree with something, explain to yourself why you do so and offer a better alternative. This will help you develop an interpretative strategy of your own. As you use this Studyguide to develop your skills, we hope that the 'Try it out' boxes will offer you practical help with the passage you are working on.

1

Where Do We Want to Go?

Introduction: using this book

This book is designed to help you become a better reader and interpreter of the Bible. It offers an integrated approach, introducing a range of critical methods to enable you to interpret biblical passages for yourself. We do not suggest it is possible to arrive at one final correct interpretation of any biblical passage. Rather, the process outlined here is designed to help you interpret the text carefully, critically and creatively. And to be open to fresh insights each time you read the text, in the light of new information about yourself, the world and the Bible.

Alongside this book, you may find it helpful to have access to a dictionary of biblical interpretation, to look up key words and concepts discussed here. One book we regularly refer to is the *Handbook of Biblical Interpretation* (4th edition, 2011) by the father-and-son team of Richard and R. Kendall Soulen. The website www.bibleodyssey.org, a project of the Society of Biblical Literature, offers short articles, maps and videos introducing biblical passages, context and interpretative methods.

Identifying our reason for reading the Bible

Each time we turn to the Bible, we do so with a particular purpose, for example, to refer to a passage as background reading for an English literature course, or to learn more about Jewish or Christian beliefs. But we may have a deeper motivation for reading the Bible: because we regard it as a sacred book, a great literary work, a useful historical source, or perhaps a problematic text that needs to be challenged or understood.

> **Try it out**
>
> Jot down a few thoughts on how you view the Bible, and then try to state your underlying reason for reading the Bible.

There are many reasons for studying the Bible, all with different goals and outcomes. As authors, we regard the Bible as a text of great importance for the academy, for faith communities and for the wider world. For all of these contexts, we seek to offer a method of reading the Bible that encourages an ongoing quest for life-affirming interpretations of the text. All readers of the Bible need to recognize that the Bible witnesses to the faith of the communities from which it arose, even though clearly not all readers will share this faith. While we both write from a Christian perspective and believe that the Bible informs, enriches and directs our interaction with God, the method outlined here recognizes that many people read the Bible with other eyes and commitments and that such readings are also valid.

Identifying our reasons for interpreting a passage

However we view the Bible as a text, it is worth answering two quite practical questions before we open it. What do we want from the Bible, for ourselves and for others? And therefore which passage(s) are we going to read?

The Bible is a collection of books, most of which have a long history of development, and all of which have a long history of interpretation and influence. This means that the Bible is a complex text that can be difficult to handle. As readers, our individual context and identity change over time and

WHERE DO WE WANT TO GO?

this also affects our reading of the Bible. To avoid getting lost in a sea of questions, each time we read the Bible we should clarify our purpose in doing so to help focus our study.

> **Try it out**
>
> Read the story of David and Goliath in 1 Samuel 17. What questions do you have for this text today, and what questions does it have for you?

The story of David and Goliath is often included in illustrated collections of Bible stories for children, and when the title is mentioned we may find that our first memories are of such a version. There are many good things about reading the Bible as a child that we should maintain as adults: children read playfully and imaginatively. But it is important to recognize that we may not have been told the whole story as children. Reading about David and Goliath later in life may raise many new questions for us, even if as adults we are still often discouraged from asking questions about the Bible.

These new questions may fall into a range of categories:

- Historical: Why were the Israelites and the Philistines at loggerheads?
- Geographical: Where are Socoh and Azekah?
- Cultural: Was David following normal military practice by cutting off the head of his dead enemy?
- Narrative: If David is presented as a skilled musician and warrior in 1 Samuel 16, why is he described in v. 42 as 'only a youth'?
- Psychological: Was the young David traumatized by having to carry his enemy's head with him, for example holding it 'in his hand' when he went into King Saul's presence (v. 57)?
- Relational: How does violence inform David's relationships, with his enemies, supposed friends, and even family members? If we acknowledge David's violence here, does it help us name and challenge his violence towards Uriah and Bathsheba, for example? A helpful resource in relation to this last question is the Bible Society's *#SheToo* Podcast series (2019).

By reading this passage attentive to these and other questions, we notice the strangeness of even this familiar story. Thinking back on our prior knowledge of the story of David and Goliath, we may notice how incompletely we recalled it, perhaps because it was told to us selectively as children. Equally, we may have heard a sermon on the passage that presented David as an example of faith. Yet, reading it now against, for example, reports of death and dismemberment in conflicts across the world, such an interpretation may strike us as inadequate because it fails to recognize the violence in the text or to relate it to the violence we must face in our own lives.

If we try to insist that this account is not really about warfare, but rather spiritual or theological matters, then we only need to look back to the end of 1 Samuel 16, which suggests that God sent an evil spirit to torment (some translations say, to terrorize) King Saul. In case we have missed this shocking statement, the next verse describes the king's servants as saying to him: 'See now, an evil spirit from God is tormenting you' (1 Sam. 16.15). We then find ourselves with a theological problem and have to ask what sort of God 1 Samuel 16—17 presents.

The above example shows how quickly our Bible reading can raise numerous questions and interpretative problems for us. To help us sort out which of these issues we are to work on and which to set aside for the present we need to be guided by our overall purpose in reading the Bible and our present goal in reading this passage. We cannot and do not need to tackle every sort of question at once.

> **Try it out**
>
> Think of your overall purpose and your immediate motivation for reading whatever biblical text you are currently exploring. These will normally be determined by some everyday need that provides you with a focus for study.

There are many reasons why we engage in biblical interpretation. We may be involved in formal teaching, and have to provide a considered answer to a matter of interpretation; for example, about what different texts might teach about human sexuality. Perhaps we are facing a personal crisis and hope that the

Bible can offer some guidance. We may have recently watched a film, listened to a song, heard a comment, or visited a building and been struck by the way a biblical theme is reflected there. Perhaps we are involved in church leadership and have been asked to preach on an unfamiliar Bible passage.

We try to interpret the Bible for all sorts of reasons but the questions with which we turn to the Bible are not always the ones it answers. The text often leads us in a different direction, provoking other questions than the ones with which we began. Because of the propensity of the Bible to send us off somewhere else, it is necessary for us to plot where we are now and where we hope to get to at the outset, a bit like a sailor setting off on a course with many potential hazards and diversions. If we know where we have started from and where we are aiming for, we can check our progress along the way. In biblical interpretation this does not, or should not, guarantee that we will arrive at our intended destination; certainly not in the sense of arriving at the conclusions that we expected at the outset. But it will help us to place limits upon our enquiry and ask the right questions of the text. If we find ourselves blown off-course by the force of the passage, at least we will know this and be able to account for it. Perhaps the original questions we began with have not been answered by the text but we may have been led to explore other questions that now seem more important.

Provisional and responsible interpretation

As authors, we do not believe that it is possible to arrive at a final, definitive interpretation of any biblical passage, but instead encourage working towards a responsible interpretation of a passage for a particular purpose and time. This is a vantage point in an ongoing journey towards deeper understanding of the Bible, of ourselves, and of the world we inhabit.

Any interpretation should be offered with self-awareness, making evident to ourselves and others that we understand the limitations of our interpretation. We should seek to read the text (and ourselves) with integrity and honesty, resisting temptations to short-change ourselves or others with simplistic or trite answers. We should try to bring our deepest and truest questions and convictions to our conversation with the Bible, and seek out the best answers we can discover.

> **Try it out**
>
> The Lord's Prayer is one of the most well-known passages in the Bible, so it is likely that you will already know something about it. Perhaps you know it by heart. If so, recite it to yourself. What seems to you to be at the heart of this text?
>
> Now read Matthew 6.9–13 carefully and attentively. In what way does this reading confirm or question your prior understanding of this passage? How does your current life situation shape your reading? How might you test out whether your reading is a responsible one?

In the years since we first wrote this book, both of us have experienced significant changes in our own lives, as well as witnessing wider social, political and environmental change. Rachel spent three years living in Buenos Aires, researching women's resistance to domestic violence and asking questions of how Christian teaching around marriage might be transformed by listening to such experiences. For the past nine years, she has taught biblical studies, feminist and contextual theologies at an ecumenical theological college in Birmingham. Revising this book has made Rachel more aware of the need to read with close attention to the multiple connections and frequent silences of the Bible.

Over the same period, David has been the principal of an ecumenical theological college and a residentiary canon for theology and mission in an urban cathedral. In the latter role, he has learned to read the Bible with people of other faiths and heard its call to work for social transformation more deeply. He often prays with others, 'Help us to work together for that day when . . . justice and mercy will be seen in all the earth.'

The text swirls around us as readers, as threat and promise, offering both life and death, but rarely a firm place to stand. Often, the Bible seems to say to us, 'Listen again. Listen with others. Listen for others.'

2

Past Experience and Present Expectations

In Chapter 1, we began to consider our overall reason for studying the Bible, as well as the particular task in hand. The next step in the process is to clarify our relationship with the Bible, so this chapter considers how our collective and individual experience of the Bible affects the interpretative task.

This chapter begins with asking where and how we might encounter the Bible in our day-to-day routine. It notes how the Bible has shaped communities and cultures. Indeed, throughout history people have used the Bible to control and oppress others as well as to encourage and support them, and it is important to take account of this mixed legacy in our interpretations. The first section of the chapter ends with the suggestion that, despite the West's cultural familiarity with the Bible, it remains an alien, mysterious text. The second section of the chapter examines differing expectations about the authority and status of the Bible. In the third section, we look at the status of the Bible as scripture in Jewish and Christian communities.

An everyday, extraordinary text

If we live in a western, nominally Christian context, we are likely to encounter the Bible in a variety of places: growing up at home or in school as story; in synagogue or church as sacred scriptures; in a court of law as a solemn witness to oaths of truth-telling; in popular culture, art and the media as shifting fragments of a (once) common language. Let's look briefly at some of these contexts of encounter.

Even in twenty-first-century Britain, where people of many faiths and those of no religious commitment live side by side, we may first encounter the Bible at a relatively young age. Perhaps we heard stories from the Bible (related as part myth, part moral instruction) at home, church or school. Indeed, as we considered in Chapter 1, it is hard to imagine how those of us who were raised in a nominally Christian context can ever read the Bible without some prior knowledge of its stories, characters and teachings.

> **Try it out**
>
> What are some of your earliest beliefs about the Bible? When did you first encounter the Bible, in childhood or later in life? Make a list of images or phrases that highlight how you were introduced to it. How has your understanding of the Bible changed during your life?

As well as being a collection of powerful stories, the Bible has been understood as a formative document, which is able to shape communities through study of it. We offer two examples here of Christian communities that see the Bible as integral to their common life.

In the early 1700s, the Moravian community at Herrnhut in Germany drew up a document called *The Brotherly Agreement*. Drawing closely from the Bible, this text, known as *The Moravian Covenant for Christian Living*, formed the basis for Moravian community life. The following extract illustrates this method of shaping social relationships according to certain biblical teachings:

> 15. We will endeavour to settle our differences with others in a Christian manner (Galatians 6.1), amicably, and with meditation, and, if at all possible, avoid resort to a court of law (Matthew 18.15–17).

Moravians established a number of communities in Britain. The Fairfield Moravian Settlement on the outskirts of Manchester was founded in 1785. It was self-sufficient with its own church, schools, bakery and farm. The community's intention to be formed according to biblical teaching impacted on all aspects of life. Women and men were treated as equals (despite the diversity of teaching in the Bible on gender relationships). Marriage partners and other key decisions were decided by the casting of lots (although lots were used in the Bible primarily in relation to inheritance and the taking up of new responsibilities, for example the selection of the replacement for Judas is conducted by lot in Acts 1.26). Today, through engagement with other aspects of the biblical tradition, the community continues to support mission and social welfare projects, including sheltered housing.

A twenty-first-century example of a community that seeks to be formed by Bible is the Community of St Anselm, a new monastic community established by the Archbishop of Canterbury Justin Welby. Each year, a group of young people form the community, which is focused on prayer, theological reflection and service. Each section of the community's Rule of Life begins with a biblical verse. The section on study begins with Proverbs 9.9–10 on the importance of seeking wisdom, and invites members to make the following commitment: 'We make time for God to speak to us through Holy Scripture. We study the Scriptures with all our heart and our mind and spirit' (Rule of Life 2016, p. 16).

Even beyond intentional religious communities, the Bible's status comes from its value as a holy object. Witnesses in an English court of law usually take an oath on the Bible or another significant or holy book to tell the truth. In 2013, a proposal to end this practice was defeated, the argument being that swearing an oath on a religious book such as the Bible still has a profound impact on witnesses. The power invested in the Bible is demonstrated in other ways around the world; for example, Brazilian Christians might bury a Bible in the foundations of their new house for blessing and protection (Schroer 2003, p. 8).

In the digital age, many of us encounter the Bible online, intentionally or unintentionally (see Michael J. Chan's article 'The Bible and the Internet' online at Oxford Biblical Studies). The number of references to the Bible made in the secular media may come as a surprise to us. For example, in 2018, the book of Leviticus was mentioned in a total of nine articles in the *Guardian* newspaper, the majority being references to its instructions on caring for neighbours and seeking justice for those who are poor and strangers; but also with reference to debate over sexuality, and, in an interview with British author, Kit de Waal, as a work of literature. In 2003, Sri Lankan-born, Birmingham-based scholar R. S. Sugirtharajah tracked biblical references in the British media. He noted the humorous irreverence of many ironic references as well as the continued cultural force of biblical quotations and allusions. He described much of the media's use of the Bible as simply 'looking for something that fits' (Sugirtharajah 2003, p. 78). However, he also noted the tremendous power appeal to the Bible can have – both as a source of comfort and as a means of oppression. Sugirtharajah described much popular usage of the Bible as 'poaching' or taking what is needed from the whole narrative as and when necessary. Although alert to the dangers of this free-form, open-ended appropriation of the Bible, Sugirtharajah suggested it offers people the opportunity to encounter the Bible on their own terms, without having its meaning restricted by academics (Sugirtharajah 2003, pp. 82–4).

> **Try it out**
>
> Do some informal research of your own – noting down any biblical references or allusions you encounter in the media, music, art and conversation during one day. Do these popular interpretations strengthen or alter your existing understanding of the text? Would you dispute any aspect of the popular interpretation, and on what grounds?

In contrast to the somewhat superficial knowledge of the Bible encountered within nominally Christian contexts, many Jewish and Muslim communities have a deeper collective knowledge of their holy books. Here there is often a living knowledge of the scriptures that comes from a regular encounter with the text during times of prayer, as well as knowledge of the original language (Hebrew, Aramaic or Arabic). In a synagogue, for example, the Torah is first read in Hebrew, followed by a translation into the local language or vernacular. The Qur'an echoes many Bible stories from both the Hebrew Bible and the New Testament, often reflecting extra-biblical and post-biblical traditions. In Chapter 5, we will consider the benefits and challenges of reading the Bible alongside other sacred texts, and in the company of people of different faiths.

> **Try it out**
>
> Ask a person of another faith to your own, or the one you are most familiar with, about their knowledge and understanding of their sacred texts.

A political text

The Bible has been instrumental in constructing, shaping and even destroying social structures. This diversity is not simply the result of interpretive differences since the Bible itself expresses a range of social views, with some traditions advocating social conservatism and others, social radicalism. Such debate is apparent in the Hebrew Bible's variant attitudes towards the monarchy; for example, 1 Samuel 7-15 includes two perspectives: that the monarchy is God's will and that it is an act of infidelity. No clear answer to the dispute over the institute of kingship is given (Brueggemann 1997b, p. 72).

Over the centuries, numerous political and religious rulers have interpreted the Bible to fit their own agenda. Some have used it to preserve so-called Christian culture, or to justify 'one nation under God'. Others have read the Bible as a mandate for persecution, colonialism and enslavement. In response, womanist scholar Renita Weems notes:

> The Bible cannot go unchallenged in so far as the role it has played in legitimating the dehumanization of people of African ancestry in general and the sexual exploitation of women of African ancestry in particular. It cannot be understood as some universal, transcendent, timeless force to which world readers – in the name of being pious and faithful followers – must meekly submit. It must be understood as a politically and socially drenched text invested in ordering relations between people, legitimating some viewpoints and delegitimizing other viewpoints. (Weems 2003, p. 24)

This history of interpretation should caution us against using the Bible destructively. It is important that we are able to assess the role the Bible has played in the past and, where necessary, be willing to challenge our relationship with it so that we can develop a more responsible and life-affirming interpretive method, for ourselves and for others. Active resistance to the harmful imposition of the Bible on a community can be seen in the following example.

The Bible constituted a central part of the Spaniards' justification of the invasion of what became known as Latin America; the conquistadors even used the invasion of Canaan as a biblical model from which to validate their actions. Almost 500 years later, local people continued to protest against this abuse of the Bible. When Pope John Paul II visited Peru, local leaders sent him the following note:

> John Paul II, we, Andean and American Indians, have decided to take advantage of your visit to return to you your Bible, since in five centuries it has not given us love, peace or justice. Please take back your Bible and give it back to our oppressors, because they need moral teaching more than we do. Ever since the arrival of Christopher Columbus a culture, language, religion and values which belong to Europe have been imposed on Latin America by force. The Bible came to us as part of the imposed colonial transformation. It was the ideological weapon of this colonialist assault. The Spanish sword which attacked and murdered the bodies of Indians by day and night became the cross which attacked the Indian soul. (cited in Richard 1990, pp. 64–5)

While cautious of its negative impact, liberationist movements have also understood the Bible to be a text for freedom. In apartheid South Africa, both sides used the Bible to justify their actions. Although the Dutch Reformed Church believed they had biblical support for racial discrimination, Desmond Tutu warned the apartheid regime:

> The Bible is the most revolutionary, the most radical book there is. If a book had to be banned by those who rule unjustly and as tyrants, then it ought to have been the Bible. Whites brought us the Bible and we are taking it seriously. (Tutu 1994, p. 72)

Writing with a Marxist perspective in the same period of South Africa's history, Itumeleng Mosala's *Biblical Hermeneutics and Black Theology in South Africa* (1989) argued for the ambiguous political nature of both the Bible itself, as a product that emerged out of a class struggle between different social groups,

PAST EXPERIENCE AND PRESENT EXPECTATIONS

and of biblical interpretation. In doing so, he challenged the oppressive claims of both text and interpretation and sought to enable revolutionary readings of the Bible that resulted in social, political and economic liberation.

> **Try it out**
>
> How would you assess the social and political impact of the Bible in your communities and contexts? What kind of impact do you think the Bible should have?

A cultural text

For over 2,000 years the Bible has influenced culture and art in many areas of the world. Indeed, religious material was the dominant subject of most art forms for many centuries. Beautiful paintings and sculptures in churches, public buildings and private homes represented the devotion of benefactors, artists and worshipers. These portrayals of biblical stories have been an invaluable way of enabling people from oral societies to engage with the Bible. The breadth of artistic styles and forms continues today: from Laura James' Ethiopian Christian iconography used to illustrate the *Book of the Gospels* (2001), to Si Smith's graphic retelling of the book of Job in *Rage, Despair, Hope* (2011); from the cartoon, *Jonah: A VeggieTales Movie* (2002) to Elisabeth Frink's statue *Walking Madonna* (1981) located outside of Salisbury Cathedral. Our reading of the Bible is influenced in turn by these portrayals: Leonardo da Vinci's *The Last Supper* has shaped western Christians' interpretation of this event for hundreds of years.

In his book, *The Return of the Prodigal Son*, Henri Nouwen recounts the deep impact of Rembrandt's painting on his spiritual journey. He spent many hours reflecting on the different characters in the painting and discovered how each one illuminated some aspect of his own story:

> When . . . I went to Saint Petersburg to see Rembrandt's *The Return of the Prodigal Son*, I had little idea how much I would have to live what I then saw. I stand with awe at the place where Rembrandt brought me. He led me from

the kneeling, dishevelled young son to the standing, bent-over old father, from the place of being blessed to the place of blessing. (Nouwen 1994, p. 139)

Nouwen's testimony illuminates how artistic interpretations of the Bible can help us explore the written text in greater depth and complexity. Paintings, plays and poems may reveal connections between ourselves and a Bible passage that may not emerge from simply reading the text.

> **Try it out**
>
> Read Proverbs 31.10–31. How do you imagine the capable woman? Do you recognize her as someone you know? Now visit the Visual Commentary on Scripture website and look at the three pictures chosen for the exhibition 'The Wife of Noble Character'. Read the commentaries on each picture and the overall commentary. How has your interpretation of the Proverbs poem developed?

Classical western literature has often been in intentional dialogue with the Bible. There are hundreds of allusions to the Bible in the works of Shakespeare. Steven Marx's *Shakespeare and the Bible* (2000) explores how the playwright used the Bible to develop his narrative and characters. He compares, for example, the book of Job with *King Lear* and looks at the impact of Matthew's Gospel on *Measure for Measure*, in which characters reference (and occasionally misinterpret) the gospel's teachings. A further example would be John Steinbeck's *East of Eden*, which explores the Genesis narrative, particularly the relationship between Cain and Abel (Genesis 4).

In turn, literary retellings of biblical stories have influenced scholarly interpretation of texts. Thomas Mann's epic novel *Joseph and his Brothers* (published 1933–46) interpreted the story of Genesis for his context. Begun in Nazi Germany, it was completed in the United States following Mann's exile. As a novelist, Mann argued for the literary coherence of Genesis. His understanding of the story of Tamar and Judah (Genesis 38) as an integral part of the whole narrative, rather than a loosely related fragment, influenced later interpretations of Genesis.

The Bible itself has been studied as literature as well as a devotional text.

In 1998, Canongate published individual books of the Bible marketing them as literary works, with introductions by writers, artists and politicians. For example, singer Nick Cave, in his introduction to Mark, commented:

> The Christ that emerges from *Mark*, tramping through the haphazard events of His life, had a ringing intensity about Him that I could not resist. Christ spoke to me through His isolation, throughout the burden of His death, through His rage at the mundane, through His sorrow. (Cave 1998)

As story, rather than sacred text, Mark's Gospel was able to speak to Cave with a freshness and directness that he had not previously noticed. In Chapter 6, we will return to the method of reading the Bible as a story and our role as story-tellers in this process.

Each generation retells the ancient biblical stories in new and different ways. The style, structure, language and meaning of a text can all be re-evaluated through new methods of retelling. Contemporary culture is crammed with biblical references: the inscription of 1 Corinthians 15.26 on a grave in J. K. Rowling's *Harry Potter and the Deathly Hallows* (2007); the exploration of gospel themes in grime artist Ghetts' album, *Ghetto Gospel: The New Testament* (2018); or Mark Wallinger's sculpture, *Ecco Homo* (1999) that for a while occupied the fourth plinth in Trafalgar Square. Even within a genre such as crime fiction we can encounter biblical texts and themes; for example, a 1940s Sherlock Holmes play that is structured around the Book of Tobit (Collins 2019).

The above are all examples of the impact history of the Bible. In Chapter 3, we will explore in more detail how biblical texts have been interpreted over the centuries. For now, let's look at one example of a conscious attempt to bring the Bible into dialogue with contemporary society, music and culture. Using the text of the *Di Jamaikan Nyuu Testament* (2012), Robert Beckford's project the *Jamaican Bible Remix* (2017) weaves together the biblical text with contemporary black British music, dance and art to offer a political commentary on violence, resistance and liberation within black British communities today. The track *Incarnation* is offered as a call for social justice in which the biblical witness confronts the multiple deaths of black men and women in police custody and prisons. In *Magnificat*, Mary's song is set alongside a piece of contemporary dance and multiple images of black women with natural hair, thus bringing together the biblical text and black women's history of political struggle.

Three useful websites for researching the Bible in film, music and literature are: Textweek, which links to visual images of different biblical passages as well as summaries of films that reference the Bible or biblical themes; Hollywood Jesus, which includes reviews of films and other media; and the Art and Theology blog, which explores biblical and religious themes in a wide range of music, visual and performance art.

Observing how the Bible is interpreted in everyday conversation and culture offers us fresh ways of looking at the text. Such interpretations can reveal the impact a passage has had on a particular community and local interpreters sometimes function as guardians of a community's understandings of a text. Popular interpretations may sometimes be judged as misinterpretations, but they can still provoke new insight, revealing nuances and angles as yet hidden to academic readers.

An unfamiliar text

There is a danger of becoming overly familiar with a text that we encounter on a daily basis: politically, culturally or through corporate worship or devotions. Texts such as Psalm 23, for example, may have lost their impact through frequent and uncritical use. Ronald Allen, who teaches preaching in Indianapolis, United States, remarks: 'In exegesis, as in life, expectation plays an important role in fulfilment. What we expect is usually what we find' (Allen 1984, p. 22). If we believe the Bible to be a friendly, uncritical voice, then that is how we are likely to hear it.

Yet, no matter how familiar some passages may seem, the worlds of the Bible are very different from those of today's world. Allen warns against the cosy relationship American civil society has developed with the Bible:

> North American culture has co-opted the Bible as a source of blessing on our values, economic and political system, and life-style . . . we have tended to regard the Bible as a word of confirmation of our way of life. In the United States it is easy to think of God as middle-class and the Bible as a kind of handbook for better family relationships. (Allen 1987, p. 23)

In contrast, biblical scholars from Asia and Africa have become more insistent that we recognize that the Bible did not originate in a western context. The South African-based translator Gosnell Yorke argues that the African context of various biblical events and communities has been hidden in Bible translations. He notes how translators have been reticent to identify Cush (Gen. 2.10–14) with modern-day Ethiopia and the Sudan, thus 'de-Africanizing' the text and denying the possibility that Eden was partially located in Africa (Yorke 2004, pp. 159–61). R. S. Sugirtharajah further challenges the tendency to westernize the Bible, highlighting, for example, the comparative work done between Buddhist ideas and biblical texts such as John's gospel, that may indicate shared patterns of thought and expression (Sugirtharajah 2003, pp. 96–113). One of the questions we should attend to as readers, therefore, is how an interpretation of a biblical passage enables us to hear the African and Asian contexts and influences present within the text.

As well as cultural differences between the modern western world and the worlds of the Bible, readers have to contend with the revelatory claims of the text. If the Bible is regarded as a divine or sacred work, this will create distance between the text and the reader. Some interpreters suggest the Bible should be read with a sense of awe to allow its distinctive voice to be heard. In the 1930s, the Swiss theologian Karl Barth sought to challenge the complacency of his fellow Christians. Against a background of a church co-opted by Nazism, he proclaimed the radically different word of God that challenges the presumption that we can meet or know God through human culture. Barth's work highlighted the strange, other-worldly nature of the Bible, which cuts across all rational human attempts at knowledge or justification. For Barth, the Bible reveals the awesome word of God to us that has the power to transform everything about us: 'Barth dared to assert the normative claim of the gospel defiantly against the landscape. What is normative is odd and peculiar, distinctive and scandalous, and can never be accommodated to the landscape of cultural ideology' (Brueggemann 1997b, p. 20).

Barth's work reminds us of the importance of allowing the Bible to speak on its own terms. As readers, we need to gain distance from the text so that we can come to it anew, willing to be surprised. For readers of faith, there is a creative tension that results from exploring the meaning of the Bible through cultural expression and human discourse, while retaining a sense of the ultimately unknowable nature of God's word that can be encountered through the Bible.

An inspired and inspiring text

We turn now to questions of authority and status with regard to the Bible. What kind of book is it: divine, human, or a combination of both? We will first consider what kind of truth the Bible has been understood to offer. We will then explore different understandings of the nature and authority of the Bible, before asking how Christian communities have debated whether the Bible alone is a sufficient guide and a source of truth, or whether it needs to be read alongside other sources of knowledge and insight, such as church tradition, reason and experience.

A truthful text

If we were asked to give our testimony, we might assume this would involve standing at the front of a local church, telling the story of our journey of faith. Or we might think of being asked to give an account of an event we witnessed in a courtroom or another public space. In many Latin America contexts, a *testimonio* is an account of both violence and resistance; for example, the account of a Guatemalan activist recorded in *I Rigoberta Menchu* (1983).

These different experiences of truth-telling, whether the truth of everyday experience or of one's beliefs, and whether told through words or actions, might help us consider what we mean when we say that the Bible is truthful. As we will explore in this section, many Christians have had a very narrow understanding of truth, which has prevented them from engaging deeply with the Bible. But debates over biblical truth often fail to recognize that the Bible is primarily concerned not with scientific facts or historical events, but rather to bear witness to God's nature and purpose, that is, to offer theological truths.

> **Try it out**
>
> How do you think the Bible does, or does not, bear witness? What kind of truth, if any, do you consider is revealed by the Bible? How does this shape your understanding of the text?

As authors, we reflected on our own response to these questions. For Rachel, the Bible emerges out of the desire of several communities to encounter God and consider the kind of relationship they might have with God. It is therefore revealing of human nature, of the struggle to belong and connect. For Rachel, the word of God can be heard in the lively debate taking place within the biblical text, in which there is always another perspective to be argued, or story to be told. It is a text in which something new emerges each time it is read or studied, no matter how familiar the passage. Moreover, it bears witness to the attention that others have given it, and can be likened to a stone polished over the centuries, each reading gradually revealing more and more of its colour and detail.

For David, the Bible is a well-known classic that has accompanied him his whole adult life. As a Christian, it is an essential point of orientation and perspective for him, encountered through study and in worship. Yet he also describes his relationship with the Bible as a long-standing friendship. This reflects his commitment to seeking a deeper and more truthful understanding of the Bible as Scripture. David contrasts his intimate knowledge of the biblical canon with a more limited knowledge of other ancient Jewish, Christian and Islamic texts. This speaks of the special importance of the canonical texts to him as a Christian. Reading the Bible in conversation with others and the wider world raises fresh questions for him each day. The Bible retains the power to surprise him, to lead him into places of mystery.

An authoritative text

In this section, we will consider debate within the Church concerning the origin, nature and authority of the Bible. Our starting point is the eighteenth century, when the culture of the Enlightenment encouraged scholars across a range of disciplines to seek out logical, provable sources of knowledge. During the nineteenth century, this resulted in the development of a range of critical approaches to the Bible (known as higher or historical criticism), which sought to discover the origin, nature and historical reliability of the biblical narrative (see Bible Odyssey's 'Key Ideas in Biblical Scholarship' timeline; and Soulen and Soulen 2011, pp. 88–90). Drawing on insights from archaeology, geology and linguistics, many biblical accounts were demonstrated to be factually inaccurate (see Nicola Denzey Lewis's article, 'Does the Bible Relate to History "as It Actually

Happened"?' on the Bible Odyssey website). For some, the logical conclusion of this work was to regard the Bible as an interesting collection of ancient texts, which had little to say to the modern world. For others, such developments were highly problematic and needed to be stopped, so that the truth of the Bible could be reaffirmed.

> **Try it out**
>
> Which statement best describes your own understanding of the Bible?
>
> - The Bible is the inspired word of God and is therefore free from error.
> - The Bible is inspired by the Holy Spirit but written by humans and it is possible that some of the divine message was corrupted in the process.
> - The Bible is a record of various communities' shared history, communal identity and faith experience.
> - The Bible is the word of God only when we enable it to be so by listening to God's word spoken to us through the text.
> - The Bible is a collection of ancient writings irrelevant to today's society.

These different views about the Bible's origin and reliability fall into three broad categories, which we now consider: the Bible as a divinely inspired text that is free from error (God's role is the focus); the Bible as a divinely inspired, authoritative but human text (the partnership between God and humans is the focus); the Bible as a human account of faith (human activity is the focus).

The belief that the Bible came directly from God and is therefore without error developed in the nineteenth century. It won a strong following among some conservative Protestants in the United States who, in the early twentieth century, became known as fundamentalists. Responding to the challenges presented by historical criticism, biblical fundamentalists sought to defend belief in the divine inspiration and inerrancy of the Bible (James 2012, p. 36). They argued that if the Bible was a direct record of God's proclamation, there could be no errors in its text or teaching. This resulted in much time and effort being used to explain apparent inconsistencies within the Bible or to respond to disagreements between the biblical account and modern scientific knowledge (for example, the challenge the theory of evolution presents to literal readings of the creation stories of Genesis 1 and 2). Fundamentalists differ as to how God worked with humans to create the Bible, with some believing that God dictated words to human writers, and others that God inspired the human authors in a more nuanced way (James 2012, p. 40).

Beliefs developed within nineteenth-century fundamentalism continue to influence Christianity today. Some denominations and Christian groups overtly express fundamentalist beliefs, as can be seen, for example, in the doctrinal statement of the Universities and Colleges Christian Fellowship (James 2012, p. 36). There are many more Christian groups and individuals whose starting point is the assumption that, if the Bible is inspired, it must therefore be without error. Christians who believe that the Bible is inspired and inerrant are often motivated by a desire to protect the Bible; although it could be argued that such a powerful book does not need protection. For many Christians, the idea that parts of the biblical narrative might be historically inaccurate raises wider concerns about the reliability of the whole Bible and the Christian faith itself.

Yet biblical fundamentalism has been widely criticized by both Roman Catholic and Protestant authorities. An official document of the Vatican denounced fundamentalism as, 'a reading of the Bible which rejects all questionings and any kind of critical research' (The Pontifical Biblical Commission 1993, section F). The Vatican argued that a fundamentalist approach to the Bible fails to acknowledge the Christian belief that God works with humans and entrusts the historical church with God's mission.

In recent decades, Catholic and Protestant denominations have sought to clarify their understanding of the Bible as an inspired and authoritative text. The Bible is understood to be a text inspired by God but written by humans, as active agents (*Dei Verbum*, n. 11). It is also read and needs to be interpreted by humans, even if this is understood as taking place with the help of the Holy Spirit (Pontifical Biblical Commission 2014, paragraph 143). The Bible is a witness to God's truth (Pontifical Biblical Commission 2014, paragraph 144), but is not identical, nor confined to it (Trustees for Methodist Church Purposes 1998, paragraphs 2.9, 3.2, 4.2, 4.9). As William Brown comments: 'What makes the Bible the Word of God does not depend on any particular theory of inspiration so much as to testify what the Bible has done and continues to do in people's lives' (Brown 2007, p. xiiii).

Finally, it is important to note that some Christians do not regard the Bible as a uniquely inspired text, believing that other texts or experiences are equally valid sources of knowledge about God and the world. We will look at such approaches to the Bible later in this chapter.

From thinking about how the Bible is understood as inspired by God, we turn to a consideration of the authority of the Bible. Although it is true that in recent decades many western societies have experienced a rejection of authoritarian figures and institutions, at the same time there has been a longing for the type of certainty promised by authoritarian leaders, fixed identities and beliefs. Unsurprisingly, the same dynamic can be seen in attitudes to the Bible, with both rejection of its authority and affirmation of the same increasingly visible in recent years (Brown 2007, p. x). Christians from a variety of theological perspectives have sought to offer more nuanced accounts of authority as a result. The 1998 report of the Methodist Church in Britain, entitled 'A Lamp to my Feet and a Light to my Path. The Nature of Authority and the Place of the Bible in the Methodist Church', sets out a range of views of biblical authority, noting the value of a diversity of perspectives.

> **Try it out**
>
> Read John 2.1–11. Which of the diverse understandings of the nature and authority of the Bible is most helpful in your understanding of the passage? What type of authority (historical, moral, theological, etc.) do you expect the Bible to have, if any? How does this passage bear witness?

Perhaps there is something in William Brown's suggestion that the authority of the Bible should be understood as 'a generative, provocative power that elicits a response, and in so doing, shapes the conduct, indeed identity, of the reader or reading community' (Brown 2007, p. xiii). It is to the relationship between the Bible and the believing community that we now turn.

A text in conversation

For some Christians, the meaning of biblical texts is self-evident and can be read directly off the page without any need for interpretation, or translation between the historical and literary contexts of the text, and the situation of the reader (James 2012, pp. 41–2). The belief that the words of the Bible are directly inspired by God and that God communicates clearly and without confusion through the Bible is sometimes called biblical literalism. John Stackhouse, an evangelical scholar, observes how some evangelicals see a direct relationship between matters of faith and the biblical teaching: 'we believe X because the Bible teaches it *right here*' (Stackhouse 2004, p. 187, Stackhouse's italics). Conservative evangelicals argue this direct application of biblical teaching is a sign of the central place of Bible in their faith.

Closely associated with a belief in the clarity of biblical teaching is the method of application known as proof-texting (citing one or several biblical verses to support a point). Proof-texting tends to be associated with more conservative sectors of Christianity and often occurs in ethical debates; for example, protesters outside abortion clinics holding placards quoting biblical verses such as, 'For you created my inmost being; you knit me together in my mother's womb. I praise you because I am fearfully and wonderfully made' (Ps. 139.13–14), the implication being that Psalm 139, which explores God's creative power and presence, can be applied directly to the contemporary context of reproductive healthcare. But as Rowan Williams points out, Christians from across the theological scale are guilty of proof-texting, or at least seeking to bend a text to their own purposes, often in a way that is a distortion of its original meaning within the wider literary context (Williams 2017, pp. 34–7).

In contrast to biblical literalism, most mainstream churches and biblical scholars would say that, as with any text, the Bible requires interpreting (Trustees for Methodist Church Purposes 1998, paragraph 4.6). For the Church of England, the Bible is 'God's living and active word' (The Windsor Report 2004, paragraph 57), and should not be viewed as a rulebook. Indeed, the Vatican notes:

> The fundamentalist approach is dangerous, for it is attractive to people who look to the Bible for ready answers to the problems of life. It can deceive these people, offering them interpretations that are pious but illusory, instead

of telling them that the Bible does not necessarily contain an immediate answer to each and every problem. (The Pontifical Biblical Commission 1993, section F)

The Church is by no means the only community in which the Bible is studied and interpreted, but, for Christians, an important discussion has been the relationship between the authority of the Bible and that of the Church. Within the Roman Catholic tradition, the Council of Trent reinforced the importance of both the Bible and tradition in theological discernment (Lamb 2013, pp. 154–5). For some time, the Bible took something of a back seat to the authority of the Church and its tradition, but post-Vatican II, there has been increased emphasis on biblical study (see *Dei Verbum* 1965). Although Protestantism has tended to place the Bible in the central position of its self-understanding, most churches would see the Christian tradition and community as important resources for interpreting the text for today (Trustees for Methodist Church Purposes 1998, paragraph 7.9.4). The Church of England frames the Church as 'witness and keeper' to Scripture (General Synod 2009) and, for many churches, the formal leadership and decision-making bodies of the church are considered key interpreters of the Bible (The Windsor Report 2004, paragraph 58; Trustees for Methodist Church Purposes 1998, paragraph 4.3). Addressing evangelical Christians, Andrew McGowan, a Scottish theologian, argues that there needs to be a refocusing on God's revelation rather than on the Bible, which is one aspect of divine revelation. McGowan argues for clearer recognition that tradition, in the form of creeds and confessions, is used alongside the Bible within evangelical theology, but that this is often not considered (McGowan 2007, pp. 207–10).

Many churches also advocate human knowledge and study of a wide range of disciplines, as essential for understanding such a complex text as the Bible (General Synod 2009; Trustees for Methodist Church Purposes 1998, paragraph 7.9.3). Many Christian traditions further recognize the insights to be gained from experience. Here experience means both lived human experience and spiritual experience, including the guidance we might find through prayer and the work of the Holy Spirit (Trustees for Methodist Church Purposes 1998, paragraph 7.9.5). Black Pentecostal churches often emphasize the inspiration of the Holy Spirit in both the formation and reception of the Bible.

This section began with debate over the authority of the Bible, provoked by developments in biblical studies during the nineteenth century. In Chapter 3, we will test out a range of historical critical and literary methods that are designed to help us pay attention to the biblical text and its contexts. Before doing that, we need to explore the relationship between text and community, which is expressed in the notion of canon. We need to ask how the Bible both shapes and is shaped by faith communities. Birch and Rasmussen suggest that the authority of the Bible for Christians is not located in the book itself but comes from the Church's recognition of the importance of these writings (Birch and Rasmussen 1989, p. 142). For this reason, scholars who use a canonical approach (a set of approaches we will explore further in Chapter 6) are interested in how the Bible is read and interpreted as sacred Scripture. They look at how the community of faith interprets the texts so that a normative interpretation emerges. Moreover, they consider the mutual impact of the canon and the community, asking how the communities of faith and the developing traditions shape each other. Thus Rowan Williams views the Bible as first a text that is read publicly, and to which the faith community is asked to listen, remaining open to God's word. It is also a text that 'summons' or calls together the community of faith (Williams 2017, pp. 30–1, 42).

A gathered and gathering text

The Bible is not a single book but a collection of texts written in many different styles, in a range of contexts, over many centuries. In this section we look at the formation of the biblical canons, and ask whether the texts gathered by earlier Jewish and Christian communities still function to define and orientate contemporary faith communities of these traditions.

The biblical canons

The word 'canon' originates from a Greek word referring to a measuring rule or standard. In biblical studies, canon describes a set collection of books granted authoritative status by and for a particular community. These texts tend to come from the formational period of the faith community and helped define it.

While it is usual to speak of the biblical canon, there is in fact no single agreed biblical canon. The Jewish community has its own collection of sacred writings known as Mikra, meaning 'that which is read', or Tanakh, an acronym referring to its three parts: *Torah* (Law); *Nevi'im* (Prophets); and *Ketuvim* (Writings). The collection includes the same 39 books that most Christians recognize as the Hebrew Bible or Old Testament (although in the Tanakh organized into 24 books). In addition to these books, Roman Catholic and Orthodox Christians include some extra Jewish texts, such as Tobit and Judith. These texts, alongside an early Greek translation of the Hebrew Scriptures, formed what became known as the Septuagint. This translation is sometimes referred to by the Roman numeral LXX, referring to the belief that it took 70 translators to complete it. As Christianity spread across the Mediterranean region, it was the Greek, rather than the Hebrew, version of the Scriptures that became widely used by the early Church, thus explaining the inclusion of these additional texts within Christianity.

Jewish and Christian canons developed over time and through debate: for example, the book of Esther was a later addition to the Tanakh and there was centuries of debate over the status of texts such as Hebrews and Revelation that were eventually included in the New Testament. Today there is widespread agreement on the makeup of the New Testament canon, with the same 27 books accepted throughout most of the Christian Church. The main exception is the Orthodox Tewahedo Church of Ethiopia and Eritrea that recognizes eight additional texts from the historic Ethiopian tradition as part of their New Testament canon.

> ## Try it out
>
> Look at a copy of the Tanakh, a Protestant Bible with Apocrypha, and a Catholic Bible. You can compare them on the Bible Odyssey website ('Three Biblical Canons'). How does the order of each collection differ? How are individual books grouped together? For example, Ruth and Daniel appear in different categories, each location suggesting a different interpretation.
>
> By looking at the final verses of each collection, we can see how the Tanakh ends with reference to the return from exile, whereas Christian editors chose to end with the prophet Malachi, as a way of connecting the Hebrew prophetic tradition to the figure of John the Baptist who appears early on in the New Testament. What difference does this ordering make to your interpretation of the Bible?

In the process of developing the canon, the early Jewish and Christian communities edited earlier writings and traditions, adapting them for their contemporary situation. This is particularly evident in the Hebrew Bible because of the lengthy time frame during which individual books, Isaiah for example, were produced. Central events and stories were retold and reinterpreted throughout as new generations adapted traditional teaching to their own situation. Mary Callaway points out: 'The very nature of canon is to be simultaneously stable and adaptable, a fixed set of traditions infinitely adaptable to new contexts by successive communities of believers' (Callaway 1999, p. 146).

Establishing boundaries

The process of canon formation was long, complex and contested for both Jewish and Christian communities. Over time, certain texts came to be viewed as trustworthy and truthful. Through recognition of such texts, communities sought to establish their identity, often in the face of internal or external threats. It is therefore not surprising that, from the beginning, there were disputes over the status of some books.

The Jewish community began to compile texts in response to the experience of being exiled in Babylon during the sixth century BCE. This new context for the interpretation of the tradition had an impact on the shape of the Torah, with Joshua's account of entering the land excluded, and a shift in focus towards the law and future fulfilment of God's promises to Israel (Callaway 1999, pp. 145–6). The Torah formed the kernel of scripture for the post-exilic community. Reference to 'the Law and the Prophets and the other books' in the second century BCE book of Sirach (see the prologue to Sirach) indicates a growing corpus. By the second century CE we encounter a familiar list of 24 books (*Baba Batra*, 14b), even though debate continued over the status of Esther and Song of Songs (McDonald 2012, pp. 59–60). As with later Christian communities, different groups within Judaism gave authority to a diversity of texts, although all recognized the Torah. A well-known example is that of the Qumran community whose library indicates that certain of the community's own writings were given similar status to more widely recognized scripture (Soulen 2009, p. 19). Indeed, the boundary between canonical and other texts was perhaps always more fluid than fixed, with Hindy Najman suggesting that what defines scripture has always been its ability to generate new imaginative texts, commentary and midrash (Najman 2012, pp. 498–9, 517).

The first Christians regarded the Torah, prophets and psalms as sacred writings (Luke 24.44), to be read during worship and studied for guidance and insight. But they began to see a need to supplement these with texts that bore witness to their experience of encountering God through Jesus. Paul's letters, written to emerging Christian communities, began to be circulated more widely; as did accounts of Jesus' life, suffering, death and resurrection known as gospels. These texts came to be seen as scripture alongside the received tradition (2 Peter 3.15–16) and by the mid-second century CE, we learn from Justin Martyr's description of Christian worship that 'the memoirs of the apostles or the writings of the prophets are read' (Justin Martyr, *First Apology* 67.3). The new testimony of the apostles did not displace the witness offered by earlier Jewish teachers and prophets. Most Christians continued to make use of a variety of Jewish writings, including those that would form part of the Jewish Apocrypha (McDonald 2012, pp. 79–80). But Marcion (more on him later) set gospel and letters against Torah and prophets, and called on Christians to reject the Jewish scriptures. It was down to other second-century theologians such as Irenaeus that the Church managed to hold together Old and New Testaments (Soulen 2009, pp. 23–4).

Early Christians were a diverse group, scattered across the Roman Empire, encountering a range of philosophies and traditions. In this creative period, writings of different styles and teaching were circulated among local communities. Matthew's gospel and Paul's letters were widely known, but so too were texts unfamiliar to many twenty-first century Christians, such as *Shepherd of Hermas*, the *Didache*, the *Letters of Ignatius*, *1* and *2 Clement*. Indeed:

> There are more surviving copies of the *Shepherd of Hermas* in the first few centuries than all of the other New Testament books except for the Gospels of Matthew and John. This book was also included in a well-known copy of the church's complete Scriptures (Codex Sinaiticus) in the late fourth century AD. (McDonald 2012, p. 5)

The early Church used a set of criteria to judge whether a book should be included within the New Testament (see, for example, Irenaeus, *Against Heresies* 3.3.3 and 3.4.1; McDonald 2012, pp. 100–4). Was the book written by, or based on the teaching of the apostles or their companions? Did it contain teaching considered orthodox by the Church? Was it widely recognized and read by the Church (see Eusebius, *Ecclesiastical History* 3.25.1)?

> **Try it out**
>
> Imagine you were tasked with reviewing one of the biblical canons today. What criteria would you use? Would you remove or add any texts? On what grounds?

The Christian canon took further shape under Emperor Constantine. He requested the scholar Eusebius arrange for 50 copies of the scriptures to be distributed to churches in Constantinople, thus requiring further decisions about content and order to be reached (see Eusebius, *The Life of Constantine* 3.34–37; McDonald 2012, p. 99). A few decades later, Athanasius of Alexandria listed for the first time all 27 books of the New Testament (*Thirty-Ninth Festal Letter*, 367 CE). Widespread recognition of these texts did not, however, prevent continued use of additional texts for several centuries (McDonald 2012, p. 92).

Canonical diversity

The diverse nature of the canon provides readers with a colourful, multi-textured work with which to engage. For Christians, the inclusion of four gospels within the New Testament, for example, enriches their knowledge of Jesus and opens up space for them to enter into the traditions and events behind the four accounts.

When we compare different parts of the Bible we notice a variety of teaching, often in response to the differing circumstances of the faith communities from which the texts emerged. For example, the characters of Joseph and Daniel respond differently to life in foreign lands. Daniel holds fast to the teachings of his faith, refusing to eat food offered to idols or to worship the king. His actions lead him into the lion's den, from which he emerges unscathed thanks to his faithfulness (Daniel 6.6–28). In contrast, Joseph adopts a 'when in Rome' approach to life. He becomes Pharaoh's confidant, settles down in the life of the court and marries an Egyptian (Genesis 41.39–45). While Joseph's actions offered insight into how Jewish communities in strange lands (such as during the Babylonian exile) could thrive, Daniel's religious faithfulness encouraged later Jewish communities who wanted to retain their distinctiveness to survive in the long term.

The canon also enables us to use other biblical texts to help us interpret a particular passage. Gina Hens-Piazza reminds us:

> The collection was established on the consensus that together these books express the faith beliefs of communities claiming them as their confessional texts. "Together" here is the operative word. The notion of canon is important for us because it suggests a further context for our story. It urges us to read and understand our tale *together* with other stories of the canon. (Hens-Piazza 2003, p. 96, Hens-Piazza's italics)

Hens-Piazza illustrates the benefits of reading a biblical text as part of the wider canon in her work on 2 Kings 6.24–33, the story of two cannibal mothers, King Jehoram and the prophet Elisha during the siege of Samaria. The brief yet disturbing story of the two women is explored with the help of other stories about two women, disputed children and powerful men – Sarah and Hagar (Gen. 16, 21.1–21); Rachel and Leah (Gen. 29–30); and the two mothers who appear before Solomon (1 Kings 3.16–28). Hens-Piazza draws fresh insights from reading the stories together, noting how in each story the women understand that children give them status, love and even life itself, and thus their struggle over children becomes more desperate. To contrast these stories of conflict, Hens-Piazza draws our attention to the beginning of Exodus, where cooperation between many women saves the newborn boy Moses in defiance of the destructive wishes of the Pharaoh. Hens-Piazza suggests that such courageous stories give readers hope and strengthen us to seek out alternate ways to the way of violence.

Beyond the canons

A number of Jewish and early Christian writings were eventually excluded from some or all of the canons, or were given secondary status. In this section, we will consider both why these texts were rejected by some communities, and whether they have anything to offer to twenty-first-century readers of the Bible.

The Apocrypha The fourth-century Christian scholar Jerome defined the Apocrypha as those writings found in the Septuagint (the early Greek translation of the Hebrew scriptures which included related Jewish writings) but not in any Hebrew manuscripts. Although Jerome identified these books as of secondary status, they continued to be widely used until the Reformation. In his translation of the Bible into German, Luther relied on the Hebrew tradition and, although he included writings from the Greek tradition as 'useful and good for reading', he differentiated them from the Old Testament proper (Walden 2007, p. 5). Other Protestants followed suit to a greater or lesser degree, with the Church of England allowing reading of these texts, 'for example of life and instruction of manners; but yet doth it not apply them to establish any doctrine' (Thirty Nine Articles, 1562). In contrast, in response to the Reformers, the Council of Trent (1546) reaffirmed the deuterocanonical status of texts from the Greek tradition for the Catholic Church. When the Protestant Reformers excluded much of these secondary or deuterocanonical texts, these books became known to Protestants as the Apocrypha. (It is worth noting that Protestant Apocrypha is slightly larger than the Roman Catholic Deuterocanonical Books, since it includes additional Greek texts accepted by some Orthodox traditions.)

> ## Try it out
>
> Look at a print or online version of the Bible that includes the Apocrypha or the Deuterocanonical Books, listed according to their standing in each denomination. Read Tobit 11. With what other biblical texts does Tobit share a similar style, themes or characters? How might reading Tobit help you explore these texts?

The Pseudepigrapha The Pseudepigrapha is a collection of Jewish and Christian writings (from as early as 650 BCE to as late as 800 CE but mainly written between 200 BCE and 200 CE) not awarded canonical or deuterocanonical status by the Church. The writings of Pseudepigrapha mostly emerged at a later stage than the deuterocanonical books, during what was to be a formative period for both Judaism and Christianity. They record and reflect a time of lively debate when these communities of faith were more receptive to influences from the surrounding cultures. Dominant themes include the origins of evil, the end of the world, the Messiah, angels and resurrection (Porter 2001, p. 8).

The Apocryphal New Testament The Apocryphal New Testament includes writings from the second to the ninth century CE, mostly of familiar genres such as letters, acts, gospels; for example, the *Gospel of Thomas*, the *Acts of Andrew* and the *Protoevangelium of James*. These texts helped develop the status of the apostles and other early followers of Jesus. Various Christian doctrines about Mary, the mother of Jesus originated in these apocryphal texts, notably the infancy gospels. Sometimes the texts increase Mary's standing, for example claiming she was a miracle worker, or embellish her earlier life, suggesting that she was brought up in the Temple (*Protoevangelium of James*). Although these gospels give greater prominence to Mary and women disciples such as Mary Magdalene, they do not offer a clear picture of a community of equals within the early Church. Indeed, Mary Magdalene's entrance into the kingdom is dependent on her becoming male in the *Gospel of Thomas* (although 'becoming male' could refer to keeping celibate) (Økland 2001, p. 74).

What do these texts offer us as biblical interpreters? They help us understand more about early Jewish and Christian communities, and the reception of canonical texts within these communities. They offer us imaginative extensions of familiar stories and fresh perspectives. And they can redress the balance of our understanding of the biblical witness, perhaps reminding us of the strong eschatological flavour of Judaism and Christianity during this.

That these texts remain relevant to twenty-first-century readers is the conviction behind *A New New Testament: A Bible for the 21st Century Combining Traditional and Newly Discovered Texts* (2013). To the established New Testament, editor Hal Taussig and other scholars have added ten texts from Christianity's formative period, in an attempt to make visible the diversity and breadth of early Christianity, and to encourage fresh conversations about Christian belief and practice. Several of the additional texts are ones which witness to women's leadership and teaching within the early Church (*Gospel of Mary*; *Acts of Paul and Thecla*). Others offer different interpretations of Jesus' ministry. Yet others provide further spiritual resources. With Natalie Renee Perkins, Taussig founded the Tanho Center, which aims to encourage scholarly, artistic and spiritual engagement with early Christian texts.

> **Try it out**
>
> Visit the website of *A New New Testament*, or that of the Tanho Center. Read an extract from the *Acts of Paul and Thecla*, or one of the other texts mentioned. What fresh insights and questions do these texts generate in relation to your understanding of the early Church? What hesitations do you have about reading texts that have been placed beyond the canon?

Feminist biblical scholars have had a particular interest in extra-canonical early Christian texts, especially those that focus on women's ministry or leadership in the early Church. Examples of this approach can be seen in Elisabeth Schüssler Fiorenza's *Searching the Scriptures* (1993) and Luise Schottroff and Marie-Theres Wacker's *Feminist Biblical Interpretation: A Compendium of Critical Commentary on the Books of the Bible and Related Literature* (2012). More fundamentally, feminist scholarship has sought to subvert fixed boundaries around authority, and singular notions of truth (Tolbert 1999). Thus it is unsurprising that some feminist scholars challenge the whole notion of canon. A third approach is imaginative and invitational: What if the canon was an ever-growing collection? By expanding the canon, other stories, experiences and encounters might be understood to bear witness alongside the Bible. It is to this idea that we now turn.

Extending the canon today

Inclusion in the biblical canons awarded certain texts authority in the life of the Jewish community and the Church. At the same time, it had the effect of limiting Christian and Jewish understandings of revelation. It was as if God had stopped communicating with the world once the last canonical book was completed. The United Church of Christ challenges this view with its testimony that 'God is still speaking', through acts of faith, justice and welcome today.

Some theologians advocate an extended written canon, arguing that we need to recognize the limitations of the canon. They point out that many people do not find themselves portrayed within the Bible, or only in negative ways (as foreigners, silenced or enslaved peoples). Therefore other stories need to be read alongside the Bible to redress the balance. Atabaque, a group of black pastoral workers in Brazil, argue that:

> The Bible is one source among many. Sometimes it is not even the main one. For the poor and the black, the stories of the saints and of miracles stand side by side, for examples, with the sung and danced stories of thee *terreiro* of Candomblé. The Bible of the *terreiro* is a story that is danced and sung. It is not written, it cannot be read . . . but it is also a story of salvation and liberation. (cited in Pereira 2003, p. 52)

Through this dialogical process, the experiences of contemporary, culturally diverse communities are allowed to interact with the biblical narrative that describes the experiences of the early Judeo-Christian community. Among scholars from Asia, Africa and Latin American there has been a rise in academic interest in local or indigenous traditions and texts. As one of many examples, Musa Dube from Botswana uses a traditional story from her own community, that of Utentelezandlane, a beautiful, beloved princess, to critique the biblical story of Judith (Dube 2003, p. 60).

From a different context, that of the city of Wolverhampton, Rachel sees in the poetry of Liz Berry a celebration of Black Country culture and dialect which helps her bear witness to some of the places and people which have formed her and in which she can ground some of her experience of God's world. The tall towers of biblical texts are never those of abandoned factories, and, while there are many doves, outside of sacrificial offerings, there is scant reference to pigeons. What would it mean to see tumbler pigeons as symbol of the Spirit, for example? Berry's poem 'Bird', in which the poet imagines her younger self as a bird taking flight, ends with a reclaiming of her voice; and in 'Homing' she writes of her resistance of the suppression of her native dialect (Berry 2014). To extend the canon can be seen as making space for silenced voices to speak, and claim their ability to bear witness to the truth of God in their experience (Oakley 2016, pp. 65–72).

African American womanist scholars have advocated an extended canon that includes novels and literature written by and about women. A classic example of this is the importance of Alice Walker's novel *The Color Purple* (1983) within womanist theology. The late Katie Cannon remarked how the oppressive use of the Bible and the limited insights it offered created this need to read texts written by and about black women alongside the Bible. She commented: 'Canon formation is a way of establishing new and larger contexts of experience within which African American women can attend to the disparity between sources of oppression and sources for liberation' (Cannon 1995, p. 76).

> **Try it out**
>
> You may already have books, songs or films that might form part of your extended canon. These might be stories that resonate with your own experience or that enable you to see the world in a new way. Draw up your own extended canon and note the ways it allows you to make use of other resources in your biblical interpretation, theology or reflections on life.

Scholars such as Dube and Cannon do not reject the traditional canon but feel it needs to be opened up to include a wider range of experiences. Of course, such moves are vigorously contested by some other Christians who do not believe that the canon can or should be extended beyond the Bible. This is particularly true of Christians who believe the Bible represents a unique unrepeated revelation. William Abraham, an American Methodist scholar, explains why moves to extend or change the canon are so divisive:

> In a real sense canonical material is actually constituted by the community. The two ideas, canon and community, are logically and reciprocally related. A community constitutes its canonical heritage, and in doing so, that community is itself constituted along certain lines. That is one reason why the development of canonical material and its subsequent rejection is so significant for a community. Once a community has formed its canonical traditions, changing, transforming, or rejecting those traditions from within is liable to be a convulsive affair. (Abraham 1998, p. 30)

However, Abraham himself argues that the canonical heritage of the church should not be limited to the Bible since it was always wider than that, including canon law, church councils and the embodied wisdom of senior cathedral staff known as canons. This breadth enables him to see the canon is a place of encounter with God rather than a measuring rule against which to judge other pronouncements about God (Abraham 1998, p. 474).

Other scholars who advocate an entirely open canon, 'declare the canonization process of the fourth century a mistake or failure of nerve' (Gnuse 1985, p. 95). They argue that the formation of the canon was a theological or political act of control, undertaken in response to perceived heresies or other threats. They feel that all canons by their very nature are exclusive and therefore suspect. On the other hand, an open canon removes any control the church might have over what understandings of God are acceptable within it.

Favouring parts of the canon

Stephen Dawes points out:

> The Bible does not interpret itself; it is not self explanatory. There is even a sense in which the Bible is silent, that it cannot speak for itself and that its users give it the only voice it has. The Bible is, after all, a book. No matter how venerable it is, it has to be opened and its chapters and verses selected before they can be quoted and used. (Dawes 2004, p. 114)

In this section, we will examine how readers select passages from the Bible for study, worship or other purposes. We may have preferred passages that we turn to for insight or interest. The Jewish community and Christian Church also have their favourites, those books that are regarded as central to God's revelation. The Torah and the Gospels are both placed at the start of the Tanakh and New Testament respectively, immediately indicating their primary importance. They are the books through which the other books in the collection are to be understood. *The Jewish Study Bible* notes: 'In Judaism, the Torah is accorded the highest level of sanctity, above that of the other books of the Bible' (Berlin and Brettler 2004, p. 1). Furthermore, Jewish and Christian worship will almost always include a reading from the Torah or Gospels correspondingly. The predominance of these texts is clear. They include the foundational stories of each faith community – the acts of creation, exodus and blessing; and the incarnation. As one such foundational event, the exodus is rehearsed time and time again in the biblical narrative. It represents the defining moment in Israel's relationship with God, and no matter what difficulties Israel experiences, this story retains the power to strengthen and shape the community.

> **Try it out**
>
> Rank these books in order of importance: Matthew, Genesis, Numbers, Ruth, Habakkuk, Titus, Romans. What criteria did you use to order the books? You may have used one of the following criterion: influence on the church or society, length, date, reference to the Torah or to Jesus.

We all inevitably favour some stories, characters or books of the Bible over others. Within Christian history, this favouring of certain texts has shaped the theological understanding of different groups. In his mission to uphold 'justification by faith' rather than 'justification by works', Luther famously dismissed the letter of James as an 'epistle of straw'! In his translation of the New Testament, Luther did include James, but separated out the letter, along with Hebrews, Jude and Revelation, from the rest of the New Testament (Walden 2007, p. 6). It can be argued that Luther's dislike for James moved social action or 'good works' to a marginal position in the theology of the emerging Protestant tradition.

> **Try it out**
>
> Do you turn to some biblical books more frequently than others? Would you disregard any books, perhaps some of the more obscure prophecies or letters? What about in your academic course or church – which texts are given priority there?

In the 1930s, some German theologians, building on the work of Adolf von Harnack, promoted a truncated version of the Bible that contained no reference to the Old Testament, which was regarded by them as a Jewish text contrary to the New Testament. This denial of the Jewish roots of Christianity was part of the wider anti-Semitic movement that led ultimately to the Shoah (destruction). The

Deutsche Christen or 'German Christians' were accused of Marcionism, a heresy named after Marcion, who in the second century rejected the Old Testament (as well as much of the New Testament, retaining only Luke and ten epistles) as a valid part of the Christian Scriptures. In fact, it was in his work on Marcion that von Harnack suggested it was time to review the canonical status of the Old Testament.

This is an extreme example of the way all readers inevitably favour some books of the Bible. We naturally prefer stories that inspire us, or characters to whom we relate. What we need to ensure, however, is that the Bible is understood as a rich and diverse testimony of human experience and faith. Those unfamiliar stories may be the ones through which we can encounter fresh and compelling insights into life and faith.

This was certainly the case for the German scholar, Claus Westermann, who wrote many books on the Old Testament, especially Psalms and Genesis. He had not intended to become a biblical scholar but, as a young pastor of the Confessing Church in 1930s Germany, Westermann was confronted with the political and spiritual significance of studying the Old Testament:

> The state's demand that we renounce the Old Testament as the Bible of the Jews became an occasion for us young theologians to do intensive work on this book. We were sent to a practical seminary (Predigerseminar) which had students from both camps. The Old Testament was hotly contested in our discussions. Was it worth it to stand up for this book as an integral part of the Bible and thereby to bring suffering upon oneself? . . .
>
> But in the middle of all that we discovered that if we wanted to hold on to the whole Bible, Old Testament and New, we could only do that by believing in a God who holds everything in his hands – where 'everything' includes the entire creation and encompasses both beginning and end. For to speak of God means to speak of the whole. (Westermann 1990, pp. 8–9)

Westermann continued to read and study the Old Testament as a conscripted soldier, a prisoner of war, and, later, a biblical scholar. He reflected on the importance of the psalms for him, recalling how in the prison camp:

> I thought about the psalms and tried to relate my own wartime thoughts to the Psalter. In doing so, I sat on a block of wood and wrote on a board held on my knees. Sometimes I traded bread for paper. (Westermann 1993, p. 340).

Westermann offers us an example of the importance of engaging with the breadth of the canons, and, in the remainder of this chapter, we explore how churches have sought to ensure this breadth of engagement, especially within services of worship.

Journeying through the canon: lectionaries

Following long-established Jewish practice, the early church drew up a scheme for the use of biblical passages during worship. Many Christian denominations today continue this practice, ordering their reading of the Bible to ensure key texts are heard by the congregation at least once every year or over a number of years on a rolling cycle. By using a lectionary in a local church, biblical passages are encountered in a systematic way. There are benefits to this process: it disciplines worship leaders to make use of a wider range of biblical texts than ones they are familiar or comfortable with; it enables churches to plan ahead and work with other local churches across denominations who use the same lectionary (for example through *Roots*, an ecumenical worship and learning resource); it adds to the structure and order of the church year; it helps worship leaders make connections between biblical texts.

Yet not all churches make use of a lectionary. Lee Martin McDonald observes the failure to engage with the breadth of the canon in some conservative churches, giving as one extreme example: Tenth Presbyterian Church, Philadelphia where one longstanding pastor preached on Romans every Sunday for seven years, only for one of his successors to preach primarily on John's gospel, for an even greater number of years (McDonald, 2012, pp. 164–5)!

The Revised Common Lectionary (RCL) is a three-year cycle of Bible readings developed in 1992 by the Consultation on Common Texts. In Britain, the RCL is used in many Methodist and United Reformed local churches. The Church of England adapted the RCL to produce the *Common Worship* lectionary. The Roman Catholic Church has its own lectionary but there are many points of contact between this and the RCL.

The RCL sought to respond to calls from the churches for more exposure to the historical books and wisdom literature of the Hebrew Scriptures. It therefore focuses on the Patriarchal/Mosaic narrative for Year A (and the Gospel of Matthew in Ordinary Time), the Davidic narrative for Year B (and the Gospel of

Mark), and the Elijah/Elisha/Minor Prophets series for Year C (and the Gospel of Luke). The Gospel of John is covered each year, particularly in the Sundays around the festivals of Christmas and Easter. Wisdom texts in the RCL include passages from Job and Proverbs, and a handful of texts from Ecclesiastes or Qoheleth, the central one being Ecclesiastes 3:1–13: 'For everything there is a season . . .' which is set for New Year's Day each of the three years. It also sets wisdom texts from the Jewish Apocrypha: the Wisdom of Solomon, Sirach and Baruch. While this represents an improvement in the breadth of coverage, there remain significant gaps.

Use of a lectionary can restrict worship leaders and prevent them from responding to dynamics within the local church or news and current events. A further concern about the uncritical use of a lectionary is that worship leaders and congregations may be guided towards particular interpretations of a text through the placing of certain texts together. For example, for the fourth Sunday in Advent in Year A, Isaiah 7.10–16, Isaiah's prophecy about a young woman with child is set with the birth of Jesus in Matthew 1.18–25. Such groupings suggest to preachers and worship leaders that a reading from the Hebrew Scriptures should be interpreted through the lens of the gospel reading it is linked with for that Sunday.

> ## Try it out
>
> Look up the set readings for the forthcoming Sunday in the RCL (see Vanderbilt Divinity Library website) or another lectionary. Read the set readings and, especially if it is a festival season rather than Ordinary Time, look at what connections are implied by the grouping of the texts on this particular Sunday. What understanding of each text is encouraged by this process? Do you agree with it? How would you explain or challenge such interpretations?

Another obvious difficulty is that the Christian lectionaries do not include the whole Bible, even over a three-year cycle, leading to supplementary reading projects such as *Year D* (Slemmons 2012). If Christians only hear the Bible read on a Sunday, the lectionary acts as a filter to their comprehension of Bible, shaping their understanding of the priorities of Christianity. So which passages are heard over and over in church? Which stories is the contemporary church embarrassed by, and does this give the church the right to ignore them?

As one example, the RCL includes just two readings from Judges: Judges 4.1–7 (part of the story of Deborah) and Judges 6.11–24 (part of Gideon's story). More challenging texts, texts that vividly describe violent acts or questionable characters, such as Ehud's trickery and murder of King Eglon (Judges 3.15–25) or Jael's role in the victory of Deborah and Barak, through the murder of Sisera with a tent peg (Judges 4.17–22), do not appear in the lectionary. Similarly, the teaching concerning the relationship between wives and husbands, and slaves and masters, from Ephesians and related texts, is not in the lectionary. Some feel that violent and oppressive texts have no place in worship (especially if not critically engaged with, through preaching or prayer). Yet, the silence over such problematic texts can be unhelpful since it reduces the opportunities for debate of traditional interpretations.

A number of feminist projects have sought to address the lack of women in readings in the RCL and other lectionaries (see Raymer 2018, pp. 189–93). A collection of liturgical readings curated by a group of Roman Catholic women scholars was prompted by asking whether the Bible was able to bear witness to the reality of women's lives (Bowe et al. 1992, p. 5). The editors not only sought to extend the scope of the readings from the Bible to include women characters who had been cut out of the Roman Catholic lectionary – women such as Phoebe, Lois and Esther – but also included non-canonical texts, early church writings and epitaphs; and later spiritual works, such as *The Acts of Perpetua and Felicitas*, *Egeria's Travels*, and Julian of Norwich's *Showings*. This collection is offered with the encouragement: 'let these tales enrich your repertoire of the ways God has moved among us and the ways women have struggled to respond with integrity – for here is the kernel of ourselves' (Bowe et al. 1992, p. 10). A further resource is Miriam Therese Winter's project, *WomanWisdom* (1991), *WomanWitness* (1997) and *WomanWord* (1990) which foregrounds women within the Bible, either by lifting up marginalized characters or by imagining women into spaces and speaking roles.

While it would be almost impossible for any one lectionary to satisfy everyone, such critical conversations about the shape and content of the Church's lectionaries are helpful in that they remind us of the Church's and our own tendency to overlook texts which disturb, or suggest the current practices of the Church might need reviewing. A question to ask might be: When it is time to renew and refresh an established lectionary?

Listening to marginalized texts and silent voices

In churches, synagogues or universities, we spend more time with a few texts than with many others. It is through these central texts that we learn much about the key beliefs of faith communities. However, we will not get the whole story from concentrating on these favoured texts alone. Sometimes we need to search around at the edges of the Bible to discover new images of God and faith. To redress the balance, some biblical scholars prioritize lesser-known passages and characters, and even spend time with the silences of the text. In these places and spaces, there are hints of alternative communities and understandings of God that have been suppressed and denied.

The Bible is an attempt by several communities of faith to offer reflections about their relationship with God. At times the people write as those with some power, and at other times as a community with little power. Most often it is the powerful within the community whose views are recorded but there are also critiques of the dominant story, such as the witness of the prophets. Often, in order to build up a fuller picture of the community's experience of God, we have to consider who or what is absent from the text. An important example of this reconstructive work is Elisabeth Schüssler Fiorenza's *In Memory of Her. A Feminist Theological Reconstruction of Christian Origins* (1983), which offers an alternative picture of the early Christian community, one in which women played a full part. The presence of female leaders in the earliest house churches offers a strong model of inclusivity for the Church today.

> **Try it out**
>
> Read through either the book of Obadiah or the letter of Jude. Now answer the following questions about this text:
>
> - Who is present or absent? (Think about communities or groups as well as individuals.)
> - How is the story or event told? What is the narrative slant? What value judgements are made by the narrator, speaker or writer?
> - Why do you think this text has been overlooked?
> - What connections can you make with other biblical texts?
> - How does this text balance other texts or movements within the Bible; namely, why might it have been included in the canon?

Unity in diversity?

As we come to the end of this section on the biblical canons, let's return to the questions with which we began this section: What binds these diverse texts together? And how do we understand difference, even tension, within the Bible?

Brevard Childs' canonical approach described the whole canon as the arena for understanding. He, and others who follow his approach, believe that the full canon must be held together. There can be a lively discussion between the different voices, but all must be heard. Other interpreters have questioned whether this attempt at unity is successful, and have argued that canonical approaches effectively push for the establishment of standard or approved interpretations, limiting the possibilities for other critical or fresh readings.

In these post-modern times, some interpreters argue that the plurality and tensions of the biblical narratives are both realistic and liberative. Walter Brueggemann suggests that the time for 'thin readings' is at an end and we should rejoice in the density of the text (Brueggemann 1997b, p. 61). Through the tension, dialogue and spaces within the material, there is room for much creativity and the emergence of many stories and many more readings of them. Brueggemann argues that the Bible itself points beyond any exclusive reading: Christian, Jewish or other; noting that even the original and still valid Jewish interpretations of the Hebrew Bible must allow room for other readings alongside them:

> In the text, there is a recurring restlessness about a Jewish reading and a push beyond that to a reading as large as the nations and as comprehensive as creation ... The text simply will not be contained in any such vested reading, which is what makes the text both compelling and subversive. (Brueggemann 1997b, p. 95)

Try it out

What tensions do you experience within the Bible? Do you seek to resolve them, and if so, how?

In this chapter, we have considered our individual and collective experience of the Bible, and the assumptions we have about its power and status. We have explored how the Church has formed and been formed by its canon. We turn now to the work of biblical criticism and consider a range of methods designed to help us better understand the text, that is to become better readers of the Bible.

3

Tools for Exegesis

Introduction: learning to do exegesis

Somewhere along the line, biblical interpreters have to deal with the fact that the text before them is an old one: written or compiled on the basis of earlier oral or written traditions, in an ancient language and in a culture very different from the globalized world of the twenty-first century.

It is a collection of classic texts, a bit like the works of Shakespeare, though Shakespeare is much, much nearer us in time and culture, wrote most of his plays himself and, of course, in English. As a collection of classic texts, the Bible has already had a long history of interpretation in our culture and has influenced the way we think, speak and even behave. Most chapters in this book make some reference to the importance of this impact history, and we discuss the concept of impact history at the end of this chapter.

This chapter deals with exegesis, demonstrating some of the tools and approaches that help us engage more systematically with whatever Bible passage is before us. There is nothing mysterious about this. It is just a matter of learning to use skills and tools, some of which we will already have: a bit like learning to do DIY or a craft.

Words such as 'exegesis' and 'hermeneutics' can be intimidating, but they needn't be. Every discipline has its own special technical language, and biblical interpretation is no exception. 'Exegesis' simply means a careful systematic study of a passage using a range of methods and 'hermeneutics' is another word for interpretation. Exegesis is an important part of the whole process of biblical interpretation, but it is not the whole of it, nor its starting point, as is obvious from the placement of this chapter some way into the overall book.

When we do an exegesis of a biblical passage we consider it from two points of view. First, we have a good look at it as it is, here and now. And then we investigate how it came to be here, in this form, in this place in the Bible. This distinction between looking at a text as it is and as it has developed was borrowed by biblical scholars from structural linguistics. The technical words for these viewpoints are synchronic (with time) and diachronic (through time). The distinction enables us to be clear in our own minds about whether we are thinking about the final form of the passage in front of us, or thinking about the history of its development.

This is one example of the way exegesis makes use of tools for studying ancient texts borrowed from other disciplines, such as history or literature. Each tool has a different purpose and orientation. Some are designed to help us explore the history of the formation of the passage, spotting, for example, where a quotation from another writer has been inserted. Other tools help us appreciate the artistic skill of the author or editor. This chapter will introduce you to some of these tools and help you to begin to use them for yourself.

Synchronic approaches

When we take a synchronic approach to a passage, we look at the final form of a biblical text. We do so knowing that the text has a long history of development, both when it was being formed and during the long period of its transmission. The synchronic approach looks at the 'final form' of the text before us, as language and as literature.

Considering the text as language, we draw on the tools of grammar and structural linguistics to see how the text is structured, that is how words have been combined into sentences and larger sense units. That is, we look at the way the passage before us either follows, or departs from the conventions of Greek, Hebrew or Aramaic literature and grammar of the same period. The way the text conveys meaning through its structure is also important. Here we look at how the text conveys meaning not just through its words and grammar, but also through the patterns and relationships within and between smaller and larger parts of the text. This disciplined examination of the way the text is organized often yields exciting insights into its meaning.

TOOLS FOR EXEGESIS

Reading a Bible passage as literature means reading it just as carefully as we do any other literature. Much of this involves the same commonsense decisions we make every time we read anything. We first decide what kind of text it is (its genre or form) to enable us to read it appropriately. Then we attend to its shape, structure and flow (how it has been composed), its theme, plot and character development, and the way it makes its impact upon us. It may try to surprise us, as many of Jesus' parables do. Or it may try to persuade us, as Paul's letters frequently do, using all his skills of argument. Or it may even try to disorientate and inspire us, using confusing patterns and bizarre imagery, as we find in the book of Revelation.

Let's begin to do some exegesis. In this chapter we will be working with a few extended examples to see how the critical tools work together.

Making the text our own

The first requirement of exegesis is to make the text our own, at least in a preliminary way. Hans-Ruedi Weber, an experienced leader of group Bible studies for the World Council of Churches, offers a number of suggestions for doing this in an excellent guide to group Bible study called *The Book that Reads Me* (1995). The first chapter of that book reminds us that before the Bible was written down, much of it was communicated from person to person orally. Because of this oral dimension to the Bible, one simple way of getting a fresh grasp of a biblical text is simply to read it aloud. This helps us to hear the rhythms of the text and to notice places where patterns or repetitions help listeners to follow and remember what they are hearing. Other ways in which we can experience a biblical passage afresh, and do justice to its oral character, are by memorizing it, retelling it or even singing it (Weber 1995, pp. 1–6). Remember that in Jewish worship and in some Christian traditions, the Scriptures are often sung by the congregation or a choir.

> **Try it out**
>
> Read Psalm 23 aloud and then – if you can – sing one of the hymns based on this psalm in a hymnbook. Compare the effect of reading the psalm aloud with that of singing it as a hymn. Why do you think people wrote hymns based on this psalm?
>
> Now see if you can memorize a short biblical passage, that of the story of Zacchaeus in Luke 19.1–10, either on your own, using actions or prompts to help you, or working with a partner. Weber (1995, p. 6) gives a simple method for memorizing a biblical story by working with a partner: read the story aloud to one another, and then divide the story into scenes, giving each scene a key word. By memorizing the key words, it is possible then to retell the story to one another, helping each other with the missing bits, until you can retell the story from memory. You will not necessarily retell it word for word, but will have made the story your own.

It is important to remember that the Bible was oral tradition before it was written down, and later printed, and that much of the Bible is structured for memorization, recitation and imagination. People who cannot read rely on hearing and memory, and are often more able to keep more of the Bible in mind and thus to be aware of 'the whole story'.

Oral criticism argues that many biblical texts were composed or edited in such a way that those listening could more easily follow the flow of the argument and remember them. Casey Wayne Davis's study of Philippians (1999) helps us see that, while Paul's letters were written texts, they were written by someone who preached and taught orally. He only wrote letters when oral communication was impossible.

Despite the importance of hearing the Bible being read or sung aloud, today we are much more familiar with the Bible as a written text. Over a long period, the oral traditions in the Bible were recorded, revised and expanded in written form. Even after the canon was substantially complete, copies of the Bible have been made by hand for most of the Bible's lifetime. Even today, copying out a Bible passage by hand is a good way of engaging with it afresh.

TOOLS FOR EXEGESIS

> **Try it out**
>
> The story of the Tower of Babel is well known and has a long impact history. But what do you remember of the whole story? Make a few notes (or even a little sketch) on what you recall of this story.
>
> Now turn to Genesis 11.1–9 and write it out in your own handwriting. As you write, you may notice things that you want to find out more about. For example: What understanding of the 'whole earth' does the writer presuppose? Does the writer assume that people have already heard or read chapter 10? Who are 'they' in v. 2 and are they moving to or from the east? (See the note in the margin of the New Revised Standard Version.) Where is Shinar in relation to 'the whole earth'?
>
> You may also want to ask questions about the character of God in this story. For a start, why does this story talk about 'the LORD', rather than 'God', and is there a difference? And, why does it think of the LORD as having to 'come down' to see the city and tower? Come down from where? Can the LORD not see everywhere? Why is the LORD apparently against human achievement?
>
> After copying out the passage, look back at your notes or sketch out what you thought the story was about. How accurate was your recollection of it?

Discourse analysis

Discourse analysis helps us to look closely at the surface structure of a passage, and to pay close attention to the way it is 'joined up' grammatically and stylistically. It arose in the early 1970s and was developed by South African and American biblical scholars who were influenced by developments in linguistics and Bible translation. Initially some thought that it might provide them with a 'scientific' way of determining *the* structure of a passage. Later, as it became clear that scholars using discourse analysis were coming up with different accounts of the structure of the same text, it was realized that it was just a useful tool for close observation. It helped scholars to explain how they thought the text was structured and how this affected their interpretation of the text.

In this section, we are going to complete a discourse analysis of Genesis 11.1–9, and then review how this approach helps us understand the passage.

First, copy the NRSV translation of Genesis 11.1–9 from an online source such as the Oremus Bible Browser. Next, divide the text into smaller sense-units. The aim here is to release the text from the much later additions of chapter and verse numbers (although in this exercise we will keep the verse numbering for ease of cross-reference).

Then identify the main verbs. Where the text is set out below, the verbs are highlighted in bold. Remember that sometimes a verb is made up of more than one word, such as 'will be'. Also, infinitives (like 'to see' or 'to do') are not verbs but verbal nouns. Marking up the verbs helps us to divide the text up into cola, which are lines that each describes a single action. So in 11.1–2, the verbs are 'had', 'migrated', 'came' and 'settled'.

> ### Try it out
>
> Mark the verbs in bold and then place each section of a sentence with a verb in it on a new line. Each line is called a colon.

With this preparation, we are ready to identify the linguistic structure of the passage. Add a dotted line each time the passage seems to start a new section. In the example below, you will see that we think this happens after vv. 1, 4, 7 and 8.

Within each of these sections, there will be cola that belong together as parts of a sentence, such as in v. 3. It is possible to indent them, to show how these parts are related to one another. In v. 3, indents the three things that the people said to one another: 'Come', 'let us make bricks', and then more detail of how they would make them. The square bracket before certain indented words just indicates that the line above is continued below.

Next, we identify the subject of each sentence (underlined as set out below). This helps to show us when there is a change of subject. For example, the subject changes from 'the whole earth' in v. 1 to 'they' in vv. 2–4. In vv. 5–7 the subject changes again to 'the Lord'. Verse 8 either continues this unit or follows it, as

TOOLS FOR EXEGESIS

indicated by 'so' – more investigation needed! Verse 9 with the subject of the city/tower, 'it', is a summary verse.

This corresponds roughly with your intuitive decisions to identify each new section with a dotted line. Look back and see if the dotted lines you inserted above do mark these changes of subject. The reason the sections beginning 'the LORD came' and 'the LORD scattered' are marked as separate sections is that it helps to show how the section in which the LORD scatters the people (v. 8) has a relationship with the people's motivation for building the tower, their fear of being scattered, in v. 4.

1 Now <u>the whole earth</u> **had** one language and the same words.
....

2 And as <u>they</u> **migrated** from the east,
   <u>they</u> **came** upon a plain in the land of Shinar
   and **settled** there.

3 And <u>they</u> **said** to one another,
   '**Come**,
     let us **make** bricks,
       and **burn** them thoroughly.'

And <u>they</u> **had** brick for stone, and bitumen for mortar.

4 Then <u>they</u> **said**,
   '**Come**,
     let us **build** ourselves a city, and a tower with its top in the heavens,
     and let us **make** a name for ourselves;
       otherwise we **shall be scattered** abroad upon the face
       of the whole earth.'
....

5 <u>The LORD</u> **came** down to see the city and the tower,
   which mortals **had built.**

6 And <u>the LORD</u> **said**,
   '**Look**,
     they **are** one people,

and they **have** all one language;
and this **is** only the beginning
of what they **will do**;
nothing that they **propose** to do
will now **be** impossible for them.

7 **Come,**
   let <u>us</u> **go** down,
      and **confuse** their language there,
         so that they **will** not **understand** one another's speech.'

．．

8 So <u>the LORD</u> **scattered** them abroad from there over the face of all the earth,
   and they **left** off building the city.

．．

9 Therefore <u>it</u> **was** called Babel,
   because there the LORD **confused** the language of all the earth;
   and from there the LORD **scattered** them abroad over the face of all the earth.

Finally, use different coloured pens to mark similar words and phrases. In this example, we have already noticed the important verbs ('migrate' and 'settle', 'make bricks' and 'build', 'scatter' and 'confuse') and subjects ('the whole earth', 'they', 'the LORD' and 'the city'). Now, using coloured pens, we identify other recurrent words and phrases. Here they are: 'the whole earth' or 'all the earth' (vv. 1, 4, 8 and 9, in each of the sections), 'language' (vv. 1, 6, 7 and 9), 'city' and 'tower' (vv. 4 and 5) and 'building' (vv. 4 and 8).

The passage is divided in half by the almost exact repetition of 'scattered abroad upon the face of the whole earth' at the end of v. 4 and 'scattered them abroad over the face of all the earth' at the end of v. 9.

Here, without using any other study aids, we are already able to identify the shape of the passage, and have a sense of how it is organized (initial situation v. 1; human action in vv. 2–4 opposed by the LORD in vv. 5–7; the LORD's response to the human desire to make a name for themselves; vv. 8–9 outcome and commentary. We have identified also the main themes of the passage through noticing the focus on the actions of settling, building and scattering and we know this is a passage about humans and God.

Discourse analysis alone cannot tell us what this information meant to earlier readers, nor what it might mean to us, but it does help us begin to grasp the text for ourselves. This is essential if we are to avoid preconceptions or rely on others to tell us what it means. For example, there is little or no indication that the human desire to build arose from a deliberate attempt to oppose or emulate God. The text states that it arose from the builders' desire to make a name for themselves and their fear of being scattered.

But the text also indicates that the LORD opposed this. As interpreters we are now left to seek the answer why. To do so, we have to move beyond looking at the surface of the text to listening to the story which it tells. This involves a shift of perspective from looking at the passage from the outside to looking at it from within. Note that we are still looking at it in its final form.

Moving from linguistic to literary approaches

The other major synchronic approach to the passage is to read it as literature. Literary criticism helps us to answer all sorts of questions about a text. What is the place of this passage within the biblical book as a whole?

What sort of writing is it? Is it history or legend, for example, and how does that affect the way we should read it? What techniques are used to portray the characters? How does the writer try to persuade his/her hearers to think or act in particular ways?

While it is useful to ask such questions of smaller passages, such as Genesis 11.1–9 above, literary approaches are particularly helpful for understanding longer passages, of which there are many in the Bible, for example in the books of Judges, Samuel and Kings in the Hebrew Bible, or in Luke-Acts, 1 and 2 Corinthians, Hebrews or Revelation in the New Testament. Literary criticism, in the sense that we use it below, has been very helpful in allowing Bible interpreters to see larger patterns and relationships within and between books of the Bible.

Narrative criticism

Literary criticism is a general term for a wide range of critical approaches which read the final form of the text from the perspective of particular groups of readers. It includes such reader-orientated methods as deconstruction and reader-response criticism (Gunn, 1999, p. 210) that we will look at in Chapters 4 and 5.

Here we use narrative criticism to focus on 'the story being told' (Soulen and Soulen 2011, p. 134). Narrative criticism in this narrower sense asks us to identify the plot, the characters, the place and time of the events presented, and so on. It attends to the way the story is told, the author's perspective as revealed within the text, and indicators of what the author expected of the readers. As much of the Bible is in the form of narrative, narrative criticism is an important tool for biblical interpretation.

Narrative criticism aims to help us be better readers. It sets aside most historical questions about the origins and development of the text: authorship, readership, time of writing, reasons for writing and so on, and focuses on getting into the story itself. It requires us to begin with the obvious: to read them as narratives. This is not 'the whole story', but unless we read stories as stories, we will never hear the whole story!

Narrative criticism is best kept simple. Alert watchers of thrillers on film or TV already have all the necessary skills. For the sake of completeness, here is a fairly full list of the kind of things that narrative critics look for when reading (see Powell 1999, pp. 244–8).

Plot   The ordering of events is important because narratives normally expect readers to bear in mind what has gone before, and to anticipate what might happen afterwards. Sometimes events are presented out of order for dramatic effect (many film thrillers do this). In addition, narratives emphasize some events by giving more detail, or by repeatedly describing them. Think of the expansion of detail in the gospel passion narratives. It is important to notice the links between events, both forwards and back; and where and when the events take place. A person takes off their clothes. It is important to notice whether this is just before taking a bath, or just before giving a business presentation.

Most good narratives involve conflict, and there are many examples of this in the Bible. What will God do after Adam and Eve disobey? Will Moses get the people out of Egypt safely? Will Pilate acquit or condemn Jesus? Sometimes the narrative resolves the conflict, at other times it leaves us to fill in the gaps. The incomplete ending of Mark's gospel begs the question: did Mark intend this, or has some of the manuscript been lost?

Characters   It is essential to identify who the characters are in a narrative. Again, if we think of television drama or live theatre, the TV guide or programme will list the characters as an aid to the intended audience. Such guides tell us who the characters are, listing them in order of appearance or importance. We expect these characters to develop through what happens in the narrative. Minor characters often do not develop and may be portrayed in a stereotypical way: tough policeman, anxious mum, and so on.

So, for example, if you were studying characterization in the Gospel of Mark, you would look at: Jesus, the Roman and Jewish authorities, the disciples (the Twelve and other friends and followers) and the people (the crowds, the 'common people', and the multitudes). You would notice that Mark allows them to develop as characters as the gospel unfolds. Other things that affect how we understand characters are: their viewpoint or motivation; whether they are named or unnamed; their place in society; what they say and do; and what others say and do to them; and, how they respond to the central characters in the story.

> **Try it out**
>
> Watch a TV drama or sitcom and explore the characters and characterization.

The narrator   Narratives have narrators. Narrative criticism is not concerned with who actually constructed the narrative historically, but with whose voice is heard within the narrative. Even a narrative that has been built up from the contributions of many authors and written sources over a long period of time will have one or more perspectives. Narrative critics attend to the values, beliefs and views of such 'implied authors'.

Remember that the perspective of the implied author may or may not be trustworthy. Even in the Bible we need to remember that the perspective of the narrator of biblical texts cannot always be relied upon. As we have already seen in the example from Genesis 11.1–9, God often appears as a character in biblical narratives. Literary critics do not agree on whether God's viewpoint is normative for truth, as Mark Allen Powell asserts (1999, p. 246). By raising the question of the reliability of perspectives within narratives, narrative criticism invites readers to make their own considered judgements about these matters on the basis of their reading.

In literary criticism the narrator is the 'voice' within the narrative telling the story. The actual identity of the person or persons who wrote or compiled the narrative is a different historical question which does not affect this. In fact, books of the Bible often fail to name the author explicitly. In addition, ancient writers sometimes wrote pseudonymously, that is using the names of more famous biblical characters. This practice is found in the Hebrew Bible (for example, Daniel), the Apocrypha and Pseudepigrapha (for example, the Wisdom of Solomon), the New Testament (for example, 2 Peter) and the New Testament Apocrypha. This was not done to deceive readers but to honour and extend the teaching of the person whose name was used. For example, by writing in the name of the apostle Peter, the author of 2 Peter claims to be a faithful mediator of the apostolic message (Bauckham 1983, pp. 161–2).

Literary strategies   As with all literature, biblical narratives use various literary devices in the course of telling their stories. They may describe symbolic language, actions or locations. In Genesis 11, what do the people in Babel mean when they say, 'Let us make a name for ourselves' (v. 4), what does their city with its tower with its top in the heavens symbolize, and is Shinar a significant place?

Narrators may also use irony. In the Babel story, the actions of the builders of the city and the tower achieves the exact opposite of what they intended. They are scattered. They make a name for themselves, but it is not the sort of reputation they wanted.

Biblical narrators often use 'intertextuality'. This technical term simply recognizes that narratives often assume that their readers are familiar with other texts and stories both within and outside the Bible. The gospels assume that their readers know many parts of the Hebrew Bible and the stories of Elijah in Kings echo those of Moses, for example. Narrative critics draw attention to such intertextuality, and suggest that this points to the narrative unity of larger blocks of text, such as from Genesis to 2 Kings.

Implied readers and the narrative world   Narrative critics identify the persuasive thrust of a story by using the concept of 'implied readers'. As with the implied author, this refers to an aspect of the narrative itself. The idea of a narrative's implied readers helps us to consider the way a narrative appears to expect readers to respond to its story, and how it tries to shape the beliefs and perceptions of its readers (Soulen and Soulen 2011, p. 134), even if this is not what happens in reality. Once we become aware of how a text is trying to persuade or direct us, we are in a better position to decide whether we want to go along with this process, or resist it.

As readers we need to distinguish the 'real world' from the 'narrative world' which is presented in the text. The narrative world is constructed by the person telling the story and is shaped by his/her values and beliefs. Think, for example, of the narrative world of a romantic novel or film: true love wins through in the novel or film in ways that don't often happen in the real world. Individual narrators may follow or depart from such conventions in constructing the particular narrative world of the story they are telling.

A worked example: Paul's shipwreck in Acts 27

In the example below we use the account of Paul's shipwreck near the end of the Acts of the Apostles to test out our understanding of narrative criticism.

Please read Acts 27. (The most fundamental principle of biblical criticism is: first read the passage for yourself!) You might note that it is part of a wider narrative unit that runs on to Acts 28.14, ending, 'And so we came to Rome'. On the face of it, this is just a vivid account of a shipwreck that could have been summarized in a few lines, as Aharoni does: 'Though late in the season, the captain decided to brave the weather. After passing Crete, the ship was caught by a tempest near the Adriatic Sea and was shipwrecked at Malta' (Aharoni 1968, p. 248). Instead of such a summary, Acts 27 offers a dramatic, first-person description of a life-changing event.

Looking at the events, we see that the story moves quickly towards the drama of the shipwreck. The trip from Sidon to Fair Havens is described quickly, then a note of urgency and danger intervenes – 'much time had been lost'. Paul advised the centurion to wait, but his advice is not followed and the ship heads out to sea, soon to be caught in a violent storm, vividly described in vv. 14–20, 27–30 and 38–43. Between these passages are two passages in which Paul assures them that they will be safe. Verse 43 ends with the whole party safely washed ashore.

The chief characters in this narrative are Paul and Julius, the centurion in charge of him. No others are named, though the narrative speaks throughout of 'we' and 'they'. God never speaks and is only mentioned, by Paul. Julius protects and cares for Paul at the start and the end of the chapter, yet fails to listen to Paul at a crucial moment in v. 11. This failure raises the theological question of providence, which is relevant to this narrative, because this story claims to describe real events. It could be argued that God would have saved and protected Paul no matter what the centurion decided. But the characterization does not stress this. The vividness of the narrative suggests that the centurion's failure to listen to Paul cost everybody dearly. Paul himself is presented only through direct speech, speaking with calm faith. When the sailors feel safe they do not heed his words, but, amidst the storm, they receive and obey his guidance.

The narrators here are just identified by references to 'we'. Their observations are important. They describe the journey in vivid but neutral detail, using language showing some knowledge of seafaring. The only glimpse of a personal viewpoint is given in v. 20, when the narrators concede that in the midst of the tempest 'all our hope of being saved was at last abandoned'. Thus, the narrator's perspective is disclosed obliquely, suggesting that people of faith share the same difficulties as other people, and that the faith of some offers resources which can benefit all. The indirectness of this perspective makes it seem all the more persuasive – a clever apologetic strategy on the part of the author.

Apart from the use of direct speech and the careful descriptions of the journey, seafaring and weather, the narrative uses other literary devices, particularly in the frequent references to time and motion. During the storm, Paul and his fellow travellers are outside the normal conditions of life. In vv. 27–43, the focus zooms in on the events of a single night. This slowing of time is a feature of the Greek novels of the same period, where narrators move from summaries, to scenes and into close-ups, using direct speech (Holgate 1999, pp. 56–60).

Finally, who are the implied readers? At the time Acts was written there was a great appetite for adventure stories that included accounts of shipwrecks. This chapter seems to have been written with such readers in mind, in the hope that they might be moved by Paul's bravery, generosity and faith.

Diachronic approaches

The word 'diachronic' means 'through time'. 'Diachronic' approaches to interpretation all look at changes in a text over a period of time, looking at how it was formed, rather than how it is now. These tools should be used after some synchronic work on the text. Every text deserves to be read carefully and attentively before questions are asked about where it came from and how it came to be the way it is. In practice, it is all too easy to be side-tracked by historical questions and to fail to read the text for ourselves, or to lose confidence in our ability to read it.

Despite the logical force of the argument that we should always begin our interpretation by studying the text synchronically, for much of the twentieth century interpreters began by looking at biblical texts historically. The books of the Bible are very old and nearly all of them have a complex history of development, so interpreters do need to think about the formation of biblical texts, including considering the 'ingredients' woven into it, whether and when it was edited, and when it reached its final form.

Historical approaches to the text fall logically into three areas. The first area looks at how the text developed until it reached its final form. This cluster of methods is known as historical-critical exegesis. The second area works towards establishing the most accurate example of this final form by studying the history of its transmission through the manuscripts that survive today. This work towards the reconstruction of the final form is known as textual criticism. In terms of the history of the text this stage comes after looking at its formation, but because it is necessary to get as close as possible to the final form of the text historical criticism normally begins with text-critical questions. The third area of historical study considers the impact history of the text. It looks at how it has been received and interpreted through the centuries and all the ways in which these interpretations have affected the world.

Using the original languages

Obviously, the best way of reading a biblical passage is in the original language. This will be classical Hebrew or Aramaic for the Hebrew Bible and *Koine* (common) Greek for the New Testament. Hebrew is a member of the Canaanite family of languages, a group of Northwest Semitic languages. Most of the Hebrew Bible is written in classical Hebrew, hence its preferred name. From the post-exilic period onwards (sixth century BCE), the closely related language of Aramaic replaced Hebrew in public use because it was the administrative language of the Persian Empire. Hebrew continued to be used for religious discussion and worship, but various dialects of Aramaic replaced Hebrew in everyday life. The New Testament contains a number of Aramaic words, and it is likely that some dialect of it was Jesus' home language. Thus, the two languages of the Hebrew Bible are the products of the social and political worlds in which the texts arose.

The same is true of the Greek of the New Testament. It is a simplified, colloquial Greek dialect called *Koine*, which developed through the spread of the Greek-speaking empire of Alexander the Great and his successors. The linguistic history of the world in which the Bible arose thus affects our interpretation of it. For example, scholars are still not agreed on whether Jesus spoke only Aramaic, or *Koine* Greek as well.

As for all literature, texts in their original languages contain layers of complexity and meaning that are not apparent in translation. Because 'meanings have words' rather than the other way round, there is seldom a direct translation for a word in another language. So, for example, a word in English will have several different translations into Greek, all with slightly different emphases, and a word in Greek may be translated by several different words in English, but none alone will capture the complete meaning of the word. Sometimes biblical writers use subtle word play to make their point and footnotes to English translations will draw your attention to important examples of this. For example, Amos 8.1–2 records a pun on the similarity of the Hebrew words for 'summer fruit' (*qayits*) and the 'end' (*qets*). Translators may try to reproduce this in English, for example, by playing on the English words summer and summary execution, but much word-play cannot be reproduced in translation.

Choosing a translation

If we have not had the opportunity of studying Hebrew, Aramaic or Greek, we have no immediate alternative but to study the Bible in translation. English speakers are fortunate in having many translations available to them, so the question then becomes, which one should be chosen for study? The *New Revised Standard Version* (1989) is generally regarded as the best English Bible translation to use for this.

It is the latest revision (hence the words New Revised in the title) in a tradition of translation which goes back to the *Authorised Version* (1611). Therefore there is a family likeness between this translation and earlier versions. Later revisions such as the NRSV make use of advances in textual criticism, and are not just more modern English translations. That is they both reflect modern English usage and are based on more faithful reconstructions of the original Hebrew, Aramaic or Greek texts. Note too, that the Authorised Version of the Bible was translated from later and less-reliable manuscripts, and so it should not be regarded as a reliable translation for the purposes of exegesis (see the following section on textual criticism).

The NRSV is a scholarly translation, which seeks to be faithful to the best modern critical editions of the Hebrew Bible and Greek New Testament, without consciously making translation decisions in favour of particular doctrinal positions, as some other translations do at times. It also makes moderate use of inclusive language, translating the Greek word for 'brothers' as 'brothers and sisters'. This is not a perfect solution. Sometimes it can be misleading, as when it hides the specifically gendered nature of some biblical arguments.

We should never rely on one single translation when studying the Bible. While using the NRSV as a base text, we should compare it with other modern English translations. We might also want to look at Bible versions which offer a dynamic equivalent paraphrase into contemporary language, such as the *Good News Bible* and *The Message*.

> **Try it out**
>
> Compare the NRSV translation and *The Message* paraphrase of Psalm 1. What emphasis and insight does each version offer?

It is also very helpful to consult Bible translations into any other modern language that we might know. This enables us to spot aspects of the text which are not evident in English, such as the distinction between 'you' (singular) and 'you' (plural) in languages where different words or forms are used to distinguish between singular and plural. Words in another language often have different resonances. For example, in Spanish translations, John 14.6 reads, 'Yo soy el camino, la verdad y la vida', and these words (camino, verdad, vida) may provoke associations with Latin American solidarity movements seeking justice and truth, thus offering an alternative interpretation to the dominant western focus on whether this verse suggests only Christians can be saved.

Being aware of text-critical issues

Textual criticism has two aims: to reconstruct the original version of the biblical text and to trace the history of transmission of the text. Neither of these goals can be finally attained, yet the work of textual critics forms the foundation for all Bible translation and interpretation. It offers a disciplined approach for looking closely at how the books of the Bible have been copied and re-copied, and provides information about (mostly small) variations between such copies at different times and places. In this way it offers us a unique window into how texts were read (and 'corrected') in earlier periods.

It is the oldest of the historical approaches to the text and in some ways the most difficult. It requires not only a sound knowledge of the biblical languages, other ancient languages into which the Bible was translated, such as Syriac, Coptic, Ethiopic and Old Latin, but also an understanding of associated matters, such as the physical properties of ancient manuscripts, how scribes and copyists worked and how scrolls and books were made, used and circulated. For these reasons, most biblical interpreters need to rely on the work of specialist scholars. Even interpreters who are able to read the Bible in the original Hebrew or Greek use critical texts which are themselves the fruit of centuries of careful textual criticism. These critical editions offer careful reconstructions of the most likely original forms of the biblical books, with extensive footnotes indicating where manuscripts differ from the text they have adopted.

For the Hebrew Bible, the critical text in use by scholars and translators is the *Biblia Hebraica Stuttgartensia*, (2nd edition, 1977), but textual critics are currently working on the *Biblia Hebraica Quintai* (due to be completed 2020). For the New Testament, the critical text is the *Novum Testamentum Graece*, edited by E. Nestle, B. and K. Aland, J. Karavidopoulos, C. M. Martini and B. M. Metzger (27th edition, 1993).

While checking textual variants is an important exegetical step, for everyday interpretation all we need to do is remember that no-one today has access to the original copies of the biblical books, and we are all dependent upon the painstaking research of textual critics. They have provided us with texts which are extremely faithful to the earliest existing manuscripts and these texts can be trusted as providing a sound basis for further critical study. Modern translations of the Bible use these modern eclectic reconstructions of the originals.

For practical purposes, when we work on an exegesis from a modern translation like the NRSV all we need to do is note any footnotes to the passage. If there are any, these either reflect different possible translations of the original Hebrew, Aramaic or Greek, or variations between different manuscripts. Remember that textual criticism itself does not deal with modern translation variations. It is concerned solely with the question of deciding which of the variations between manuscripts is more likely to reflect what was originally written. If the footnote does identify a variant, usually with the words, 'Other ancient authorities add/omit . . .', the textual criticism section of a critical commentary sets out the pros and cons of such variation(s).

Textual criticism (like all critical work) is an art which is developed through practice and experience. For this reason, interpreters should usually be willing to be guided by the conclusions of experts. The experts are usually willing to indicate their degree of certainty about their conclusions, as in the textual commentary edited by B. Metzger, which classifies each judgement listed in the commentary with the letters A, B, C or D, where A indicates certainty, B a high degree of certainty, C doubt about which variant to choose, and D that none of the variants are likely to be original (Metzger 1994, Introduction, p. 14).

Metzger's *Textual Commentary on the Greek New Testament* provides enough information for most everyday exegesis of the New Testament and is an essential tool for studying books of the New Testament which have a complicated textual history, such as the Acts of the Apostles. There is no similar reference work for the whole of the Hebrew Bible, but critical commentaries provide full discussions of text-critical matters and there are guides to textual criticism of the Hebrew Bible (Brotzman 1994) and guides to using the *Biblica Hebraica* (Wonneberger 1990).

> **Try it out**
>
> Look at the text of the Lord's Prayer recorded in Luke 11.2–4 and look at the footnotes to the NRSV. Identify which refer to text variants and which suggest different translations. Where the differences are between manuscripts, the longer version of the Lord's Prayer found in Matthew's Gospel (Matt. 6.9–13) was and still is more widely known. The text-critical guideline of preferring the shorter reading means that this text does not include the longer variant readings of some manuscripts, such as 'Our father in heaven' and 'Your holy spirit come upon us and cleanse us'.
>
> Incidentally, this example helps us see the point of all historical criticism, which starts with textual criticism. We need the tools of historical criticism to answer important questions like: If the gospels record two versions of the Lord's Prayer, which is closest to the prayer Jesus taught? By what processes, and for what reasons, did the Gospels of Matthew and Luke develop these two different versions of that original prayer?

The history of the language being used

In our discussion of discourse analysis above, we found that by paying close attention to the text we were able to identify key words. Look back to your study of Genesis 11.1–9 and make a note of the main verbs (in bold) and subjects (underlined) there. These important words guided our synchronic reading of that text.

A historical approach now asks: What do we need to find out about the history of these words and word patterns to deepen our understanding of the passage? To think historically about them, we ought to think of the words in the original Hebrew. If we cannot read Hebrew, we need to consult commentaries written by those who do.

If we are able to read Hebrew or Greek, or at least know enough to use theological dictionaries and lexicons, we can look up the key words in the passage. This will enable us to ensure that we are sensitive to the particular meanings that are, and are not, likely to be represented by them. For example, what is the significance of the pun on the Hebrew word for 'confuse' (*balal*) in Genesis 11.9 and the name of the tower (Babel)?' To take a New Testament example also beginning with 'b', the meaning of the Greek word translated 'barbarians' in Romans 1.14 does not have the same strongly negative connotation that it has in modern English. Paul simply uses it as a dismissive Greek expression for non-Greeks, which imitates what a foreign language sounded like to them: 'bar-bar'.

Interpreters need to be meticulous about locating the meaning of words in their historical context. It is not responsible to review all the possible meanings of a word and then to translate it with the one meaning that most closely suits your purpose! Because words change their meaning over time, we need to find out what a word was likely to mean and imply at the time it was originally used. If the text has a long history of development, we will also need to consider possible shifts in the meaning of the word at the various stages in the formation of the text, for example, where an older text has been woven into a later one, or edited for a new purpose.

> **Try it out**
>
> Make a note to yourself to see how commentators either are, or are not, sensitive to thinking historically about the meanings of words and ideas in Genesis 11.1–9. For example, do they consider *making a name for oneself* to be a good or a bad thing? Does this phrase mean that the people in the narrative wanted to be remembered (that is, not completely forgotten) or famous (better remembered than others)? There is no simple answer to this question, yet it is necessary to make a decision about this in order to offer an interpretation of that passage.

Form criticism

We have already seen that in order to read a passage sensibly we have to make a preliminary judgement about what kind of literature it is. That is, we need to identify its genre. Broadly speaking this means registering the obvious: for example whether our passage is a historical narrative, a parable, an apocalypse, a gospel, a letter, or whatever. Such a general identification is essential for any literary approach to a passage.

It is also essential for thinking historically about the passage: people don't write gospels today, so we have to think historically about the common features of this genre for those who wrote gospels. What conventions governed their construction and interpretation at the time they were originally written and read, or spoken and heard? However, even a genre as familiar as a letter needs to be thought of historically, because the conventions governing the structure and contents of letters were different in the Hellenistic world of the first century CE.

Determining the genre of a passage is part of form criticism. But form criticism also asks historical questions of biblical texts: is there any evidence that all or part of the passage first existed in an oral form before being included within this written document, and can we identify the actual situation (*Sitz im Leben* is the technical German term) where and when this oral form might have been used?

In trying to answer these two questions, form criticism builds on the answers already offered by synchronic readings of the text about its structure, shape and genre. Often an analysis of the structure reveals elements which suggest their earlier use elsewhere, whether in oral or written form, such as proverbs or hymns. Other examples of pre-literary forms or patterns include laments, parables, proverbs, laws, tales, myths, legends, 'call' stories, beatitudes, healing stories, nature miracles, resurrection accounts, creeds, slogans, blessings and curses.

In this brief outline of form criticism, we come up against an issue which recurs throughout this book: should methods of interpretation developed at particular times for particular purposes continue to be used in changed circumstances? We ask this because methods of interpretation are naturally affected by the spirit of the age in which they arise. Form criticism rightly reminds us to consider the relationships between the genre, the shape and the function of units of tradition, particularly units of tradition which appear to have been shaped by oral usage. However, older examples of form criticism of the New Testament were unduly limiting when they assumed that units of oral tradition mainly arose in worship situations ('cultic occasions'), such as baptisms, the Eucharist and sermons (Berger, in Hayes 1999, p. 414). Older examples of form criticism have also been accused of 'historical scepticism and sociological determinism' by assuming that communities adapted and even generated tradition to suit their immediate needs (Muddiman, in Coggins and Houlden 1990, p. 242).

Clearly we should not assume a simple, direct relationship between the forms of units of oral tradition and their origins and purposes. Yet, such objections should not prevent you from using form-critical questions to gain insights about the oral basis of much of the Bible. It does contain oral traditions which were both as fixed and as influential upon the faith of the first readers and writers as popular hymns are upon people today.

Form criticism today is more focused on the literary structure and genre of a passage, than on hypotheses about when and where the oral unit might have arisen or been used historically. The structure of the unit helps us to identify where it starts and finishes, and the genre may be obvious from the content and structure. For example, the hymn in Philippians 2.6–11 is clearly evident as a distinct unit, with a separate structure and feel from the surrounding material. It is harder to say where this hymn came from and how it was first used, though form critics may make some proposals. More important for our purposes, is noting where, how and why these oral units are included in the final text we have.

> **Try it out**
>
> Read Deuteronomy 26 and identify the earlier confession of faith incorporated in it. How does your identification of this earlier oral tradition affect your reading of this chapter? Consider why the prophets and priests who assembled Deuteronomy might have wished to include this creed here.

Source criticism

All that we have said about the importance of thinking about genre, shape and function is relevant to source criticism too. As the oldest of the historical critical tools (excluding textual criticism), it has a long and distinctive history of development. Like form criticism, it also raises a simple and crucial question about the composition of a passage: does it incorporate any pre-existing sources? While form criticism looks for evidence of oral sources, source criticism looks for evidence of written sources. If it finds evidence of these, it seeks to classify them according to genre, and ask where they come from, what their perspective is, and why the author has incorporated them within the passage under consideration.

When we identify a written (or oral) source, it is important to note that it may well have a different character from the passage in which it is now embedded. It may, for example, have a different view of God, or embody a different ethical principle. The next question that arises is: why would an author incorporate a passage expressing views that differ from their own? There are various reasons for this. They may wish to show their awareness of other views, or show their respect for older traditions, in order to gain the sympathy of their readers. Whatever the reason for this, when authors create texts from other sources they raise questions in the minds of readers about the author's own perspective.

Well-known examples of multiple source usage in the Bible are the Pentateuch, in which a number of sources have been detected, and the Gospels of Matthew and Luke, which each appear to use Mark's Gospel, together with another hypothetical written source, known as Q, and possible written sources of their own, which are tagged M and L for short. This data alone shows that source criticism is an important tool for biblical interpretation. This also creates problems for those who wish to interpret the Bible literally, resulting in questions such as: Which of the two creation narratives in Genesis 1-2 describes how God actually created the world? Did Noah take two pairs (Gen. 6.20) or seven pairs (Gen. 7.3) of every kind of bird into the ark?

Try it out

Using a Gospel parallels book or online resource, compare Jesus' teaching on divorce in Matthew 5.31–32 and in Luke 16.18. These passages have some shared features that suggest a common source.

First, note the common features (and that a related passage in Matthew 19.19 relates better to Mark 10.11–12) and judge for yourself whether these do imply their use of a common source.

Then, consider the very different use made of this material in

> Matthew and Luke. What does this tell you about their different concerns and emphases? For example: why does Luke tuck away this unit of tradition amidst a large section on the use of riches, while Matthew embeds it within teaching on anger, lust and oaths? In Matthew's mind, is looking at a woman lustfully the same kind of adultery as marrying a divorced woman? In Luke's mind, is the abuse of riches far more important than the question of divorce and adultery? This question of the theological interests of the different gospel writers is dealt with further by redaction criticism (which we look at below).
>
> Finally, notice how this historical thinking makes it clear that it is not easy to say 'what Jesus actually taught' on this topic. Similarly, notice the way source critical analysis distances you from feeling the persuasive force of each narrative. Does this matter?

Tradition criticism

A further dimension of how texts use traditional material is considered by tradition criticism. While traditions are relatively fixed, they also change and develop over time: for example, consider how and why patterns of shared family meals have changed over a generation. Tradition criticism traces the development in traditions over the period before they become incorporated into the passage under consideration. Hebrew Bible scholars have tended to use tradition history as an overarching method to trace all the developing stages of the text from early parallels in other cultures and religions to the place of the tradition within the biblical canon.

Gnuse (in Hayes 1999, vol. 2, p. 586) applies the five stages of tradition history analysis to the story of the call of Samuel (1 Sam. 3). He shows how this story can be fitted into wider and wider cycles of tradition or narrative. To get the most from his example, as always please read the passage first.

- Analysis of comparable prophetic narratives and dream reports from other literature of the Ancient Near East offers examples of similar experiences to the one recorded in 1 Samuel 3, especially night-time prophetic dream

reports at shrines in Mari (1800 BCE) and auditory message dreams from Egypt and Mesopotamia.
- Form criticism of the passage indicates that vv. 1–18 contains the original form of the text, identifies literary devices in the plot development (for example, contrast between the aged Eli and the young Samuel, and the threefold call pattern which heightens suspense). Similarities between this and other call narratives in the Hebrew Bible (such as Moses in Ex. 3 or Saul in 1 Sam. 9) are noted. In contrast, 1 Samuel 3.19—4.1a seem a later editorial comment.
- The passage is then located within the wider context of 1 Samuel 1—3. This larger narrative cycle compares the young Samuel with the evil priests of the time and has common themes with the Elohist cycle in the Pentateuch which also has auditory message dreams, a positive view of prophets and a distrust of priests. This larger unit of tradition is then located within a wider narrative cycle about the rise of the monarchy (1 Sam. 1—15). This further supports the view that prophets are better than kings, a view which seems to come from the final Deuteronomic editors. In this way, 1 Samuel 3 can be seen to play an important role in stressing the authority of the prophetic word.
- The whole Deuteronomistic History can then be related to the theological themes of the entire Hebrew Bible and the contribution of 1 Samuel 3 can be related to them.

New Testament scholars also recognize the importance of tracing lines of development within important New Testament traditions, for example in the words of institution that Paul passes on regarding the Lord's Supper.

Try it out

Compare the forms of wording of Jesus' institution of the Lord's Supper in Mark 14.22–25 and 1 Corinthians 11.23–26 below.

What are the differences between them, and how would you account for them? 1 Corinthians was written in 56–7 CE and Mark about 10 to 15 years later. Can we talk about the development of this tradition over such a short time, or are the differences between these two uses of the tradition more determined by the theological purposes of the two writers?

1 Corinthians 11.23–26	Mark 14.22–25
23 For I received from the Lord what I also handed on to you, that the Lord Jesus on the night when he was betrayed took a loaf of bread, 24 and when he had given thanks, he broke it and said, 'This is my body that is for you. Do this in remembrance of me.' 25 In the same way he took the cup also, after supper, saying, 'This cup is the new covenant in my blood. Do this, as often as you drink it, in remembrance of me.' 26 For as often as you eat this bread and drink the cup, you proclaim the Lord's death until he comes.	22 While they were eating, he took a loaf of bread, and after blessing it he broke it, gave it to them, and said, 'Take; this is my body.' 23 Then he took a cup, and after giving thanks he gave it to them, and all of them drank from it. 24 He said to them, 'This is my blood of the covenant, which is poured out for many. 25 Truly I tell you, I will never again drink of the fruit of the vine until that day when I drink it new in the kingdom of God.'

Redaction criticism

The final stage in the historical development of a text is the revision work done on it by later editors. Redaction criticism arose as a reaction to the tendency of form criticism to fragment biblical texts into small units. It attempts to redress the balance by considering the whole picture, looking particularly for evidence of the perspective of the final author(s) or editor(s) in the way the work has been shaped and assembled.

Redaction criticism arose particularly out of gospel research, by looking closely at the final form of the gospels. It looked at how the writers of the three synoptic gospels had assembled the oral and written traditions they had inherited and added to these, to present their own perspective on the life, death and resurrection of Jesus. Redaction criticism looks for the theological perspective of 'Matthew', 'Mark' or 'Luke' by noticing what editorial changes they have made to the material they have inherited, what additions they have made and what changes they have made to the order of the materials they have received. By considering the additions and changes made by the final writer(s) or editor(s), redaction criticism is able to identify the theological emphases and convictions of those responsible for shaping the final form of the text.

> **Try it out**
>
> Compare the two passages from Mark 6 and Luke 9 below with two redactional critical questions in mind. First, note what changes Luke makes to the Marcan tradition which identifies John the Baptist with Elijah. Next, try to suggest why Luke might have made these changes (Soulen and Soulen, 2011, p. 178).
>
> ### Mark 6
>
> *14* King Herod heard of it, for Jesus' name had become known. Some were saying, 'John the baptizer has been raised from the dead; and for this reason these powers are at work in him.' *15* But others said, 'It is Elijah.' And others said, 'It is a prophet, like one of the prophets of old.' *16* But when Herod heard of it, he said, 'John, whom I beheaded, has been raised.' *17* For Herod himself had sent men who arrested John, bound him, and put him in prison on account of Herodias, his brother Philip's wife, because Herod had married her.
>
> ### Luke 9
>
> *7* Now Herod the ruler heard about all that had taken place, and he was perplexed, because it was said by some that John had been raised from the dead, *8* by some that Elijah had appeared, and by others that one of the ancient prophets had arisen. *9* Herod said, 'John I beheaded; but who is this about whom I hear such things?' And he tried to see him.

Notice that redaction criticism works with little clues or hints. Here it probes the text for hints of what Mark and Luke respectively thought of Herod, or what the people believed about the resurrection of the beheaded John, and in what respects they thought that Herod (or the people) thought that John (or Jesus) was the new Elijah. What this process reveals is that Luke's view of how Jesus' ministry is related to that of the line of prophets is different from that of Mark.

Historical background

This discussion of redaction criticism concludes the range of diachronic critical methods that are normally termed historical-critical. However, there is a wide range of information which interpreters need to assemble if they are to apply these methods in an informed way. Often a circular approach has to be adopted here, namely, the interpreter begins by tentatively locating the formation period of the text and then adjusts this in the light of information yielded by historical critical research.

For all texts that claim to describe historical events, other dates have to be considered, such as, the time when the events described took place, the period(s) in which the passage was first spoken, then written and later edited. It may be that the passage was edited to address issues relating to a much later time than the time of the original events or the time(s) when it was first written.

For passages with lengthy development histories, interpreters need to consider the relevant background information for the whole periods. For the Hebrew Bible, see *The Old Testament World* (2005) by John Rogerson and Philip Davies; or Lester L. Grabbe's *Ancient Israel: What Do We Know and How Do We Know It?* (2017). For New Testament studies, the best single volume is Everett Ferguson's *Backgrounds to the New Testament* (3rd edition, 2003). A more detailed publication is the two-volume *The Biblical World*, edited by John Barton (2002).

Such general volumes need to be supplemented by books on Israelite history, and the history of the world in the Hellenistic era for the intertestamental and New Testament period, the geography of the region, and books on the social, economic, political, cultural and religious world of the Ancient Near East. For this purpose a bibliographic guide is helpful, such as *An Annotated Guide to Biblical Resources for Ministry* by David Bauer (2011).

When it comes to specific passages, we often need to refer to more specialist reference materials too. For example, for Acts 27 we need to know not only about the geography and archaeology of the relevant places in the Mediterranean, and first-century seafaring practices, but even about the conventions of the Hellenistic novel. The Greek novel *Chaereas and Callirhoe*, written roughly at the same time as Acts, gives one a good idea about sea travel in the first century. Such primary sources also give modern readers a helpful window into the popular mind of the first century CE.

Social scientific approaches

Social scientific approaches use the tools and assumptions of the social sciences to understand the social dimension of the Bible more accurately. The most traditional way of doing this is to retain a historical approach to the text. Social historians seek to build up their understanding of the social world of the texts through a close reading of the text read against the background of information from traditional disciplines such as ancient history, classical studies and archaeology. In this way they build up an informed but limited idea of the social worlds in which the texts were written, edited and used. This social-historical approach to the world of the Bible has much to commend it as a focus, as the work of New Testament scholars such as Abraham J. Malherbe on the Thessalonian letters (1987, 2000) or David Aune on Revelation (1997–8) shows. Malherbe's comparison of Paul's approach to pastoral care with those of other moral teachers of the time, for example, shows Paul to be consistently mild and self-giving in a way that moral philosophers would have considered to be dangerously close to compromising their integrity (Malherbe 1987, p. 109).

However, other scholars criticize this approach for being neither social nor historical enough. These scholars use methods borrowed from the social sciences – sociology, cultural anthropology and psychology – to do social-scientific criticism of the Bible. While still remaining interested in history, these approaches read the text using modern social scientific methods. They differ from the older social history method by being synchronic. They take snapshots of the complex web of relationships between social actors in the text, and look for meaning in the 'complex web of culturally-determined social systems and patterns of communication' between them (Barton 1995, p. 69).

Sociological critics are interested both in the social background of the text and what it describes, and the social context and location of the initial author(s) and their audience(s). Greater knowledge of the social context has moved biblical interpreters away from seeing simple parallels between the Bible and their own context. Such critics also ask questions about the social function of the text: for example, does it appear to encourage social conformity or try to resocialize its readers?

Anthropological critics use models drawn from anthropology to study phenomena in the Bible such as social structure, myths, magic or sacrifice. Jerome Neyrey (1988), for example, uses a model developed for studying societies in which witchcraft accusations occur to shed light on Paul's relationships in Galatians, providing new insight into Paul's provocative language in Galatians 3.1, 'You foolish Galatians! Who has bewitched you?'

Fewer critics have used psychological models to interpret the Bible. Gerd Theissen, a pioneer of sociological approaches, was one of the first biblical critics to draw upon models from the psychology of religion to interpret Paul's theology. He used learning theory, psychodynamic models and cognitive models to interpret Romans 7 and 8. Learning theory showed that, through Christ, Christians could 'un-learn' their anxiety response to the law; psychodynamic theory helped to show how Paul's encounter with Christ enabled him to face repressed conflict; and cognitive models showed that when Paul understood his inner conflict in a new light, he was able to change (Theissen 1987, pp. 222–75). Further illustrations of this approach can be found in *Psychological Insight into the Bible: Texts and Readings* (Rollins and Kille 2007).

Margaret MacDonald argues that models derived from the social sciences can be effective thinking tools:

> They can bring hitherto unconscious levels of thought into awareness; they enlarge our control over data. Models can also facilitate understanding for the [modern] reader by clearly identifying the writer's frame of reference and by making it more readily available for criticism. The use of models can lead to greater comprehensiveness when doing interpretations by providing categories and suggesting relations between categories. (MacDonald 1988, p. 26)

Social scientific models can therefore be used to fill the gaps in the often limited historical information we have about what life was like, say, in the cities and churches of Paul's day. Clearly the success of this approach depends on the appropriateness of the model being used and the amount of data available. Critics of this approach warn that models developed on the basis of social interactions today may be anachronistic. There are also concerns that social scientific approaches do not work well when interpreting narratives that describe unusual or unique events, such as Moses' encounter with God on Sinai or Jesus' resurrection.

There is a further ideological concern. The social sciences are rooted in the Enlightenment view that we should not understand human behaviour, even religious behaviour, with reference to belief in God. Stephen Barton points out that this ideological framework prefers to account for theology and religion as 'the products of other forces and interests, whether the human unconscious (Freud), economic relations and class interest (Marx), the maintenance of society (Durkheim), or the legitimation of patriarchal domination (feminism)' (Barton 1995, p. 76). While these kinds of ideological challenges are helpful, and often provoke fresh insights, we should be aware that the secular ideological roots of social scientific approaches to the Bible can downplay some issues of prime importance to biblical writers, such as a character's encounter with God.

Social scientific approaches are diverse and controversial, but they have deepened our knowledge of social aspects of biblical texts: the material culture (such as food, clothing, work and institutions); the social history of groups; the social organization of movements; and their social worlds (Soulen and Soulen 2011, pp. 195–7). Many biblical scholars draw information from all four of these research areas, without necessarily applying social science methods rigorously. Their use of insights from social scientific approaches is eclectic, intuitive and pragmatic. For most, sociological models are suggestive, rather than analytic tools, and they continue to rely heavily on historical criticism to verify their findings.

For the practical task of biblical interpretation, social scientific approaches offer two other benefits. They remind us that the original authors and readers of the Bible lived in a material world, and so do we. They also remind us that our own experience of reality, including our experience of reading and interpreting the Bible, is socially constructed.

> **Try it out**
>
> Baptism is a central initiation ritual for Christians, and there are a number of descriptions of its significance in Paul's letters, for example Romans 6.3–12, 1 Corinthians 6.9–11 and Galatians 3.26–9.
>
> Read one of these passages, noting that social-scientific criticism would bring questions such as these:
>
> - What did this rite look like in action, and what would members of the Roman, Corinthian or Galatian churches understand by it?
> - What social relations (internal relations, boundaries and the like) was this rite used to promote?
> - What interpretation does Paul give to this rite?
> - How does the Christian's participation in this rite shape or reinforce his or her experience of everyday life, worldview and priorities?
>
> This exercise is adapted from David de Silva's *Introduction to the New Testament* (2004, p. 631) which contains many useful examples of exegetical methods and a number of worked illustrations of social-scientific readings of New Testament texts.

Impact history

So far, we have looked at tools for reading a passage in its final form and tools for tracing the history of its formation. As a historical discipline, textual criticism serves both of these approaches because it is the tool we rely on to provide us with a copy of each book of the Bible which is closest to what the authors wrote.

Before we leave diachronic approaches, however, there is one further aspect of the history of the text that we need to note. That is the effect that biblical texts have had on people down the centuries since they reached their final forms. All great works of art and literature have such an impact history, which is more than a history of interpretation. Think for example of the difference between musicological study of the roots of Elvis Presley's new brand of rock and roll, and the effect that his music, and the rock and roll it gave birth to, has had on the world since the 1950s.

The critical tools we have used so far have produced a variety of results, and have all tended to keep the text at a distance. Discourse analysis and literary criticism are both rather analytical, though they can give us the satisfaction of feeling that we are reading the text attentively. The historical critical approaches all look 'behind' the text for information about the text, rather than allowing the text to speak for itself. While recognizing the value of this historical information, many Bible interpreters today have become dissatisfied with this distancing effect. There has been a shift of interest away from looking 'behind' the text to looking 'in front' of it: to what the Bible has meant and said to people down the centuries.

Impact history (sometimes known by the German term *Wirkungsgeschichte*) is the study of all the different ways in which each passage of the Bible has been received and has influenced human life. As such, it is clearly a way of looking at the Bible, rather than a method for interpreting it. It explores how the Bible has influenced human history and the ways in which all sorts of people, known and unknown, have contributed to this process through the centuries. Precisely because of its breadth, impact history has the capacity to draw in a wide range of data that is normally excluded by other approaches to biblical interpretation. One way of handling this quantity of material is by focusing on a particular strand of impact history; for example, Christopher Rowland's work on Revelation (1998, with Kovacs 2004 and 2005) pays close attention to the book's impact on western art.

At the end of the last century, Markus Bockmuehl wrote that impact history was one of the few contemporary approaches to the New Testament that was able to integrate the academic study of the New Testament and prevent it from 'going down the plughole' (1998, pp. 295–8). Similarly, the Swiss scholar Ulrich Luz included a major focus on impact history (sometimes called the history of effects) in his commentary on Matthew's gospel (2007, 2001 and 2005), showing that social and political circumstances have always affected how the Bible is interpreted and that these interpretations in turn affect the course of history.

Impact history shows us that interpreters frequently do not prefer the plain meaning of the text, and asks us to consider why this should be. By making us face the fact that all biblical texts have had a wide variety of interpretations through history, it supports the postmodern view that texts have many possible meanings. At the same time, it moderates this view by showing that there are limits to the range of meanings of each text. Texts can be interpreted in more than one way, but they also robustly resist being assigned arbitrary or alien meanings. Impact history shows both that differing circumstances reveal different aspects of the range of meaning within a text, and that some attempts to assign meanings beyond this range have been later shown to be irresponsible and illegitimate.

As an approach to the interpretation of the Bible, impact history is helpful in moving us back to the question of why we are interpreting a passage. Seeing the range of possible meanings that a passage has had over its history, we are forced to make a decision about which interpretation we prefer, at least for here and now. By alerting us to the effects that good or bad interpretations have had on human life, they also require us to consider the implications of our preferred interpretation for the world or the Church. They require us to take responsibility for the consequences of our interpretations. We cannot claim to be merely disinterested scholars. As we shall see, when we look at Scriptural Reasoning in Chapter 5, such awareness is particularly important when we are reading the Bible with people of other faiths.

Impact history works with three hermeneutical principles: the context of interpreter is important; interpretations in turn affect the context in which they are made; and human history, the history of the text and the text itself should all be valued. It shows that interpreters often adopt interpretations which cannot be defended on historical-critical grounds. Overall, it gives abundant proof that the meanings of texts are profoundly affected by the identity and purposes of those using them.

Try it out

The Internet is a good place to get an initial impression of the range of effects of a biblical passage. If you review the results of a search for 'the good Samaritan', you will discover that:

- It is the name of many caring institutions: hospitals, churches, crisis centres and service organizations in the United States and Canada, usually with a Christian foundation.

> - There are many paintings representing this parable: e.g. the painting by Hogarth (1737) that hangs in St Bartholomew's Hospital, London.
> - It is the basis of a number of urban legends, following a similar format in which a mechanic helps someone whose car has broken down as an act of kindness. Having reluctantly given the person their name and address, they learn later that the person in distress was very rich and are sent a large reward.
>
> There are some common features associated with the impact history of the phrase 'the good Samaritan'. The main effect of this parable seems to have been to inspire acts of compassion and care. The key question by which these results should be evaluated is: do they intensify or help to focus or direct this important effect? For example, it should be able to explain that disinterested compassion is a core value of the parable, and in this respect the urban legend fundamentally misunderstands it.

Whether we try this out with a well-known or little-known passage, we may be surprised to notice that many older Bible commentaries pay almost no attention to impact history. However, newer commentaries do refer to it, or make it a major focus. Apart from Ulrich Luz's work on Matthew's gospel, the *Blackwell Bible Commentary* series is devoted entirely to this approach.

Not surprisingly, there are some difficulties with it. The main ones are:

- how to select and order the vast amounts of disparate material and how to evaluate interpretations;
- whether to include interpretations that are clearly wrong or immoral (for example, the many anti-Jewish statements found in biblical interpretations of late antiquity and the medieval periods);
- and how to ensure that each commentary is more than just a catalogue of effects and actually sheds light on the biblical text.

Despite these problems, many researchers and readers find it deeply satisfying to explore the moments of performance or impact when biblical passages meet the world.

TOOLS FOR EXEGESIS

> **Try it out**
>
> Investigate the impact history of a Bible passage for yourself. Remember that impact history is not a method or tool, but an approach to the Bible. It invites us to come to it with more of ourselves: 'The understanding of a biblical text happens not only through the elucidation of its statements but beyond that by practising and suffering, by singing and poetry, by praying and hoping.' (Luz 1989, p. 98)

The impact history of the Bible reminds us that Bible interpretation is a relational task in that it is done by, with and for others. Our interpretations should 'help others to experience joy, freedom and identity' and also help them 'in their external needs, in their hunger and sufferings' (Luz 1994, p. 94). To help us do this, the next chapter offers us ways of looking more closely at ourselves and others.

4

Our Reality

Reading the Bible well requires understanding not only what we are reading but who we are as readers. We have to learn to read ourselves as well as the text. This chapter offers some ways into thinking about the way we create the meaning of a text as readers; our identity as readers; where we read from; and the communities with whom we read. We end the chapter by encouraging reading the Bible across different identities, contexts and communities, in order to benefit from the many meanings we create as readers.

This chapter, therefore, is about asking the necessary questions of ourselves as we stand before the text, recognizing how:

> different readers, shaped in diverse ways by the interaction of such variables as religious tradition, gender, national origin, race and ethnicity, socio-economic class, political affiliation and a host of comparable social factors, attribute multiple and even contradictory meanings to the 'same' biblical texts. (Stone 2002, p. 78)

> **Try it out**
>
> Think of a recent film you have seen and discussed with other people. How did your interpretation of the film differ from theirs? Consider how your own life experience influences your interpretation of films.

The role of the reader

The importance of the reader in biblical interpretation has become more widely recognized in recent decades. Biblical scholars, especially those using literary and contextual approaches, are concerned with who is doing the reading as well as what is being read, recognizing that the meaning of any text depends on the reader as well as the writer.

Reader-response criticism

As we noted in Chapter 2, the Bible is dependent on people to open, read and respond to it. Reader-response criticism is interested in the process of reading, and recognizes the work the reader has to do to make sense of the text. The meaning of the text emerges through reading and is therefore reliant on the reader as well as the text. From this perspective, the reading of the text is an activity in which the reader has a vital role to play, from making literal sense of the text, to supplying gaps in the narrative and ironing out repetition (Gillingham 1998, p. 183). As you will already be aware, this book accepts many of the assumptions of reader-response criticism, including a concern for the ethical responsibility of the reader in their meaning-making.

Readers' expectations and life experiences guide their reading of a text in many ways. They may linger with one aspect of the story more than another or make a moral judgement based on their own value system. Gina Hens-Piazza notes also the role of the reader in character formation, describing the text version as 'only an initial draft' (Hens-Piazza 2003, p. 11) from which the reader builds up a fuller picture. She suggests this process happens more often with minor characters who have only a few lines in a story since there is more scope for the reader's imagination. The reader reads ideas and associations into the story to flesh out such characters. However, Hens-Piazza and others argue that characters cannot be moulded into any shape we choose, since the text and its context set limits to our interpretation (Hens-Piazza 2003, pp. 12–13).

The obvious implication of reader-response theory is that each new reader responds to the text differently, creating the possibility that a biblical passage has more than one meaning, or no stable meaning. Among reader-response critics, there is a divergence of opinion as to whether the biblical text is free to be interpreted without constraint, or whether it had a meaning for its original audience, one which should be given precedence today (Soulen and Soulen 2011, pp. 175–6). As we shall see in Chapter 5, some scholars believe the meaning of the text is fluid and wholly dependent on its readers, none of whom are able to give a definitive reading. But if a text can be interpreted to mean anything, on what grounds can a reading community (such as the academy or a faith community) challenge inaccurate or harmful readings? A helpful overview of these and other debates within reader-response criticism is offered in the article 'Reader-Response Criticism' at Oxford Biblical Studies online.

> **Try it out**
>
> Read 1 Corinthians 12.14–31. How would you test the validity of new or divergent readings of this passage? Are there any boundaries to interpretation and if so, what are they?

Reading for ourselves

Tiffany and Ringe (1996, p. 25) encourage us to begin our journey with the Bible 'at home', paying attention to our own situation first. What are the defining characteristics that give us our unique shape? How do we identify ourselves when others ask us, 'Who are you?' There are so many different elements to our identity; some we are comfortable talking about, and others we hide.

> **Try it out**
>
> Begin by listing, in no particular order, the different ways you describe yourself. You can include anything you like – serious or silly, something quite unusual or something you share with millions of others. This is just a quick identity sketch that only you need to see. Once you have spent a few minutes on this, read through your list and see if there is anything that surprises you. Have you forgotten anything important?

In 2006, Rachel made the following identity sketch:

> I am a feminist; a Wolves fan; of white ethnic identity which awards me unearned privileges in life; I'm still listening to Radio 1; a vegan; my theological perspective is most influenced by Latin American liberation theology; I wear glasses.

Working on the revision of this book in 2018, Rachel observed that while some aspects of her identity have remained consistent, others have changed or become less significant, describing herself thus:

> I am a feminist, in it for the long haul; from Wolverhampton and in recent years deeply aware of the value I attach to being a European; I love that I can speak Spanish; I'm of white British ethnic identity which awards me unearned privileges both at home and around the world; I tend to listen to Radio 6 music; a vegan; my theological perspective is most influenced by Latin American feminist theologies; I wear glasses.

Not all of these characteristics will have equal bearing on her reading of the Bible, but all shape her perspective in some way or another. She will be able to see some things in the texts more clearly because of her identity and experience (provided she's wearing her glasses!) and other aspects of a passage will remain hidden or irrelevant to her.

Randy Litchfield points out that our identity provokes both contact and distance between people since:

> identity forms at the boundaries and intersections of social locations as much as at their centers.... Individuals uniquely embody the intersections of many social locations. Thus, difference among individuals is a given. Yet people *do* share particular social locations with others, which suggests commonalities. (Litchfield 2004, pp. 232–3)

Some aspects of our identity are more likely to create wider connections with others (for example, our gender) while other more unusual qualities mark us out as different, until we encounter others who share those specific marks of identification (such as left-handed people).

There are three more things to note about this self-identification process: we identify ourselves differently depending on where we are, who we are with and for what purpose we are being asked; we can never fully describe ourselves (and similarly, we can never adequately sum up the reality of another person); we are always all, and more than, our defining characteristics.

We have multiple and fluid identities that develop through time and experience. To illustrate this, Robert Beckford draws parallels between identity formation of young people in New York City and the technical layering of sounds within hip hop. Sounds are built up to create a new track, just as young people deconstruct and mix up traditions and cultures to form new identities (Beckford 2001, p. 106).

In this section of the chapter we focus on five key aspects of our identity that have been recognized as affecting our interpretation of the Bible in recent years: gender, sex and sexuality; ethnicity and colour identity; age, ability and well-being; socio-economic status and political commitments; and denominational, spiritual and theological traditions.

Despite the multi-faceted nature of our identity, any one person is only able to read from one place at a time. Yet for a long time, western biblical scholars, predominantly white men, failed to acknowledge the restricted nature of their readings until liberationist movements, through naming their own location, forced them to recognize their specific identity. Even then, some theologians failed to fully acknowledge their particularity. For example, early feminist theology was primarily based on the experience of middle-class white women and it was only through painful dialogue with black and Asian women that this was properly acknowledged. Soulen and Soulen note how readers who explicitly identify their location believe they are less vulnerable to ideological distortions (Soulen and Soulen 2011, p. 1).

Many first-world theologians and biblical scholars have come to recognize the importance of naming their location. One example would be Eleanor Haney, a theologian who lived and worked with church communities in Maine. Shortly before she died, she described herself in the following way:

> I am white, of northern European ancestry and culture, female, academically trained with a Ph.D., in a lesbian relationship, a member of a largely white and middle-class Protestant denomination, from a lower-middle-class background, sixty-five years old, representative of the culture's understanding

of mental and emotional normalcy, physically able-bodied, and an easterner who deeply loves the ocean. (Haney 1998, p. 6)

Moreover, she noted: 'As a white middle-class Christian feminist, I can only do white middle-class Christian feminist theology and ethics. My experience and perspectives, though limited, can nevertheless contribute to a larger, rainbow-hued understanding of justice, theology and ethics' (Haney 1998, p. 1). Haney recognized the demands that her location placed on her theology and the authority that came from an authenticity of place. In locating the particularity of her interpretation, she enabled her contribution to be an honest part of the dialogue between people of different locations.

From a different location, Gale Yee reflects on her own gradual integration of multiple aspects of her identity into her work as a biblical scholar, as over time she came to identify within her academic work as an Asian American feminist and class activist. Such awareness helped her to see connections between the portrayal of the biblical character of Ruth, and how Asian-Americans are problematically viewed as both 'perpetual foreigner' and 'model minority' (Yee 2006).

It will be obvious from these two examples that the different aspects of each person's identity cannot be isolated from each other, but are united in a single individual. Intersectional theory, which builds on the work of African American legal scholar, Kimberlé Crenshaw (1989), draws attention to the complex, interdependent and fluid nature of identity and structures, as well as forms of oppression and resistance. Biblical scholars who are intentional in naming their own context and identity are increasingly aware of the need for an intersectional approach, which takes account of intersections of power across gender, ethnicity, sexuality and other aspects of identity (for example, see Randall C. Bailey, Tat-siong Benny Liew and Fernando F. Segovia, *They Were All Together in One Place: Toward Minority Biblical Criticism*). However, for simplicity in the following sections, we will focus as far as possible on one element at a time.

We turn now to a closer examination of each of the five areas of identity listed above, recognising that it is artificial to treat each characteristic separately, since we retain all these aspects of our identity at all times.

Gender, sex and sexuality

> **Try it out**
>
> At the beginning of each of these five sections, you are encouraged to reflect on some aspect of your identity. For this section, you will find it helpful to note down a description of your gender identity, expression, biological sex and sexual orientation, all of which may be more fluid and contested than commonly assumed. A helpful resource to explore these aspects of your identity is the *Genderbread Person* resource kit, developed by activist and educator Sam Killermann. How do you feel about these aspects of your identity? How do you think they might affect your reading of the Bible?

We cannot read the Bible as non-specific human beings, but only as people of a particular biological sex, gender identity, expression and sexual orientation. Our embodied readings might result in some readers being better able to understand the experience of the women with haemorrhages (Mark 5), and others more able to relate to the discussion concerning male circumcision in Galatians. This does not prevent insights that cross such boundaries, for example both men and women can relate to a biblical passage that describes hunger or friendship or joy – although there will no doubt be nuanced understandings of even such a basic human experience as hunger (for example, in many western societies, a man might consider hunger through the lens of pressure they may feel to be the 'bread winner' and a woman might reflect on established, if contested, female roles of cooking food and providing nourishment).

Dominant interpretations of the Bible restrict roles for men and women, and offer fixed ideals of male and female identity; notably in dominant readings of Mary, the mother of Jesus, that work to encourage sexual purity and sacrificial motherhood among Christian women. Furthermore, texts such as the Household Codes (Col. 3.18—4.1; Eph. 5.22—6.9; 1 Pet. 2.13—3.7) have been used to prescribe a hierarchical model of gender relationships. Readers may need to search out alternative role models, even crossing gender lines to discover new ways of being. In Chapter 5, we will explore further how feminist and womanist scholars have challenged dominant readings of gender roles and relationships in the Bible and its interpretation.

The biblical texts are dominated by male characters, with fewer women named or given speaking roles. Unfortunately, the marginalization of women continues in many societies today. Women have pushed for greater representation in politics, the Church, culture, etc. In film, for example, the Bechdel test is used to challenge women's continued underrepresentation. To pass the test, a film must have at least two named women in it, who talk to each other about something other than a man (Bechdel 1985).

> **Try it out**
>
> How many books of the Bible pass the Bechdel test? Were you surprised at what you discovered? How might you as a reader of the Bible increase the visibility of women in the text for yourself and others?

Women and lesbian, gay, bisexual, transgender, queer or questioning, and intersex plus (LGBTQI+) people often have to imagine themselves into the biblical text. This has led to a greater alertness to minor characters caught in the shadows of the stories. One example of this is the reclaiming of Hagar (Genesis 19—21) as a central biblical character within womanist theology, particularly through the work of Delores Williams (1993).

Another example is the work of queer interpreters (the description chosen by many LGBTQI+ readers) in calling attention to visible sexual outcasts in the Bible such as eunuchs, Nehemiah being one example of a character who may be identified as a eunuch through his role as a cupbearer (Neh. 1.11). Eunuchs are also considered potential ways into the text for intersex readers, particularly those 'from birth', who, with other eunuchs, are lifted up as an example of discipleship through their location on the margins of power (Matt. 19.12; DeFranza 2014, pp. 55–7, 68). In addition, gay and lesbian biblical scholars have argued that the relationship between David and Jonathan or Ruth and Naomi may have included a sexual dimension. Goss and West note the need to be:

> resistant readers who struggle against heterocentric privilege that erases us from the text. As queer readers, we want to befriend the Scriptures to find

our voices and allow subversive memories and diversities to emerge. (Goss and West 2000, p. 6)

In Chapter 5, we have the opportunity to explore further some of the methods and insights offered by queer biblical interpretation.

There is no shortage of male characters within the biblical text! But it was not until the work of scholars such as Randall Bailey, David Clines and Stephen Moore in the 1990s that masculinity within the text began to be explored. Building on feminist and womanist studies, these scholars recognized that male characters in the Bible needed to be seen as men rather than as normative humans (Smit 2017, p. 2). As a still emerging discipline, we might wonder what kinds of questions scholars ask about the portrayal of maleness in the Bible. A particular focus has been certain male characters (especially David and Jesus). In addition, scholars have sought to understand models of masculinity present within ancient Israel and early Christianity, how these related to neighbouring societies, and what opportunities for subverting and resisting such models existed (Moore and Anderson 2003; Creanga 2010). More recent studies have explored how gender intersects with ethnic identity, age, sexuality and social status.

Biblical texts have been used to legitimate certain models of masculinity (the authoritative patriarch, heroic leader, strong warrior, etc.) often through inaccurate simplistic interpretations of the Bible (Moore 2014). Rather than accept such limited and limiting models, we might do better to recognize the dynamic, complex models of masculinity present in the Bible, developed by marginalized communities in relation to dominant imperial powers, and in relation to a God who is often portrayed as 'hypermasculine' (Smit 2017, p. 67; Moore 1996; Sawyer 2005).

Studies of masculinity within the biblical text might help us resist normalizing maleness and masculinity within either text or our own contexts. They might help us to ask questions about gender roles and relationships. They should certainly invite us to challenge readings of the text that portray Abraham, David or Paul as uncomplicated heroes and models of faith. It is better to allow such characters to be flawed individuals who wrestled with their own gender identity and role, as we as readers might also. Finally, they might help us explore some of the challenges facing men today, including in some western societies issues such as poor mental health, loneliness and violence. One example of this might be David Tombs' (1999) exploration of Jesus as a victim of sexual violence.

In comparison to studies of masculinity within the biblical text and its reception, feminist and womanist interpretation of the Bible is well established in breadth and depth. Early survey works include the North American one-volume *Women's Bible Commentary* (first published 1992, revised edition, 2014), and a similar project by German scholars, *Feminist Biblical Interpretation: A Compendium of Critical Commentary on the Books of the Bible and Related Literature* (first published in German 1999, English publication 2012). A number of long-term projects enable deeper analysis, notably: Athalya Brenner's edited *Feminist Companion to the Bible* series and the Society of Biblical Literature's series, *The Bible and Women. An Encyclopaedia of Exegesis and Cultural History*, each volume of which is published in German, Italian, Spanish and English. Finally, the *Wisdom Commentary* series published by Liturgical Press seeks to offer diverse feminist and womanist perspectives on every book of the Bible, with each commentary including insights from several contributors.

Such approaches seek to honour women's diverse experiences, both within the text and among the community of readers. They demonstrate a greater awareness of the silences within the text, and a sustained interest in marginal characters and stories. When lived experiences and commitments are not reflected in the Bible, feminist and womanist scholars may draw non-biblical texts and traditions into the conversation, as we explored in Chapter 2 when thinking about extending the canon. There is a strong commitment to exposing and challenging violence within texts and interpretations. Perhaps most controversially, feminist and womanist biblical scholars, including those of faith, are more willing to deny the validity of a biblical text if it is experienced as oppressive. Finally, there is often resistance to fixing an interpretation, and instead the offering of tentative, open-ended conclusions.

Wilda Gafney's *Womanist Midrash* project offers plentiful examples of such approaches. Gafney explores Torah and throne texts (from Samuel and Kings), seeking out women characters, and reviewing legal teaching concerning women's lives (Gafney 2017). She asks questions both about the women within the text, and of black women readers of the Bible, seeking out, or creating fresh interpretations that reveal and challenge inequality and oppression, and which enable the texts to function as God's life-giving word for black women today (Gafney 2017, p. 8). In dialogue with Jewish midrash, Gafney seeks to hear the voices of silenced characters. Thus deep in the heart of Numbers (23.46), we are invited to meet Asher, a woman who the Rabbis suggested lived for generations and led

Moses to the bones of Joseph, and who, Gafney notes, made a name for herself without becoming a wife or mother (Gafney 2017, p. 165).

We can take one further example to illustrate some of these points. Joy Mead is a member of the Iona community and her poem on the story of Shiphrah and Puah (Ex. 1) explores how the midwives open up possibilities of acting differently from what was expected, collaborating rather than competing, 'trusting vulnerability' and disobeying orders (Mead 2002, pp. 43–4). Mead's reading of the story draws out the possibilities available to us when our power seems to be restricted. It encourages us to question dominant thinking and to see disobedience as a valid ethical choice. Mead explores how these two women worked together to ensure the survival of the babies and asks how we might also be midwives to hope through small everyday actions.

> **Try it out**
>
> Read through a text you are working on and note down any ways in which you think your interpretation is affected by your gender, sex and sexuality. At the time of writing, David tried this out with Isaiah 66.6–14, a passage set in the lectionary for the day, and he was struck by the deep relevance of this issue. With reference to your own passage, or this one, consider the following questions. What is hidden? What aspects of the text are brought into focus? What conversation about this text would you want to have with someone of a different gender identity, expression, biological sex or sexual orientation?

Ethnicity and colour identity

> **Try it out**
>
> At the start of this section you are encouraged to spend time thinking about your ethnicity and colour identity before reading on. You might also want to explore your nationality and family background. How do you feel about these aspects of your identity? How do you think they might affect your reading of the Bible?

The importance of ethnicity is demonstrated in a comment by Ghanaian theologian Mercy Amba Oduyoye: 'I am first and foremost an Akan, a member of a matrilineal society speaking the language of Akan . . . In fact it is as an African that I am a Christian' (Oduyoye 1990, p. 245). For Oduyoye, her ethnic identity is primary, even mediating her relationship with God. However, many white, western Christians are not used to thinking about their ethnic and colour identity and might struggle to describe how it influences their reading of the Bible. If white people do have any ethnic awareness, it tends to be accompanied by guilt about their own or others' racism or denial that it makes a difference to their interpretation. The predominantly white ethnicity of biblical scholars from the dominant tradition has been hidden but has nevertheless had a huge impact on the way the Bible has been interpreted and taught. Randall Bailey warns fellow African Americans:

> we read the text with the interests of whites, who are our oppressors, in mind. We, who have had our land stolen and have been enslaved by the people who stole our land, read the promise to Abraham to be given someone else's land and don't see our own story. We identify with Abraham. (Bailey 1998, p. 78)

How then does our ethnic identity shape our reading of the Bible? Again, we note a few suggestions of how this aspect of our identity might influence our interpretation. To begin with, an awareness of ethnic identity (particularly for white people who have been socialized into assuming they do not have a skin colour) should help readers acknowledge the ethnic reality of the biblical context. The ethnic identity of biblical characters and communities can go unnoticed unless the text reports a conflict situation between different ethnic groups. But the Bible is not without place. Its context is North Africa, Asia, the Middle East and, in later New Testament texts, some southern Mediterranean regions. For white European readers, recalling this geographical reality should guard against the domestication and Europeanization of the Bible.

While the people at the heart of the biblical narrative are mainly defined by their faith identity, as people of the covenant, as Jews and Christians, it is important to note that they are also defined in other ways. Abram is from Ur, which, if anywhere, is geographically located in modern-day Iraq; Moses is a Hebrew raised with an Egyptian name and family, who marries a Midianite; Rahab of Jericho, Tamar a Canaanite, Ruth a Moabite and the wife of Uriah the Hittite are named in the genealogy of Jesus (Matt. 1); Paul is from Tarsus in modern-day Turkey. Ethnic boundaries are frequently disrupted, those who are ethnic outsiders often bring blessing, offer wisdom or demonstrate great faith. Examples of such characters include the Ethiopian eunuch (Acts 8), the centurion Cornelius (Acts 10) and the Syrophoenician woman (Mark 7). The geographical dispersion of all those who identify as Jews is dramatized by the list in Acts 2.5–11.

Descriptions of ethnic conflict within the narrative will be experienced differently by readers living in regions marked by historic or ongoing ethnic conflict, or who live in what appear to be stable regions, but whose ethnic or colour identity means they have to negotiate hostility and discrimination daily. Such readers may be more alert to the violence and disruption that accompanies such disputes, than those readers whose ethnic identity is perceived as normative or 'national'. Readers might reflect on how the Bible understands the catalyst for division between groups and how conflict is triggered by poverty and exclusion. Within the Bible, the relationship between ethnic groups is ever-changing. The identity of the dominant and oppressed fluctuates throughout biblical history. At times the Israelites are oppressed by imperial powers such as the Egyptians, Babylonians and Romans. But at other times it is they who attack and subjugate other ethnic groups such as the Canaanites or Samaritans. Some communities have found it necessary to read the Bible from a counter-position. Osage Nation scholar Robert Allen Warrior comments that he reads the Exodus and conquest stories 'with Canaanite eyes' (Warrior 1989, p. 262), informed by the traumatic experience of First Nations peoples whose land and lives were taken by Europeans who believed they had been given the 'promised land' of North America. This narrative of conflict and oppression continues into readers' own lives and this should encourage them to explore whether the Bible offers appropriate models of reconciliation (perhaps making use of texts that remind the reader of the gifts of the stranger, such as the book of Ruth; or the claim in Psalm 24.1 that the earth belongs to God; or the focus on unity across difference in texts such as Galatians 3.28).

Anti-Semitism has been a shameful feature of Christian biblical study since early on in the history of the church. Christian readers of the Bible will need to be alert to the impact history (see Chapter 5) of the complex presentation of the Jewish leaders within John's gospel, for example. The village of Oberammergau in south Germany is an example of a community that has begun to critique its anti-Semitic legacy of interpretation. Earlier versions of the Passion

Play (held every ten years in Oberammergau) were marked by anti-Jewish interpretations and Hitler demonstrated his support for the play when he attended a performance in 1934. However, building on changes introduced in 1990, for the performance in the year 2000, the village made use of biblical scholarship to offer a more nuanced and accurate account of Jesus' relationship with Judaism. The millennium version made Jesus' Jewish identity and beliefs more visible, and differentiated between the ordinary Jewish people, and the high priests and Roman authorities who opposed Jesus. Such changes continued in 2010, with Jesus frequently speaking Hebrew, being addressed as Rabbi, and participating in Jewish prayer and traditions (Wright 2011).

Christian and Jewish readers both need to engage responsibly with the doctrine of election, which has been used to justify the suppression of a range of religious and ethnic groups. Readers of dominant ethnic communities and nations need to be alert to the dangers of an uncritical doctrine of chosenness. Yet even within the canon, there is a clear tradition that relates the Israelites' election to a responsibility to serve the wider world. This strand endorses a theology of God's universal care.

Black and Asian Christians suffering under white supremacy have challenged dominant interpretations that have validated racist oppression, for example readings of the curse of Ham in Genesis 9.20–27 that identify Ham as black. These communities have also recovered positive identifications of black ethnic identify. They have argued for Song of Songs 1.5 to be accurately translated as 'I am black and beautiful' rather than former interpretations of the verse as 'I am black but beautiful' (Mukti Barton 2004). There is a counter-tradition of interpretation that upholds the Bible as a source of liberation for groups suffering racism. Randall Bailey notes the long-standing identification of African Americans with the Exodus narrative. He cites as example the spiritual *Go Down Moses* sung by slaves in ante-bellum America:

> When Israel was in Egypt land,
> Let my people go.
> Oppressed so hard they could not stand,
> Let my people go.
> Go down, Moses, way down to Egypt land.
> Tell ole Pharaoh to let my people go.
> (cited in Bailey 1998, p. 67)

To demonstrate further how ethnic identity and inequality have shaped biblical interpretation, we turn to a sketch from the BBC3 comedy *Famalam* in which a white man prays for Jesus to help him. When Jesus appears, the man is surprised to discover he is black, despite, as Jesus points out, the Bible making it clear that he is a Middle Eastern man, unjustly arrested and beaten by government officials, something that rarely happens to white people ('There is no white Jesus', 12 April 2018). The sketch makes the point that Jesus has falsely been portrayed as white over the centuries. How so? Richard Dyer in his book *White* notes how from the Renaissance period, Christ was increasingly rendered as paler than other figures who took on darker appearances, becoming darker the further they were from Christ, both physically and symbolically. This period of art reflected European expansion and conquest of other lands, notably in the Crusades against Arab Muslims. The Crusades added to European associations of white with Christianity and salvation; and black with other religions and peoples, with sin and death. Over the centuries the whitening of Christ increased, reaching a climax by the nineteenth century of a fair-skinned, blond-haired blue-eyed Christ (see Stephen Moore's *God's Beauty Parlor and Other Queer Spaces in and Around the Bible*, 2001). Enlightenment theories placed white-skinned people at the pinnacle of human development. Thus Christ's perfection was taken to mean that he too must be whiter than white. Contemporary readers of the Bible often need to work hard to overcome such racist identifications in their interpretations.

> ### Try it out
>
> Read or listen to a passage from one of the gospels, while looking at a picture of a Christ of a different ethnic identity to you. How is your imagining of the passage transformed? There are several excellent websites offering a diversity of biblical images: for example, Art and Theology, BAME Anglican, and the Asian Christian Art Association.

Black scholars have worked to make visible the African and Middle Eastern context of the Bible (Yamauchi 2004; Adamo 2006). They have interrogated and rejected racist interpretations of biblical texts, used to legitimate enslavement, colonization, apartheid and segregation (Jennings 2017; Thomas 2010; West and Dube 2000; Wimbush 2000). As noted in the previous section, womanist scholars in particular have placed marginal characters central to their work, for example the character of Hagar and the enslaved girl of Acts 12 (Williams 1993; Aymer 2016). Two significant one-volume commentaries or introductions to African American interpretation of the Bible are: *True to Our Native Land: An African American New Testament Commentary* (2007) and *The Africana Bible: Reading Israel's Scriptures from Africa and the African Diaspora* (2009).

Contemporary African-American biblical interpretation seeks to connect the complex and diverse lived experiences of African Americans, with the complexity and diversity of the biblical text, in order to offer relevant, authentic and liberating readings (Smith 2017, pp. 75-6). Womanist scholars Gay Byron and Vanessa Lovelace comment, 'our black bodies and our black lives cannot be left outside of the interpretive process' (Byron and Lovelace 2016, p. 15). From a Black British perspective, Anthony Reddie argues that, 'the realities of black suffering and struggle provide the interpretive framework for how I interpret the scriptures' and encourages readings that are liberative, subversive and holistic (Reddie 2016, p. 153).

Scholars from many global contexts and ethnic identities have considered how their ethnic and colour identity impact on their reading of the Bible. Yet, as womanist scholar Mitzi Smith observes:

> Most mainstream, Eurocentric biblical scholars... explicitly or implicitly exercise the privilege to ignore and/or rationalize racism and its intersecting-isms while doing biblical interpretation and theological reflection. (Smith 2017, p. 50)

There is very little scholarship that directly explores the impact of whiteness on biblical interpretation. One significant contribution is the collection of essays by black and white scholars entitled, *Christology and Whiteness: What Would Jesus do?* (2012), edited by George Yancy, which explores and disrupts the imaging and identification of Jesus with whiteness. In the British context, initial work has been undertaken by David Horrell (2017) on Galatians, Jayme Reaves (2018) on the figure of Sarah as both victim and perpetrator (the relationship between Sarah and Hagar and how it relates to contemporary ethnic divides is also explored in Jewish writer Ruth Behar's essay, 'Sarah & Hagar: The Heelprints upon Their Faces', 1997), and Al Barrett (2018), building on the work of Jennifer

Harvey, on the need for white people to dis-identify with Jesus in order to move from the centre to the margins of the story.

Since whiteness is often hidden within 'western' scholarship, it may be relevant to note the work of white scholars such as Neil Elliott, Richard Horsley, Ched Myers and Leo Perdue on making visible the imperial contexts of the Bible and its readers. Here we might see how white scholars have sought to engage responsibility with political, social and economic dynamics of power, even if they have not focused specifically on whiteness.

How then might white readers of the Bible be alert to this aspect of their identity and related issues of power and privilege? The first step is to recognize that there are few, if any, white Europeans in the Bible! Perhaps some of the Roman characters of the New Testament were of southern European origin but on the whole, white readers need to recognize that they are not the centre of the story. Second, a critical white reading of the Bible needs to challenge historic and contemporary racist interpretations of the text. Third, as we encourage in this book, it is important to engage with a diversity of voices both within the text and interpretation, especially those often not heard. In an article entitled 'Black Scholarship Matters', Tat-Siong Benny Liew notes the paucity of reference to black biblical scholarship in introductory textbooks (Liew 2017, p. 243). This failure of engagement with diverse readings of the text is problematic. Finally, a good question to ask would be how the text might help reveal and challenge unearned privilege and unjust power structures.

> ### Try it out
>
> Read through a text you are working on and note down any ways in which you think your interpretation is affected by your ethnic or colour identity. What is hidden? What aspects of the text are brought into focus? What conversation about this text would you want to have with someone of a different ethnic identity?

Age, ability and well being

> **Try it out**
>
> Begin this section by noting your age, mental and physical abilities and state of health. How do you feel about these aspects of your identity? How do you think they might affect your reading of the Bible?

In the past two decades, there has been significant exploration of how age, physical ability and lived experience may affect a reader's interpretation of Scripture. These characteristics are fluid in nature, since we change physically, mentally and emotionally as we journey through life. This fluctuating element to our identity offers us a number of different perspectives on a passage. We will understand a story differently as a child, a young person, a parent or a retired person. Furthermore our physical and mental state will leave us open to different responses to the text. For example, biblical scholars have begun to explore how texts such as the psalms of lament and the book of Jeremiah might bear witness to traumatic experiences, and thus how they might be read attentive to trauma and recovery (Boase and Frechette 2016).

> **Try it out**
>
> Read one short biblical passage every day for a week. How does your own changing physical, mental and emotional state affect your reading of the text?

We have different needs and desires as we move through different states of age, ability and health. Consider, for example, how mourners at a funeral respond to biblical texts such as John 14.1–7 at a time when they seek comfort and hope; or how the mixed emotions of new parents (joy, trauma, tiredness, pain, hope, etc.) might shape their reading of the gospel infancy narratives. The Bible offers stories about a range of characters and life situations: Samuel, a boy waiting for guidance in the temple; Sarah, an old woman surprised by her ability to have a child; a nameless widow offering what little she had; Elijah, hungry and dependent on the kindness of ravens. While culturally specific, there are few human rites of passage or life stages not reflected within the canon.

Children in the Bible are often overlooked or romanticized, and the same could be said of children as readers of the Bible. Studies of the place of children in ancient Near Eastern, Jewish and Greco-Roman societies have helped clarify and complexify our interpretation of texts in which children are visible (Bunge 2008). While many biblical texts uphold family hierarchies based on age and gender, Jesus' ministry was disruptive of family life and structures, notably in his placing of children at the centre of the community of faith (Betsworth 2016, pp. 1–4). In the Bible, children are longed for and loved, but also rejected and oppressed. They are both in need of knowledge, yet also signs of wisdom (Prov. 8.30–31) and hope (Zech. 8.5). We encounter a variety of child characters in the Bible, often in moments of vulnerability and need, such as Jairus' daughter and Job's children, but also active as leaders and teachers, such as both David (1 Sam. 17) and Jesus (Luke 2.40–52) as boys, and perhaps less well known, the enslaved girl who helps heal Naaman (2 Kings 5).

Moving from text to reader, a number of studies have criticized how children's Bibles and animations over-simplify biblical passages, either because children's capacity for nuance and imagination is underestimated; or in order to make the passage (wrongly) serve a moral lesson, often one that establishes obedience as a Christian virtue, with no awareness of how such teaching can undermine children's ability to challenge abuse (Vander Stichele and Pyper 2012; Dalton 2007).

> **Try it out**
>
> Look at several versions of the story of Jonah in children's Bibles or animations. What is the focus, and where are the gaps in this version of Jonah? Where does the story end, and how does this shape how the message of the book is understood?

The portrayal of older characters in the Bible and the process of aging are also more nuanced and diverse than we might expect. Alongside growing interest in the experience of aging in relation to faith, for example through the work of

Richard Rohr (2012), we might ask whether there are insights to be gained from the Bible. Like the depiction of children, older characters are often portrayed as vulnerable and in need, at the mercy of family members or strangers. Thus for example we read of a blind and aged Isaac who is tricked by his wife Rebekah and son Jacob (Gen. 27). But we also encounter characters such as Anna and Simeon whose age gives them wisdom and insight (Luke 2). Older readers might be drawn to texts that explore reconciliation and blessing in the later part of life, for example the reconciliation of Joseph with his father and brothers (Gen. 46.28–30).

Despite the lasting ability of the Bible to bear witness to the changing nature of human experience, the biblical assessment of different life events may differ from contemporary readers' understanding of similar situations. We may no longer accept the cultural interpretations of the Bible. Children may not be understood as a reward or childlessness as a curse. Few people in western secular society regard disability as the result of sin. As readers therefore we need to negotiate the cultural attitudes of the narrative in order to let it speak to today's context.

Awareness of their physical and mental state should help readers question methods of exclusion practised within the biblical context and employed today. The HIV/AIDS pandemic has created new readings of biblical texts. While some churches have excluded people with AIDS, rejecting them as sinners, others have taken Jesus' special concern for lepers as their model of engagement, exploring texts of healing and community integration, and the need for prophetic voices in challenging the poverty, violence and exclusion that cause and accompany this health crisis (Dube 2003). There is a further example of such a reading in the section on globalization. As another example, the purity laws of Leviticus should alert readers to the dangers of demanding physical perfection and enable them to challenge western society's 'body fascism' and fascination with the beautiful. In the same book, readers might note instruction that people with disabilities are to be cared for within society (Leviticus 19.14; Stewart 2017a, pp. 86–7). And elsewhere readers should note the tradition that chooses the younger, weakest or disabled person over the obvious heroes, for example, the young David is the surprise choice in the search for the new king (1 Sam. 16). What does this tradition suggest to readers of the text?

Readers from different cultural contexts may also have different responses to the healing stories in the Bible. In reading the story of the man with the withered hand (Mark 3.1–6), Tiffany and Ringe suggest that educated western readers apply their medical and scientific world-view to the story and are sceptical about the miraculous nature of the event. Their reading becomes a search for a rational explanation. However, readers from contexts where traditional medicine is practised are usually more accepting of the story and make connections between methods of healing practised in their own community.

Both temporarily and permanently disabled characters can be encountered in the Bible, characters such as Mephibosheth (2 Sam. 4.4), Jacob (Gen. 32.31) and the suffering servant, whose disability is often overlooked (Schipper 2011). Such characters continue to play an active role in the life of the community. Moreover, it may not be accidental that the legal prescriptions concerning bodies (in Leviticus, Numbers and Deuteronomy) are located within a narrative that features a trio of disabled siblings: Moses, Aaron and Miriam. Moses' speech impediment results in his reliance on Aaron; Aaron, a priest whose body continually needs to be ritually purified; and Miriam is inflicted with a skin disease (Stewart 2017a, pp. 79–82, 85–6). Do these characters disrupt some of the boundaries established by the legal codes? In a radical reinterpretation of the significance of disability in the Bible, Sharon Betcher asks whether lameness and other disabilities might be understood as the result of conflict and enslavement and therefore whether it is possible to understand circumcision as an act of solidarity with those wounded (Betcher 2007; see also Raphael 2014, pp. 215–16).

People who are differently abled have provided new insights into these and other passages. Some have argued for the need to take pride in their physical state and the unique insights it offers. For example, John Hull reflects on the insights his blindness have given him as a reader of the Bible in his book, *In The Beginning There Was Darkness: A Blind Person's Conversations With The Bible* (2001a). Elsewhere, Hull explores the impact of realizing that Jesus is blindfolded while he is mocked and beaten by the Roman soldiers (Luke 22.63–5), the 'sighted saviour' becoming for a moment his 'blind brother' (Hull 2001b).

Finally, people with disabilities might challenge the assumptions of the narrator that the goal for each individual is to be able-bodied (Tiffany and Ringe 1996, pp. 182–3). Jennie Weiss Block notes: 'Sometimes people with disabilities feel as though they are objectified in the disability Scripture passages, as if the only purpose they serve is to be healed' (Block 2002, p. 105). Block and others challenge the healing tradition within the church that can lead to judgements on a sick person's faith if they are not healed. She argues the main focus of

Jesus' ministry was the restoration of wholeness to people rather than making people physically better. Block also notes how Jesus' wounds are not removed in his resurrected state: 'He showed his scars openly and without shame for they were, and remain, a sign of his humanity and the fullness of his life experience' (Block 2002, p. 109). As a further example, Elizabeth Lain Schell in her imaginative reading of Luke 13.10–17 suggests that the bent-over woman of the story became so through her attentive care towards her local community and, once healed, mourned the loss of her closeness to the ground. In this reading, the woman says about her healing:

> I'm glad to be straight again, glad to look beyond my home, glad to look beyond the hills . . . to feel the sunshine on my face. But I'm glad to feel my feet upon the ground. Glad to remember to look down now and then and see the things around me . . . I've been here, stooped or straight, looking to God in my different ways. (Schell 1998, p. 52)

Try it out

Read through a text you are working on and note down any ways in which you think your interpretation is affected by your physical and mental state. What is hidden? What aspects of the text are brought into focus? What conversation about this text would you want to have with someone of a different age, ability or state of health?

Socio-economic status and political commitments

Try it out

Describe your social status and economic situation. What are your political beliefs and commitments? How do you think these features of your identity affect your reading of the Bible?

We have already explored how, according to liberation theologians such as Elsa Tamez, 'The poor find that the Word reaffirms in a clear and direct way that God is with them in their fight for life' (Tamez 1995, p. 50). Furthermore, we have observed how liberation theologians argue that reading from the margins enables us to see things hidden from those nearer the centres of power. We have also considered how politics and ideology have shaped the use of the Bible over the centuries. We turn now to a few further examples of how these realities might impact on our reading.

Inevitably, socio-economic context impacts on how we read the Bible, for example readers who have become caught up in a cycle of debt, perhaps through government cuts to benefits and irresponsible loan companies, may be more able to understand the despair of the debtors who feature in one of Jesus' parables (Matt. 18.21–35). There has been much work done on recovering the socio-economic reality of the Bible to help prevent misreadings of the text. We look at these interpretative methods in Chapter 5.

Politicians from across the spectrum value the Bible and even refer to it in support of their (opposing) policies. Some see in the Bible encouragement to be self-reliant and family-focused, while others note the concern for a just and caring society present throughout. Political arguments about the relationship between personal and social responsibility shape the reading of the text. For example, the Evangelical Alliance draws on a range of biblical texts to offer its vision of a loving, just, truthful and free society, seeing in the Bible, teaching around community cohesion, political integrity and freedom of religious expression (Evangelical Alliance 2017). Taking a somewhat different approach, the Joint Public Issues Team, co-ordinating the social policy work of a number of non-conformist churches in Britain, makes use of a range of biblical texts to explore the need for housing reform and better housing provision for those who are vulnerable in society. Drawing on both Matthew 6.25–27 and Isaiah 65.21, the report notes: 'God's vision of society is one where everyone is cared and provided for, not where some place their own needs and priorities above the well-being of all' (JPIT 2017, p. 6).

> **Try it out**
>
> Read Matthew 22.1–14, the parable of the wedding feast. How might a reader's political persuasions influence their reading of this parable? You could think about the different interpretations that may be offered by a monarchist, a republican, a member of the military or a pacifist. Why do you think some interpreters avoid using the term 'kingdom of God?'

Wealth accumulation and possession are regarded in a variety of ways in the Bible, with different voices and perspectives woven through the text. Even within a single book, there is debate over the causes of poverty and appropriate response to those in need. In Proverbs, a book which offers a great deal of instruction about everyday life and relationships, poverty is considered both a sign of laziness and of virtue; an occasion for justice and for charity (Prov. 6.10–12; 14.23; 15.15–17; 19.1; 31.9, 19–21).

To explore some of these themes further, consider how a financially secure person might read the story of Jesus' encounter with the rich young man (Mark 10.17–22). A wealthy reader might be deeply challenged by this story. Jesus' teaching on wealth is consistent throughout the gospels: riches inhibit a person's discipleship. The rich reader might reflect on how their wealth affects their faith journey. How has their wealth enabled or prevented them to live rightly before God?

Yet an American scholar, Sondra Ely Wheeler, argues the New Testament is not anti-wealth. Rather:

> Material wealth is problematic because it is often a hindrance to heeding the gospel; it is dangerous because it is a temptation to the sin of idolatry; it is suspect because it is frequently the result or the means of social injustice; finally, its disposition is a matter of great moral weight, as the response to human needs is a sign of the advent of God's kingdom and the text of love that identifies Jesus' true followers. (Wheeler 1995, p. 134)

Wheeler suggests that if these concerns are adequately dealt with, there is no reason why the rich cannot be true followers of Christ. However, she points out the pivotal importance of sharing resources within the early church and warns affluent communities to take seriously this model of being church.

> **Try it out**
>
> Read through the text you are working on and note down any ways in which you think your interpretation is affected by your socio-economic status and political commitments. What is hidden? What aspects of the text are brought into focus? What conversation about this text would you want to have with someone of a different socio-economic status or political views?

Denominational, spiritual and theological traditions

> **Try it out**
>
> If you belong to a faith community, describe your denominational identity and the spiritual and theological traditions that have shaped you. How do you think these features of your identity affect your reading of the Bible?
>
> While this section is limited to Christian denominations and traditions, Jewish readers will be shaped by their belonging to diverse movements (such as Orthodox, Reformed and Liberal Judaism), and familiarity with a range of spiritual and theological traditions of interpretation. Readers of the Bible who are from other faith or spiritual traditions will bring their own assumptions and approaches to the text, something we explore in Chapter 5 when we consider Scriptural Reasoning.

The attitude of Christians to the Bible is no longer divided along denominational lines, with each denomination encompassing a broad range of theological perspectives. Christians may change denominations as often as they move congregations or attend services at churches of different denominations concurrently. Thus denominational identity has become less significant, at least in the UK. However, denominational tradition and culture may still shape attitudes towards the Bible and key texts within it. Taking account of denominational attitudes towards Scripture increases readers' awareness of the accepted interpretations of a text within a faith community, and whether they wish to question them.

Although all mainstream Christian denominations regard the Bible as authoritative, they differ in the way they relate the Bible to other sources of knowledge. Roman Catholics place greater emphasis on the Church's teaching (tradition) alongside Scripture. Reformed traditions proclaim *sola Scriptura*, although this does not prevent Protestants from bringing the Bible into dialogue with Church tradition and human reasoning. As an example of this, Methodist thinking has been compared to a mobile with the Bible at the centre and the three other elements of Wesley's Quadrilateral (experience, tradition and reason) suspended around the Bible. For Methodist theologian Tom Greggs, the Bible is a text that is first heard and interpreted in the context of the congregation, through preaching, song and prayer, but the reading of which remains deeply personal (Greggs 2016, p. 79). Readers need to take account of such understandings of Bible as a source of revelation and recognize how they prevent or enable dialogue with the text.

Pentecostals consider the Bible to be full of God's potent and transformative word. Members of Pentecostal churches in Britain will usually bring their own Bible to church services, following closely both the passage and preacher. There is a deep knowledge of the Bible, gained through private devotions, small group Bible study, preaching, singing and ministry. Pentecostal Christians often speak of the importance of being guided by the Holy Spirit in their interpretation of a passage, as well as the need to test out insights with the wider community of faith (Bradshaw 2013, pp. 58–9; Archer 2009, pp. 260, 264). Pentecostal interpretation of the Bible is marked by openness to God's powerful presence and action in the world, and a desire to hear how the text speaks into the reader's life (Davies 2009, pp. 219–20, 224). For members of the Windrush generation, and for subsequent generations of black Pentecostals, the Bible has served as a text of survival, offering comfort and encouragement to sustain them in the face of institutional racism. In summary, Cheryl Bridges Johns describes how the testimony of believers is brought alongside the biblical text, in openness to the promptings of the Holy Spirit and with a desire to respond in action (Johns 1998, pp. 139–40).

Each Christian tradition holds some texts closer to its heart than others. These are texts that have been formative in the shaping of the denomination's identity. The Reformed tradition is profoundly influenced by Paul's letter to the Romans, because of its importance in Luther's development of the doctrine of justification by faith. Pentecostals, unsurprisingly, look to the story of the founding of the Church through the coming of the Holy Spirit for their own self-understanding (Acts 2). Roman Catholic identity is embedded in Jesus' confirmation of Peter as the rock on which the church is built (Matt. 16.17–19).

Within each denomination and tradition, creeds, confessions and theological doctrines have a huge impact on readings of a text, although this is often not acknowledged (Stackhouse 2004, p. 188). Walter Brueggemann suggests that the Protestant reformers wrestled the biblical text from controlling church dogma, seeking to discover what was said about God and faith in the Bible, not what the church taught should be said (Brueggemann 1997b, p. 2). However, this moment of emancipation was not sustained and a more open interpretive approach was compromised in turn by the reformers' own theological arguments. A prior commitment to defend church doctrine can prevent us from taking seriously texts that challenge these claims. Brueggemann warns, 'some of the most interesting and most poignant aspects of the Old Testament do not conform to or are not easily subsumed under church theology' (Brueggemann 1997b, p. 106). A similar point is made by Tom Greggs who criticizes efforts to smooth out the complexities of the Bible for the sake of doctrinal clarity (Greggs 2016, pp. 83–4).

Changes in church practice have also impacted biblical readings. For example, new readings of passages relating to the early church have arisen from changing patterns of ministry. The report to the British Methodist Conference (2004) on the diaconate illustrates how developing understandings of this ministry have led to a revision of traditional interpretations of a biblical word. While a deacon's ministry was traditionally associated with humble service, more recent interpretations suggest that deacons in the New Testament also had an ambassadorial role, acting as a bridge builder and provoking change (The Methodist Church 2004, p. 4.5). In this example, ecclesiology influenced the way a passage is read, challenging long-accepted translations of a word in an attempt to free up new ways of ministering in the world.

We conclude this section with a brief word about the impact of spiritual traditions on our reading of the Bible. Richard Foster (1999) identifies six broad spiritual traditions within Christianity: Contemplative, Holiness, Charismatic, Social Justice, Evangelical and Incarnational. We will consider how spiritual practices such as *Lectio Divina* might inform our engagement with the Bible in Chapter 5. For now, let's consider how a spirituality which places holiness at its heart might shape the interpretation of a biblical passage. Methodism has long been influenced by a desire for spiritual and social holiness, and a recent project developed by the Birmingham Methodist Circuit aims to encourage 'Holy Habits' (based on a reading of Acts 2.42–47), including regular Bible study. Study of the Bible, in small groups, is set within a wider context of discipleship and mission. Reading the Bible is understood as formative, both the practice itself and the passages studied.

> **Try it out**
>
> Read through a text you are working on and note down any ways in which you think your interpretation is affected by your denominational identity and theology and spirituality as appropriate. What is hidden? What aspects of the text are brought into focus? What conversation about this text would you want to have with someone of a different denominational, theology or spiritual tradition?

Reading our contexts

This next section explores how biblical interpretation is influenced by our context, where we are located in the world, as well as who we are. By location, we don't only mean geographic location, but more broadly our social, economic and political contexts. In this section, we begin to explore how we might pay attention to our context, exploring its relationships and dynamics in order to discover relevant insights and questions to bring into conversation with the biblical text. All biblical interpretation is contextual: every reader and reading community is located in a particular context. However, in recent decades there has been greater acknowledgement of and interest in the impact context has on the shape, aim and outcome of biblical interpretation.

Social analysis as a resource for biblical studies

In order for us to speak coherently and meaningfully as biblical interpreters, we must try to understand the context for which we interpret. We might think, for example, of the kind of support a local church should offer a family in which the breadwinner has been made redundant through the closure of a local manufacturing plant. The church would need to have some understanding of social and economic issues such as global employment patterns, social security and state provision, retraining and vocation. The community should then be more able to bring the biblical narrative (teaching and stories about work and community) into dialogue with their contemporary social reality.

Joe Holland and Peter Henriot define social analysis as, 'the effort to obtain a more complete picture of a social situation by exploring its *historical and structural relationships*. Social analysis serves as a tool that permits us to grasp the reality with which we are dealing' (Holland and Henriot 1983, p. 15). They further note that such analysis can focus on particular issues, policies or underlying structures. It takes into consideration political order, economic systems and cultural foundations. Social analysts may also consider how the social context has changed over a period of time and what conclusions can be drawn about the possible shape of future social developments.

One of the fundamental differences between liberation theology and classical theology is that liberation theology takes action in the world as its starting point, rather than reflection or theory. Indeed, Gustavo Gutiérrez's *A Theology of Liberation* was heavily criticized for being too concerned with social analysis rather than traditional theological themes. For Gutiérrez, theological reflection is the 'second step' that can only take place after active engagement with the world, or praxis. Contextual theologians today continue to explore their daily reality as a viable starting point for their theological reflections.

> **Try it out**
>
> Look at a publication or the website of one of the following organizations to see how theologians use experience, dialogue and social analysis as a basis for theological reflection:
>
> Church Urban Fund; Circle of Concerned African Women Theologians; Council for World Mission; World Council of Churches.

How then do we accurately read the 'signs of the times' (a phrase popularized by Latin American liberation theologians)? What skills do we need to acquire in order to do this? The see-judge-act method used by liberation theologians arose from Catholic social movements in the 1960s. It begins with being attentive to a situation (sometimes using social analysis tools such as interviews and other methods of data collection). This observation is followed by evaluation and critical reflection, often through a specific lens, such as economic or gender justice issues. Finally an active response is required in order to enable social change. While liberation theologians initially used Marxist theory for their analysis, contemporary social theologians are not wedded to any one method of social analysis.

If this all sounds too complicated, let's take a simple example of social (in this case environmental) observation, analysis and action. Tove Jansson's *The Summer Book* (first published 1973) records the relationship between an elderly woman and her six-year-old granddaughter as they spend the summer on a tiny island in the Gulf of Finland. In the following extract, we have an example of close analysis of the natural environment and human impact on it:

> Except for the magic forest, the island became an orderly, beautiful park. They tidied it down to the smallest twig while the earth was still soaked with spring rain, and, after that, they stuck carefully to the narrow paths that wandered through the carpet of moss from one granite outcropping to another and down to the sand beach. Only farmers and summer guests walk on the moss. What they don't know – and it cannot be repeated too often – is that moss is terribly frail. Step on it once and it rises the next time it rains. The second time, it doesn't rise back up. And the third time you step on moss, it dies. (Jansson 2003, pp. 28–9)

Careful observation and a commitment to the well being of the island enabled the protagonists to make judgements about the actions of the farmers and guests and to modify their own behaviour accordingly.

Beginning with observation

All social analysis begins with careful observation. Paying attention to the world around you is something we all do, but often without noticing, or realizing how it shapes our reading of the biblical text.

> **Try it out**
>
> Think of your day so far. Note down five words that give a snapshot of your everyday reality. What difference might speaking from your everyday experience and surroundings make to how you read the Bible?

Let's look at an example. Preparing a sermon for Epiphany, Rachel began to consider how the story of the magi might be made visible in her local context, a 1950s housing estate. From an observation that the church at the edge of the estate was both named the Good Shepherd and had a single star set on top of its spire, she began to notice other ways in which the story was made manifest in her local context, observing:

> In the windows of the estate houses, the old gold of the Wolves shines out. Triumphs hard won, treasures long sought. Come celebrate with us, they proclaim.
>
> In the doctor's surgery, with its dandelion clock, people bring their ailments and fears, seeking answers and healing balm. Their prayers rising like incense.
>
> In the postman's bag, Christmas cards bring news of the year past. Greetings rewritten, family groups reshaped. We mourn the ones we must leave behind in the old year. Yet our sorrow and thanksgiving accompanies us across the threshold.

And on the lunchtime bus, young mothers, grandfathers and carers arrange babies on their laps, faces hidden in furry hoods and hats. And, with one heart, we lean forward, in joy and wonder, to catch a glimpse of these small treasures.

There is encouragement here to pay attention to both context and biblical text; to see the connections between the two, in small details and grand themes. One method of paying attention that is increasingly popular among theologians is that of ethnography. Mary Clark Moschella describes ethnography as immersion in people's lives, through careful listening and observation, in order to create a narrative account of a particular lived experience (Moschella 2008, p. 4). Ethnography recognizes the importance of stories: how we shape them and how we are shaped by them (Moschella 2008, p. 5). To write the story of a people or culture requires being present to that community or context, and in addition, to be attentive to ourselves as story tellers (Moschella 2008, pp. 25, 31). Congregational studies (Cameron et al. 2005; Tubbs Tisdale 1997) draw on similar methods to explore the shape, structure and story of local church communities.

One figure stands out as instrumental in developing a method of socially-committed observation and evaluation. Paulo Freire was an influential Brazilian educationalist whose ideas (outlined in *Pedagogy of the Oppressed*, first published 1973) were tested out during literacy programmes among rural communities. Freire observed how the local people he was working with had lost trust in their own ability to evaluate their reality:

> They call themselves ignorant and say the 'professor' is the one who has knowledge and to whom they should listen . . . almost never do they realize that they, too, 'know things' they have learned in their relations with the world and with other women and men. (Freire 1993, p. 45)

He therefore developed a method of education that enabled participants to describe their reality and thus provide the basic resources for their own education. Freire's method highlights the importance of beginning with lived experience. This means that our analysis of a situation must begin with those who live in it by asking them about their hopes and concerns. The next step is to identify emerging patterns between each individual's experience. The group is then helped to see wider social patterns and their impact (conscientization) that empowers them to work for social change.

Although there are many specialized tools and skills involved in academic social analysis, this does not prevent us from having a go for ourselves. We can begin with careful, thoughtful observation of a situation via our own experiences and through dialogue with others. Of course, other resources such as census returns, local records and social analyses completed by different organizations or academics are very valuable when available to complement our own observations. There are also a number of books on practical theology that include guidance on social research, for example *The Wiley-Blackwell Companion to Practical Theology* (2012).

The following checklist offers some initial areas for consideration when attempting to read a situation:

Environmental context
- Ecological systems.
- Access to water, land and food.
- Energy sources and production, including the development of alternative methods.
- Environmental change: destruction, protection, restoration.
- Climate change and impact, including environmental migrants and climate refugees.

Social context
- Demography (population make up and distribution), including changing patterns (in gender balance, ethnic mix, age, etc.) and relationships.
- Migration, patterns, causes and impact on sending and receiving communities.
- Characteristics of, and relationships between, urban, rural and suburban areas.
- Judicial process, security, crime and punishment.
- Housing provision and the level of homelessness.
- Education provision, access and standard.
- Health and healthcare.
- Food production and eating patterns.

Economic context
- Economic structures, systems and philosophies.
- Economic health and the availability and distribution of resources: natural, financial and human.
- Wealth distribution, the difference between rich and poor, and the number of people living below the poverty line.
- Employment, under-employment and unemployment; average wage levels; the power relationship between workers, management, owners or shareholders.

Political context
- Political process and legislation.
- Political spectrum.
- Dominant ideology.
- Lobbying and advocacy groups.
- Level of democracy and freedom of expression.
- Distribution of social power and influence.
- Politics of inclusion or exclusion; human rights.

Cultural context
- Dominant values, cultural practices and influencers.
- Media ownership and output, social media and networks.
- Religious presence and influence; religious diversity, conflict and dialogue.
- Cultural diversity and the amount of dialogue between different cultural groups.
- Art and expression.
- Sport and recreation.
- Fringe or sub-cultures; excluded groups; definition of anti-social or counter-cultural.

From description (itself a form of analysis), we move to social analysis of underlying systems and dynamics (Cimperman 2015, p. 80). Holland and Henriot (1983, pp. 98–100) offer one method of social analysis for theologians: first, the mapping of social development and change; next, analysis of the underlying structures of a situation; and finally the imagining of future developments and social change.

There are a number of resources available to help us develop our social awareness and begin to be able to read a situation. Evaluative methods tend to be rooted in particular ideologies (such as Marxist analysis) that govern how they interpret social data and the social changes and goals they advocate. Theologians, including biblical scholars, will also want to reflect on the situation, using theological themes (for example, sin, salvation, grace) and resources (biblical texts, liturgy, theological traditions, etc.) to evaluate the context. A theologian might ask how an economic or political system enables everyone to be valued as humans made in the image of God. Or they might ask if an environmental policy allows for the flourishing of all of God's creation.

Having spent time observing, mapping and analysing our context, what then? How does contextual analysis inform our reading of the biblical text?

As an example, we turn to Rachel's book *Reimagining Theologies of Marriage* (2018), which explores how women's experiences of domestic violence challenge the idealized image of marriage often presented by the Church. Rachel built up a picture of women's experience of domestic violence through spending time with local women's groups and activists, as well as looking at statistics and social scientific studies (observation). She drew on insights from other researchers and activists to develop her understanding of patterns of violent behaviours (analysis). Building on previous work by scholars such as Renita Weems (1995), she looked at prophetic metaphors of marriage in the book of Hosea from the perspective of work to prevent domestic violence. By reframing the text in this way, she was able to identify how Hosea presents God as a male perpetrator of domestic violence, perhaps motivated by a desire to prove his masculinity to other gods. This enabled her to ask what this God might need to do in order to recover from violence, noting:

> in these prophetic texts, God performs masculinity through violence, perhaps to prove his masculinity to the leaders of ancient Israel, or even to his rivals – other male gods. Reading these texts alongside research concerning male perpetrators of domestic violence, the process of rehabilitating this husband God appears complex. The jealous husband must learn to communicate in a way that is mutual and respectful (allowing Gomer, Zion and other female metaphorical figures to speak and act for themselves); he must stop enact-

ing sexual and physical violence; and he must develop his awareness of both others and himself. (Starr 2018, p. 77)

> **Try it out**
>
> Identify three key aspects of your context. What resources might help you analyse your context? What connections do you identify with the biblical text (for example, hunger, corruption, access to adequate housing)?

Reading the Bible in a global context

Any discussion of our social context, however brief, must make mention of globalization – a determinative factor in our contemporary reality. Charities like Christian Aid and CAFOD define globalization in the following way:

> Globalisation is a process of increasing interconnectedness of individuals, groups, companies and countries. The technological, economic and political changes which have brought people closer together have also generated serious concerns over the terms of that integration. These concerns have been generated by the realisation that while globalisation has led to benefits for some, it has not led to benefits for all. The benefits appear to have gone to those who already have the most, while many of the poorest have failed to benefit fully and some have even been made poorer. (Green and Melamed 2000, p. 1)

As evidence of still increasing disparity, in 2019, Oxfam noted: 'Seven out of ten people live in countries where the gap between the rich and poor is worse than thirty years ago.'

In a globalized world, we read the Bible from a global perspective – our location is the whole world. This does not mean it is possible to read the Bible in a way that suggests everyone has the same experience and desires as oneself. Living in the world as a global citizen actually increases the need to be specific about social and economic location. We become acutely aware of the great differences between the world's inhabitants. We therefore have to understand how we stand in relation to others, while at the same time recognizing the common links and therefore our common interests.

> **Try it out**
>
> Identify one particular environmental concern (such as climate change, deforestation, access to clean water) and then read Genesis 1 through that lens. What response do you have to the text when you focus on the reality of your environmental location? We discuss ecological criticism in Chapter 5.

We offer two examples for this section on reading the Bible attentive to the global context. First, we consider the impact of the AIDS pandemic on reading the Bible. We noted earlier the work of Musa Dube who brings to the Bible questions of gender, healing, sexuality and community as they arise in context shaped by HIV/AIDS. Writing from Botswana, Dube comments:

> Perhaps HIV and AIDS hermeneutics can be summarized as relating to a world that is infected and affected by an infectious, incurable, deadly and stigmatized disease that functions through social injustice. The search for healing – the healing of our bodies and social relations – is key to such a context . . . The question in such a context for biblical scholars is: Does the Bible say anything about infectious, incurable and deadly diseases that are sustained by social injustice and which evoke stigma and discrimination from the wider public? How do we build healing communities and relationships? (Dube 2010, p. 220)

In his article, 'Reading the Bible in the Light of HIV/AIDS in South Africa', Gerald West draws on the experience of popular Bible study groups attended by people who are HIV positive. West notes how even the group's choice of passage is affected by their situation:

> The group usually chose texts in which Jesus was speaking and/or acting over against the prevailing views of society. In other words, the texts chosen for

> Bible study tended to be those texts in which socially normative views victimized certain people, who were then affirmed and dignified and reinserted into a reconstituted society by Jesus. (West 2003, p. 338)

He observes how the group members seem to suffer more on account of emotional rejection than physical illness. They are judged by society; even when they die their funerals become arenas of judgement. However, the gospels' portrayal of Jesus helps them challenge their social exclusion. As an example, through studying the story of Jesus's encounter with the woman allegedly caught in adultery (John 8.1–11) members of the group were affirmed and accepted. 'The Jesus of this text had entered into and reconstituted the counselling encounter, bringing forgiveness, healing and acceptance' (West 2003, p. 343).

Our second example is related to the ongoing migration crisis facing many global regions. The UNHCR suggests 68.5 million people are forcibly displaced, either internally or as refugees and asylum seekers (2018 figures). The Bible includes many stories of migration, exile and displacement. For example, the Bible Society's booklet, *On the Road: A Journey through the Bible for Migrants* (2008) explores biblical stories of journeying and exile as well as the biblical mandate to welcome the stranger.

How might our global context of migration impact on our reading of the Bible? In Genesis 35.8, we read: 'And Deborah, Rebekah's nurse, died, and she was buried under an oak below Bethel. So it was called Allon-bacuth.' This would appear to be a passing reference to a minor character. Yet if we stay with this verse, we might discover a number of connections to some of the challenges facing migrants today. The text reminds us that Deborah is Rebekah's nurse. She does not live with her own family, and as Rebekah's wet nurse, may have left behind children of her own. Such a possibility reminds us of the many women who have to leave their children in order to care for those of a richer family and the establishment of care-chains that stretch across countries and continents. The story takes place on the road, and we cannot fail to be aware of the difficulties and dangers facing many migrants, as they cross deserts, forests, rivers and seas to find safety and security. Death is a constant companion, and for many vulnerable migrants the possibility of being buried on the roadside is very real. Yet the story is also one of the few occasions in the Bible when a woman's death and burial is recorded, as well as the mourning of her companions (the site is called the Oak of Weeping). Moreover, through her name and location beneath a mighty tree, this Deborah is connected to the judge and prophet Deborah (Judges 4), perhaps suggesting that this migrant woman had much wisdom to offer.

Our social reality shapes our selection of passages to study, the questions we bring to the text and the interpretation we place on it. As we learn about our location in the world, we come to understand how we are placed within the structures of our social reality. Are we one of the powerful? How is our power restricted? Who do we form our allegiances with? Are we comfortable with our position in society or do we wish to challenge it?

Reading in community

All of us belong to groups that, even if not communities of faith, influence how we interpret the Bible. Our belonging offers us opportunities and responsibilities. We commit ourselves to particular groups within society; these are our communities of accountability. Our communities are those people we journey with. They are the people with whom we test out our interpretation of scripture. It is these groups that we most often bring into our dialogue with the text.

> **Try it out**
>
> Identify your communities of accountability. Now consider some of these diagnostic questions:
>
> - Are these communities based on gender, sexual orientation, ethnicity, denomination, profession and/or class?
> - Does loyalty to one group create tension with another group?
> - How might you be a prophet within these communities?
> - How is your interpretation influenced by these communities? What responsibilities do you feel towards these communities when interpreting the Bible?

Many anthropologists and theologians regard humans as fundamentally relational and social beings, existing only in relation to others. This relational aspect to human identity has an impact on the location and method of biblical interpretation. Sandra Schneiders comments:

> Since the Bible is the product of a community experience and is meant to nourish and guide the community of believers, it is helpful to share biblical study and prayer with others. Because every great text has multiple meanings and layers of significance, different dimensions of meaning will be discovered by different readers. Furthermore, sharing interpretations minimizes the chances of totally erroneous or idiosyncratic reading. (Schneiders 1997)

> **Try it out**
>
> When and where do you read or discuss the Bible with other people? Your list might include: lectures; Bible study groups; family meal times; worship; down the pub. Reflect on the process of reading with others. What new insights are enabled? How does the group deal with conflicting interpretations of a passage?

The Church as an interpretative community

For Christians and Jews, the believing community is the primary group in which the Bible is explored. As we saw in Chapter 2, the Bible as Christian canon was formed by the church and, in the first instance, for the church. In response, the church is formed and transformed around the Bible. Because of this special relationship, the church has a responsibility to interpret the Bible. Interpretation of the texts is part of its calling and identity.

The church interprets the Bible in its preaching, teaching, worship and action, proclaiming it in fresh and relevant ways (World Council of Churches 1998, p. 19). One of the most important ways the church lives out the Bible is in the celebration of Holy Communion (also called the Mass, Eucharist or the Lord's Supper). This central act of worship recalls the last supper of Jesus with his disciples and is a time of fellowship, renewal and recommitment. The service traditionally follows the pattern of the biblical accounts with believers participating in the sharing of the bread and wine, as the first disciples did:

> Holy God, we praise you
> that on the night in which he was betrayed
> our Saviour Christ took bread
> and gave you thanks.
> He broke it, and gave it to his disciples, saying,
> 'Take, eat. This is my body, given for you.
> Do this in remembrance of me.'
>
> After supper, he took the cup of wine,
> gave thanks, and gave it to them, saying,
> 'Drink from it, all of you.
> This is my blood of the new covenant,
> poured out for all people
> for the forgiveness of sins.
> Do this in remembrance of me.'
> (The Methodist Church 1999, p. 193)

Most Jews and Christians would say that reading, studying and preaching on the Bible together in worship is an important context for interpretation. Sometimes, however, such a community-focused method of interpretation can leave such communities open to collective error rather than collective wisdom. In Chapter 6, we will consider the question of whether we can read the Bible against ourselves. For now, it is worth noting how difficult it is to do this.

Richard Bauckham points out the need for individual members of a community to have freedom to offer new and challenging readings, to 'allow for the Jeremiahs and the Luthers' (Bauckham 1999, p. 22). Again, we should note the difficulty of ensuring this safeguard. It is hard for individuals to go against the group mentality and perhaps harder for the community to hear and respond to criticism.

The Church's diverse nature inevitably creates diverse readings. Randy Litchfield advocates a middle way between extreme individualism in which no-one has anything to say to each other, and enforced uniformity which suppresses real complexity of different identities. The Bible should act as a 'centering force' in Christian communities (Litchfield 2004, p. 226), holding diverse people together and recognized by all as a text to attend to. 'This Bible-mediated conversation weaves individuals together into a tradition and community' (Litchfield 2004, p. 228).

In recognition of the diverse contexts and local communities that make up the worldwide church, the World Council of Churches notes the importance of both contextuality, that is interpretation in response to the local situation, and catholicity, that is shared, binding beliefs (World Council of Churches 1998, p. 31).

> **Try it out**
>
> The sixth commandment, 'You shall not kill' (Exodus 20: 13) is agreed teaching for all Jews and Christians. Yet there is much division over the application of this notion of the sanctity of life. Think how the commandment is interpreted by Christians who advocate the death penalty, vegetarianism, pacifism or the 'pro-life' movement, which seeks to restrict access to (often life-giving) reproductive health care. Can even such a central teaching as this one function as a 'centering force'?

The benefits of reading together

Despite the difficulties, there are great gains to be had from studying the text together. The important thing is to commit to listening and learning from another's interpretation:

> The reading from another's location creates an awareness in me of the particularity, brokenness and implications of my own reading – and very likely also the associated discovery of commonalities. Issues of the truth of the text are thus located in a particular reading community but are also connected to other communities. (Litchfield 2004, p. 235)

As biblical interpreters, it is vital that we seek out other perspectives on a text. We need to remain open to the diversity of interpretations and this requires us to accept the reality of another person's location as well as the impact this has on their interpretation. The *Global Bible Commentary* argues that: 'It is only when we recognize the differences between our interpretation and those of others that we learn from them, and thus truly respect them – rather than co-opting them by pretending they are the same as ours, or rejecting them as meaningless' (Patte 2004, p. xxxvi).

We offer two examples of reading together; both are intentional long-term projects that seek to enable people from a range of contexts and perspectives to share insights, find common ground and honour difference.

The *Bible in the Life of the Church* project began in 2009 with the aim of exploring beliefs and practices of biblical interpretation across the Anglican Communion. It notes the many ways in which the Bible is 'read' through song, study and worship. It recognizes the profound impact of context on how a passage is interpreted (Anglican Consultative Council 2012, p. 10). In the regional groups, participants paid close attention to their context, the biblical text and to each other. Although disagreement about biblical interpretation, especially around sexuality, continues to threaten the unity of the Communion, the project celebrates the diversity of ways in which the Bible is read and understood. Indeed, the 2012 report explicitly resists offering an agreed approach or set of answers, but rather seeks to encourage deeper, ongoing engagement with the Bible.

A similar project, but this time focused on women's interpretation, is *Tsena Malalaka* which brings together women theologians from African and European contexts. The book, *There Is Something We Long For – Nous avons un désir* (2015), explores cross-cultural theological dialogue and is written in both French and English, a symbol of the polyvalent nature of theology and biblical interpretation. The authors engage with the Bible in a variety of ways, but common themes that emerge are the importance of belonging and dignity, the need for peace and healing, and the gift of creativity and community. To give one example from the book, Yvette Rabemila of Madagascar draws on texts such as the blessing of Numbers 6.24–26 to consider how peace is created through relationships, which, just like a garden full of flowers, needs constant care.

David Rhoads (2005, p. 226) warns us never to trust ourselves to interpret the Bible correctly on our own. While recognizing the complexity of negotiating differences and redressing power imbalances between interpreters, Rhoads argues that reading interculturally is most likely to result in valid and relevant interpretations. In this section we have considered the differences within our own communities. By naming our community, diverse as it may be, we also acknowledge those groups to whom we do not belong. In the next chapter, we consider how best to hear the insights of those with alternative experiences and commitments to ours.

5
Committed Readings

In this chapter, we consider how our commitments affect the way we interpret the Bible. Our commitments arise out of our experience of our reality, and our awareness of our own needs and the needs of others. In recent years, many new critical tools have been developed to allow interpreters to read the Bible in a way that meets their and others' needs. This is a welcome change, as people have become impatient with ways of reading the Bible that yield nothing that is relevant to them, the people they care about or the society they live in.

> **Try it out**
>
> Think of a current situation in your life, which you would like to reflect on more deeply with the help of the Bible. Write it down, noting how doing this brings your own life to the forefront of your mind. Consolidate this awareness by reviewing the notes on your identity that you developed in Chapter 4.
>
> Now, look for a passage that seems to be related to your situation and your identity. Read it with your identity and situation at the forefront of your mind, deliberately setting aside historical-critical questions. Write down any thoughts, observations or insights that come to you. Write quickly without censoring what comes to mind. When you have finished writing your thoughts take a short break.
>
> After the break, reread the passage and your notes. In what way(s) might this passage give you insight into your situation? Does this

> process reveal important gaps between you and the passage, perhaps showing that something important about your situation is absent from the passage, or that the passage contains beliefs and convictions you do not share?

It sometimes seems as if both diachronic and synchronic approaches to the Bible (as explored in Chapter 3) never get round to addressing real-life questions. This is a consequence of the long-standing tradition of interpreting the Bible historically. For example, in the second volume of John Barton's *The Biblical World* (2002, p. 437), William Telford lists 68 methods and approaches to biblical interpretation, classified into three categories: historical, literary and theological. These categories follow the normal order taken by historical criticism which begins with literary and historical questions about the Bible before tackling questions about the beliefs and commitments of the original writer(s) and reader(s). But this historical-critical approach stops there, leaving us to make up our own minds about how such ancient beliefs and commitments relate to our lives today.

Happily, this situation is now changing, and in this chapter we look at some of the approaches which bring contemporary concerns and commitments into conversation with the Bible. These approaches are sometimes collectively called 'existential readings' (Gorman 2001, p. 202). Gorman's map of these approaches divides them into two categories: those which trust the text, and those which are suspicious of it. But this distinction is unhelpful insofar as it conceals the fact that we all approach the Bible with varying degrees of suspicion and trust. We therefore prefer to speak of committed approaches. We accept that all written texts, including the Bible, are products of their time and place and hence need to be read with historical awareness. But, equally, classic texts, including the Bible, also have the ability to illuminate and inspire later readers, whether or not they share the perspectives of the original writers and readers.

When we consciously consider the commitments of others we realize that all interpretations, including those that claim to be impartial, are affected by certain commitments. This is particularly important to remember when reading commentaries, the format of which can lead us to forget they are also written by people with particular beliefs and commitments. Commentaries are important for biblical interpreters because they are the genre which biblical scholars most often use to share the results of their biblical study with others. Fortunately, as we noted in Chapter 4, western interpreters have increasingly recognized the degree to which their location and interests do affect their interpretations. They have often learned this through listening to interpreters living in other places, who interpret the Bible through their experience of suffering, oppression or discrimination.

For example, as the struggle for majority government gained impetus in South Africa in the 1980s, there was a corresponding struggle between scholars focused on ever more intricate synchronic analyses of the Bible and those who insisted that it should provide resources to support the struggle for liberation. With hindsight, it becomes evident that those who were trying to limit the study of the Bible to literary questions about its structure and form were trying to distance themselves from the life experience of people who were striving for social and political liberation.

Approaches that address real contemporary interests and commitments fall into three broad categories:

1. Cultural and contextual perspectives.
2. Ideological perspectives, developed to bring the core concerns of other disciplines into dialogue with the Bible.
3. Faith perspectives, concerned to interpret the Bible in ways that meet the needs of individuals seeking spiritual and moral guidance, and groups wishing to use such guidance to inform their collective public action.

Such individuals and groups can be followers of any living faith, not just the biblical faiths of Judaism or Christianity. These approaches do not all assume or endorse one another, yet we shall see that they have much in common and there is considerable interaction between them.

Commitment to culture and context

The term 'world music' became popular in the western world in the 1980s as people there became excited about the musical riches to be found in other parts of the world. Today, music lovers in the West are just as likely to enjoy the music of Ali Farka Touré and Ziggy Marley as the music of musicians coming from the United States or Europe. A similar shift has taken place in the realm of biblical studies, with more scholars engaging with scholarship from diverse regions of the world. This marks a shift in emphasis, rather than an interpretative method, though a number of critical perspectives have risen to prominence as a result. Below we look at three types of cultural and contextual interpretation: global interpretations, postcolonial interpretations and vernacular interpretations.

Global conversations

Major reference works and commentaries have begun to reflect this shift towards global perspectives on the Bible. One of the first one-volume commentaries to draw contributions from all over the world was the *International Bible Commentary: A Catholic and Ecumenical Commentary for the Twenty-first Century* (1998) edited by William R. Farmer. Although the approach of most of the contributors still showed the strong influence of the historical-critical approach, the inclusion of voices and perspectives from all over the world widened its scope to include concerns such as healing, the family, workers' rights, violence, anti-Semitism and ecology. These pastoral concerns were also considered in supplementary articles within the commentary.

Another pioneering example of this trend was the *Global Bible Commentary* (2004) edited by a team of five scholars and offering readings on sections of each book of the Bible chosen on the basis of their relevance to the life contexts of the interpreters drawn from all over the world. Each entry began with the life context of the interpretation before offering a contextual commentary and demonstrating how reading the text with the concerns of the context in mind had a profound impact on what was seen. For example, John Riches' reading of Ephesians was affected by reading the epistle in Scotland. The prevalence of domestic violence in that context led him and his co-readers to resist interpreting Ephesians 5.21–23 in a way that endorsed views of headship or subordination in marriage (Riches in Patte 2004, p. 479).

A similar new worldwide perspective was evident in the *Dictionary of Biblical Interpretation*, edited by John H. Hayes in 1999, which contained articles on biblical interpretation from all regions of the world. This marked a real shift from the major dictionary on the same subject published just a decade earlier, *A*

Dictionary of Biblical Interpretation, edited by R. J. Coggins and J. L. Houlden in 1990. Hayes not only included African voices (which were absent from Coggins and Houlden's dictionary) but recognized that it was no more possible to cover African biblical interpretation in one article than it would be to do so for Europe. Thus, it included articles on different aspects of biblical interpretation from around the world: articles considering how the Bible is interpreted in different geographical regions; and articles reviewing interpretive approaches arising out of:

- particular cultures, reflecting the complexity of readers' identity (for example, Afrikaner interpretation, African American interpretation, African Caribbean interpretation and Calypso interpretation);
- religious commitments (for example, multi-faith interpretation, Muslim interpretation, Jewish interpretation and Rastafarian interpretation);
- experiences of oppression (for example, Dalit interpretation, Burakimin interpretation, Minjung interpretation, and South African black theology); and
- ideological concerns (for example, androcentric interpretation, Black interpretation, decolonial interpretation, and globalisation and interpretation).

In the same vein, John Levison and Priscilla Pope-Levison's *Return to Babel: Global Perspectives on the Bible* (1999) offered a Latin American, African and Asian perspective on ten well-known biblical passages (Ex. 20; Ps. 23; Matt. 5; John 1; etc.). Each contributor looked first at his or her own context, before looking at the text and producing a reflection on the passage. The process of starting with context acted as a filter for what was looked for exegetically within the text, and this in turn shaped their final hermeneutical reflections.

Walter Dietrich and Ulrich Luz edited a short collection called *The Bible in a World Context: An Experiment in Cultural Hermeneutics* in 2002, which explored cultural hermeneutics through Latin American, African and Asian readings of Luke 2. Elsa Tamez, in her contribution, reminded readers that for many people in the world, the context in which they were living was becoming more life-threatening and hostile. At the start of the twenty-first century, unlike earlier decades, Latin-American Christians now had to interpret the Bible in a context in which even belief in the possibility of social change had become absent. She warned that biblical scholarship alone did not have the resources to address this profound experience of powerlessness and loss of hope. Speaking poetically, she described her context as living under 'a sky without stars' and said that 'stars', as signs of hope, had to be sought everywhere: 'Search for them in the house, in the street, in institutions and organizations, within oneself and in the other' (Tamez 2002, p. 6).

Other studies aimed to show how world biblical interpretation could affect popular interpretations of the Bible, thus taking account of the fact that there are different cultural perspectives on a biblical book within countries. Thus, David Rhoades' collection of intercultural studies of Revelation, *From Every People and Nation: The Book of Revelation in* Intercultural *Perspective* (2005), showed that there is a 'worldwide' breadth of perspectives within countries too. His collection, intended for group study, included appendices to help study groups to engage in intercultural Bible study. He also included a checklist for readers to identify their own reading profile (similar to the process we describe in Chapter 4).

This way of interpreting the Bible has accelerated in the twenty-first century, with recent collections which aim to bring a diversity of global interpretations into conversation including: Roland Boer and Fernando F. Segovia's *The Future of the Biblical Past: Envisioning Biblical Studies on a Global Key* (2012), Craig S. Keener and R. M. Daniel Carroll's *Global Voices: Reading the Bible in the Majority World* (2013) and Michael Gorman's *Scripture and Its Interpretation: A Global, Ecumenical Introduction to the Bible* (2017). Such developments caution us against withdrawing into individualism and becoming desensitized to stresses on our neighbours or environment. Remember that global Bible interpretation does not neglect older historical-critical tools or other newer approaches. Interpreters may use sociological and rhetorical criticism to identify correspondences between the situation addressed by the originators of the text, and contemporary readers.

> **Try it out**
>
> How might you explore the theme of home within the Bible in conversation with biblical interpreters from a range of different global contexts?

Postcolonial criticism

Postcolonial criticism interprets the Bible through a commitment to make the damaging effects of colonialism visible. It focuses on 'expansion, domination and imperialism as central forces defining both the biblical narrative and biblical interpretation' and covers the overlapping areas of 'race, nation, translation, mission, textuality, spirituality and representation' as well as 'plurality, hybridity and postnationalism, the hallmarks of the postcolonial experience' (Sugirtharajah 2002, p. 25). It is both a perspective, which views biblical texts through the experience of the colonized, and a critical method, which uses postcolonial theory, poststructuralism and semiotics to critique other approaches to interpretation, as well as the biblical texts themselves. By facing up to the ways in which domination, colonial expansion and its ideological manifestations have defined the practices of biblical scholarship, it seeks to reshape the way the Bible is studied.

R. S. Sugirtharajah pioneered this approach in the UK. Around the start of the new millennium, he argued that it was a way of moving beyond liberation theology, which he believed had lost its liberatory edge. In its appropriation of the Bible, in its expositions, in its obsession with Christ-centred hermeneutics, it remained within conventional patterns and ended up reflecting upon the theme of biblical liberation rather than being a liberative hermeneutics (Sugirtharajah 2001, p. 242–3).

Other postcolonial interpreters agree with him. For example, Kwok Pui-Lan contrasts the insights of white feminist interpreters with those of postcolonial critics when studying the story of the Syrophoenician woman in Mark 7.24–30 and Matthew 15.21–28:

> White feminist critics have moved her from the margin to the center by either reclaiming her as a foremother of gentile Christians or by praising her faith and her wit, which enables her to win the argument over Jesus and broaden Jesus' perspective towards the Gentiles. Postcolonial critics, however, emphasize that she is a woman of other faith and her story is inscribed within the master discourse of the Christian canon and interpreted to justify mission to the Gentiles. (Kwok 2005, p. 65)

Similarly, when examining the history of interpretation of the characters of Rahab and Ruth, Kwok and other postcolonial interpreters, such as Musa

Dube, note how Rahab and Ruth are only accepted as foreign, sexually active and resourceful women through their assimilation into the Israelite community (Kwok 2005, p. 82). Postcolonial interpreters ask why that imperialist perspective within the text is not critiqued by feminist interpreters, as it is a problem for the many Asian, African and Latin American women who have had little choice but to assimilate into a dominant culture through marriage, work or migration.

> **Try it out**
>
> Look up one of the passages describing the experience of non-Israelite women referred to above: Rahab from Canaan (Josh. 2), Ruth from Moabite (Ruth 4.7–12) and the unnamed woman from Tyre (Mark 7.24–30 and Matt. 15.21–28).
>
> Ask yourself how these passages treat topics such as invasion, colonization and conquest. How do these texts view 'foreigners'? What is their view of the religious and cultural heritage of outsiders? Then consult a standard historical critical commentary to see if it discusses these politically important topics. Consider the ethical consequences of neglecting the challenging questions raised by postcolonial critics.

Postcolonial criticism also exposes the way anti-Semitic biblical interpretation has been used to encourage conversion in colonized nations. For example, during the evangelization of local women in Africa, Asia and Latin America, Jesus' egalitarian relationship with women has sometimes been presented as superior to patriarchal Jewish culture, whereas work by Jewish New Testament scholars has demonstrated how much Jesus had in common with his contemporaries. Many postcolonial critics are more open to working across religious divisions, and particularly value local living faiths.

It is interesting to see the way postcolonial biblical interpreters use western exegetical tools, both historical-critical and literary, against the very cultural traditions in which they were developed. Kwok notes that 'oppressed women have turned the Bible, a product introduced by the colonial officials, missionaries, and educators, into a site of contestation and resistance for their own emancipation' (Kwok 2005, pp. 77–8). Thus the approach calls into question both western cultural supremacy and the cultural supremacy of the Bible itself. Sugirtharajah writes:

> The purpose is not to recover in the biblical texts an alternative, or to search in its pages for a fresher way of coming to terms with the aftermath of colonial atrocity and trauma, and the current effects of globalisation. The purpose is to interrupt the illusion of the Bible being the provider of all the answers, and to propose new angles, alternative directions, and interjections which will always have the victims and their plight as the foremost concern. (2002, pp. 101–2)

Postcolonial theory can be a powerful tool for interpreting the Bible in the light of the ongoing political and military conflicts, such as that between Palestine and Israel. The Palestinian Lutheran theologian Mitri Raheb points out that, viewed from Bethlehem, Palestine has been invaded and occupied by one colonial power after another throughout its history. Informed by postcolonial theory, biblical scholars have considered how the stories and production of the Bible take place in the context of empire: Assyrian, Babylonian, Persian, Greek and Roman (see Perdue 2015 and Winn 2016). But they often fail to see that the invasions did not end with the Romans in the first century CE. Since then, Palestine has been occupied by the Byzantines, Arabs, Tartars, Crusaders, Ayyubids, Tartars (again), Mamluks, Mongols, Ottomans, British and Israelis (Raheb 2014, p. 10). If the last two names come as a shock to British or American readers, postcolonial theory reminds us that, 'the empire tries to control the storyline'.

Vernacular hermeneutics

Postcolonial theory says that we are all subject to control by one empire or another and that this determines which cultural values are prized and which are despised, or at least neglected. For this reason, it encourages us to revalue local culture and to use it for biblical interpretation. Vernacular hermeneutics is the discipline which invites interpreters to use their own local, popular cultural and religious heritage as a resource for understanding biblical ideas and narratives. Vernacular Bible interpretation has a long history, rooted in the ongoing work of Bible translation. One of the earliest examples of this is the translation of the Hebrew Bible into Greek, the Septuagint, to enable it to be understood by Greek-speaking Jews living in the Hellenistic world created by the empire of Alexander the Great and his generals. Later, in the fourth century CE, Jerome and his successors translated the whole Bible into the Latin Vulgate for use in the Roman Empire. Vulgate simply means, 'the language of the common, uneducated people'. Centuries later, one of the great drivers of the Reformation was the process of translating the Bible into the vernacular, that is, the languages spoken by the people in Europe.

Translation always involves finding textual and conceptual correspondences between the original languages and cultures of the Bible, and the cultures of the languages into which the text is being translated. As this process continues, there is the opportunity to find correspondences between the traditions and practices reflected in the Bible and those of the cultures of the languages into which the Bible is translated. Sugirtharajah (1999) has drawn attention to ways in which this process continues throughout the world. He argues for favouring the indigenous and the local, to encourage self-affirmation and self-esteem, and to resist centralizing systems and theories. By doing this, vernacular interpretation can give strength and visibility to those most in danger of being swept away by the controlling, but often subtle, effects of western cultural imperialism.

Vernacular Bible interpretation is often practised by seeing how ordinary people express their understanding of a biblical passage in art. For example, the South African theologian Gerald West has used Azaria Mbatha's woodcut depicting the Joseph story for the contextual Bible study of Genesis 37—50 (West in Sugirtharajah 1999, pp. 43–8). Mbatha's art is an example of the complexity of identifying what is local in our postmodern and globalized world. South African-born and educated Mbatha has lived in Sweden for nearly 40 years, yet he still feels himself to be close to the little village of Mabeka in Mahlabathini district of Kwazulu-Natal where he was born.

Try it out

Find a Bible passage to interpret in the light of your own local culture. Think about what art forms are important to you and others around you locally, and explore links between them and your text. If possible,

> discuss your thoughts with local artists. Don't put limits on what you define as art. As well as music, dance, graffiti or quilting, remember that art and culture are also expressed in the physical landscape. What light can gardeners shed on biblical passages on the natural world, for example?

Ideological commitments

Ideology is not a dirty word, and does not only describe the beliefs of fanatics or extremists! Soulen and Soulen define it as 'a set of attitudes and ideas . . . that reflects or shapes understanding (and misunderstandings) of the social and political world, and that serves to justify collective action aimed at preserving or changing it' (2011, p. 95). In this sense, everybody works with an ideology, and it is important that we are aware of the ones that shape our thinking and the thinking of others.

Ideological criticism considers three areas in which ideology affects texts: the ideological context(s) in which it was produced; the ideology or ideologies expressed within it; and the ideology or ideologies of those who read and interpret it (Soulen and Soulen 2011, p. 96). In each of these areas, ideologies affirm and uphold the interests of some at the expense of others. Ideological approaches to the Bible help us to see this, so that we can act in ways that overcome the effects of this distortion. We become more aware of the blind spots in our own perspective and can interpret the Bible in ways that are more respectful of the needs and interests of others. Moreover, this approach encourages us to notice ways in which established methods of interpretation neglect important issues. In this section we introduce deconstruction, queer criticism and ecological criticism as representative examples of the wide range of theories that can be thought of as ideological criticism (Moore and Sherwood, 2011, pp. 3–5).

Deconstruction

One of the most radical ideological approaches to the interpretation of texts is deconstruction, a poststructuralist perspective associated with the philosophy and literary criticism of Jacques Derrida. This approach is radical because it unsettles and decentres all readings of texts. It shows that there is no such thing as the centre of a text because every centre depends on the margins to exist as a centre! In this way it shows that the margins are as important as the centre, and cannot therefore be ignored. This internal contradiction undermines the coherence of all texts. Those who have seen this realize that the messages conveyed by texts are much less stable than they thought. Texts can be read playfully and subversively.

How does this affect the interpretation of the Bible? While some interpreters are unsettled by deconstruction, others welcome it, since it weakens the position of those in power who try to preserve their power by imposing oppressive interpretations of the Bible on others. Segovia comments, 'The process of deconstruction is going on in Third World theologies without using the term; indeed, decolonizing theology is a form of deconstruction' (Segovia in Fabella and Sugirtharajah 2000, p. 67). It alerts readers to the way that the Bible also de-centres readers in ways that open them to new discoveries about themselves or God.

Gina Hens-Piazza observes how postmodern approaches to the Bible similarly increase our interest in marginal texts and characters:

> As postmodern literary criticism pays attention to the seams, unanswered questions, or cracks in the narrative, it often uncovers competing voices, values and centres of power in the story. It raises unaddressed questions lurking in the margins that disrupt the integrity of a unified reading. Attention to these contradictory, contestatory, or incongruous elements in texts often leads to interpretations that challenge the prevailing wisdom about a biblical story. In the process we discover how rhetoric is not just artistic or innocent but may participate in the violence of exclusion. (Hens-Piazza 2003, p. 74)

She observes how contemporary literary critical methods give us greater freedom to choose where to focus our attention. While once we were expected to follow the lead of the narrator or line of the story, now we have the option of ignoring such guidance and linger with the background incidents or minor characters. There are new and important insights to be gained for this shift in our attentions. In recent years, for example, there has been a wealth of popular devotional literature created about minor characters in the Gospel stories, especially women. Through first-person narratives, short dramas or poems, new perspectives and points of contact with these figures have been developed for Christians. Often, the fictional extensions of these biblical characters relate their encounter with Jesus, thus encouraging a devotional response from readers.

Paying attention to the margins of a story challenges traditional readings, destabilizing the centre to allow new aspects of the story to emerge. This should not lead us to reject older readings, but rather help us bring together central and marginal perspectives to gain a fuller sense of what a passage is about.

> **Try it out**
>
> Read Matthew 21.12–17 and focus on either the children in the temple or the chief priests and scribes. What is their role and perspective in the story? Do you feel drawn to develop a 'background story' for these characters?

Queer criticism

Writing on Deuteronomy, Deryn Guest observes:

> a queer commentary, focused upon fluidity, the questioning of the two-sex model, the exploration of transgender, transsexual and intersex experiences presses hard against a scriptural text that is most resistant to such explorations and which is used in current religious rhetoric to condemn lesbian, gay, bisexual, transgender, transsexual-identified people and their choices. (Guest 2006, p. 142)

As ideological methods of interpreting the Bible have multiplied, a wide range of LGBTQI+ readings have developed. In a recent survey of queer readings of the Bible, Stewart (2017b) observes a progression from initial work responding to anti-gay interpretations of selected 'anti-gay' biblical texts; to looking at parts of the Bible that show loving same-sex relationships; before moving on to using the Bible to explore gay and lesbian experiences, especially related to the suffering caused by the HIV/AIDS crisis of the 1980s and 1990s. The problem remained that many of the established interpretative methods only took LGBTQI+ re-interpretation so far. Stewart comments, 'Perhaps different interpretations are simply rearranging the evidence' (Stewart 2017b, p. 298).

Queer interpretation takes a deconstructionist approach by questioning the idea of normality, and of fixed categories such as homosexual or heterosexual. Rather than seeking better normative interpretations, queer interpreters question the very idea of norms. They point out that the more different people study the Bible, the more they accumulate interpretations and questions. While this approach might seem unsettlingly open-ended, it has the important benefit of being very inclusive. Queer interpreters welcome all those who find themselves excluded by prevailing social norms, including people of different physical ability or state of health, different ethnicity and those of indeterminate gender or sexual orientation. Queer interpretation makes place for those seen as the exception or special cases, including those exceptions that will come in the future, such as cyborgs. These approaches are the natural outcome of the recognition that people have different experiences of being embodied, of gender identification and sexual orientation, as considered in Chapter 4.

Queer biblical scholars have seen how questioning boundaries of gender and sexuality has enabled further questioning or 'queering' of the biblical text. As one example, Ken Stone describes the book of Job as a 'cacophonous argument, incorporating multiple points of view and conflicting positions' (Stone 2006, p. 302). He sees in Job's complexities and challenges something 'queer', a witness to the messy realities of bodies, relationships and lived experience. Stone concludes:

> If we come to recognize, with Job, that the world around us is too vast and too complex to conform to our own, all-too-human, rigid ordering principles, we may be less inclined to insist dogmatically that other human beings so conform their lives ... And even when our individual and collective lives, like the book of Job itself, fail or refuse to resolve all conflicts and tensions, they can be put together in such a way as to end with an affirmation of hope, laughter, life and beauty without thereby denying the existence of chaos and pain. (Stone 2006, p. 303)

Ecological criticism

Ecological biblical interpretation takes the widest of all critical perspectives by locating all human-orientated interpretations within concerns for the wellbeing of the planet and, ultimately, the entire cosmos. It is committed to helping Bible interpreters to be better ecological citizens. It requires us to broaden our perspective beyond human-focused concerns. This includes all the previous ideological readings which address human issues of gender, race, colonialism, etc. It also asks us to recognize that those most impacted by environmental destruction and climate change tend to be those who are poor or otherwise marginalized.

Ecological critics remind us that we human beings share the earth with all other forms of life, and are made of the same physical elements as the rest of the cosmos. Such interpretations challenge the assumption that we humans are here to use the resources of the earth for our own profit and power. Rather than offering a single interpretative method, ecological critics weave together insights from all the previous methods, while showing up the weaknesses of readings which focus on human concerns and neglect many forms of human oppression. *The Earth Bible* project, begun initially in Australia, produced five volumes of ecological readings of the Bible between 2000 and 2002 (see Elvey 2010, p. 465). Work continues in this area, for example with Marie Turner's commentary on Ecclesiastes (Turner 2017).

Ecological critics remind us that those who create texts, the texts themselves and those who receive and use the texts are all material entities, located in particular places and times and connected with the material environment in which they exist. They use the concept of 'habitat' as a reminder that all our knowing happens somewhere, materially, physically and socially. The texts themselves are material, are transmitted to us via human speech, memory and writing and are recorded on physical objects made of clay, stone, papyrus reeds, animal skins or wood pulp. As physical beings, we humans use our bodies and our senses to interpret these physical texts. For this reason, our interpretations are inevitably bounded and subjective. Also, we use our bodies to live out the meanings we derive from the texts.

Ecological interpretation uses one or more of three approaches: suspicion, identification and retrieval (Habel 2008, pp. 1–8). Suspicion warns us that the interpretations we have made, or will make, often overlook the habitat of texts. Identification invites us to recognize the stories of the materials which are often left in the background of human stories: the wheat of loaves; the industry of fishing; stones quarried for cities; trees, seas, landscapes, rocks, mountains; even the microbes in yeast or those that cause the decay of bodies and texts. Retrieval attends to the earth perspectives, either those which are visible within the text or made visible when the physical aspects are overlooked or suppressed. For example, interpreters point out that *ruach* in Genesis 1 denotes the atmosphere of the earth, weather, wind, human and animal breath, sacredness and inspiration, and that, in Hosea and Amos, the earth itself mourns or prophesies.

> **Try it out**
>
> Read Genesis 1—3 and Romans 8.18–27 and notice all the information in these texts about God's relationship with the world, rather than just with humanity.

The above examples are just a few of the many recent ideological approaches to biblical interpretation. One of the great benefits of these approaches is that they open up spaces for people to read the Bible with their own interests and needs in mind. This includes the many Bible readers who read the Bible with a faith commitment.

Faith commitments

A third cluster of committed approaches all interpret the Bible from the perspective of religious faith. Here we focus on examples of reading the Bible from a Christian perspective, and do not include many examples from the Jewish tradition. Towards the end of this section, however, we look at Scriptural Reasoning, an approach to interpreting the Bible with people of other living faiths.

While Christians view the Bible in many different ways, there is widespread agreement that the Bible plays an essential role in guiding Christian belief and behaviour. Looking at the relationship between Christian understanding and the Bible from the other direction, many Christians would agree with Augustine of Hippo that the Bible should be interpreted in the context of Christian commitment and worship. Towards the end of the first book of *On Christian Doctrine*, he insists that the purpose of Scripture is to enable people to love God for God's own sake and their neighbours for God's sake. And so he is able to say:

> Whoever, then, thinks that he understands the Holy Scriptures, or any part of them, but puts such an interpretation upon them as does not tend to build up this twofold love of God and our neighbour, does not yet understand them as he ought. (Augustine, *On Christian Doctrine*, 1.36.40)

Augustine suggested that since the Bible was written from a faith perspective which places the love of God and others as the supreme value, it is best understood by readers who wish to share that perspective. In the following section we look at methods Christians use to interpret the Bible from this loving perspective. While individuals can practise some of these methods, they are all essentially communal, because Christian faith is held and expressed communally through the Church.

Meditative, prayerful Bible reading

In the city of Santiago in Chile, a group of Christian women have been meeting regularly since 1991 to discuss their faith and their world. Known as the *Con-spirando* collective, they pray, act and reflect together. To 'conspire' is literally to 'breathe with', and these Christians think of their study of the Scriptures as breathing with God. For the women of *Con-spirando*, this breathing together has led them to new ways of worshipping and following God, for example through caring for the earth.

Many traditional methods of biblical interpretation are rooted in prayer and meditation. Ignatius of Loyola's *Spiritual Exercises*, for example, were designed to help readers enter more deeply and imaginatively into the story of Jesus. Jewish and Christian readers tend to begin Bible study with an opening prayer. Some traditions understand this opening prayer as a plea for God to guide them to a correct interpretation of the passage. For others, this prayer expresses their commitment to remain open to God as they approach the Scriptures afresh, bringing with them their current questions or concerns.

> **Try it out**
>
> If you do surround your reading or study of the Bible with prayer, think about how this affects your understanding of the text and your relationship with it. What does it 'do'?

Lectio Divina is a prayerful and meditative way of reading the Bible that goes back to the earlier days of monastic life in the Christian tradition, and was also practised by early Jewish communities. Hans-Ruedi Weber describes it thus:

> It consists of a daily attempt to listen to God's word within a prescribed biblical text. This happens at regular hours according to a lectionary which covers the whole Bible, so that for example the whole book of Psalms or all four gospels are read consecutively. Sensitivity to resonances from the whole Bible is needed so that the scripture itself interprets the meditated scripture passage and so that God's word heard shapes human thought and life. (Weber 1995, p. 48)

Note that Weber distinguishes between God's word and the biblical text. The two are not directly equated. God's word is heard through a process of prayerful meditation on a Bible passage. Supporters of this process often describe it in colourful similes: the readers' thoughts are like bees buzzing around a sacred hive; the pages of the sacred book being read are like rows of a vineyard; and each letter of the text is like a juicy grape to be chewed.

Lectio is not an academic investigation of the Scriptures, but a process of encounter with God's word. It requires readers to adopt a patient, humble and open attitude to the Bible. In a sense, we have to let go, even lose control of the quest for meaning. We do not set the agenda here, but wait for God's word to come to us, which may be consoling, affirming or demanding. Of course this leaves us vulnerable – particularly to problematic or violent texts. But it can also provide a deep encounter with 'good news'.

> Significantly, for the modern reader *lectio* is a form of surrender, of letting go. God leads the way and sets the agenda; we are never sure where the practice of *lectio* will lead. In a very real sense, we give up control to the sacred text,

and only then are we free to enter into that quiet part of the self where we meet God – that place where we can truthfully say whatever needs to be said and listen to Truth in return. . . . This mingling of prayer and reading that we call *lectio divina* brings us into contact with God, and through the liberating power of the Word of God we begin the journey into wisdom. (O'Donnell 1990, pp. 49–50)

> **Try it out**
>
> Begin by finding a quiet space and becoming more focused and attentive. Choose a psalm to read and then read it slowly and attentively, ideally reading it aloud so that you 'hear' with your ears as well as your eyes. When you come to a phrase or word that seems significant, pause and begin to meditate on it. Repeat the word or phrase until you know it 'by heart'. If you wish, move into prayer, discussing the meaning of the word or phrase for you, with God. End the time of meditation by responding to God, and deciding what you will do on the basis of what you have heard. Later, apart from the process, reflect on how *lectio* enabled you to know the psalm 'by heart'. Did you find this reading method comfortable or challenging?

Lectio was originally an individual exercise for people to seek to hear the word of God for them in that moment. The classic description of this is in Part 2 of Francis de Sales' *An Introduction to the Devout Life*, first published in 1609. In more recent times, people have developed methods of corporate *lectio* where groups hear and reflect on Scripture together.

Lectio Divina can also be used to reflect on place. Kathleen Norris is a journalist and writer who reflects on her faith and life in the context of the Great Plains of North America. During her stays at a local Benedictine monastery, she learned the practice of *lectio* and began to apply it not only to Scripture but also the plains surrounding her. In *Dakota: A Spiritual Geography* (2001) biblical passages become lenses through which to read the landscape before returning to a richer understanding of the biblical text.

Reading in worship

Readers more naturally follow meditative approaches to the Bible when reading alone. However, when approached with faith, the Bible is best read and interpreted with others. This can happen in a variety of situations, including public worship, church or synagogue Scripture studies, workshops or theological college seminars. Each of these contexts affects how the Bible is heard.

When a passage from the Bible is read during Christian worship, it is read in the context of the canon and the Christian faith. We saw in Chapter 2 that there is a close relationship between canonical boundaries and the faith they are intended to uphold. Thus, when a passage is read in church (or synagogue) it is heard in relation to other Bible passages which are read on the same occasion and in relation to the faith of the hearers. In Christian worship, the reading is normally introduced and/or concluded with a statement which urges the congregation to hear the passage as 'the word of the LORD' or 'the holy gospel'. Moreover, the readings are usually accompanied by a sermon exploring an aspect of the Christian faith, and a summary of the Christian faith, such as a creed or hymn. There may be other associated actions too, such as standing when the Bible is brought into church or read, or burning incense to indicate the holiness of the text being read.

This worship context is intended to help people adopt a receptive attitude to the text out of reverence for God. This can have similar benefits to those noted for *lectio*. On the other hand, it can have the effect of discouraging them from thinking critically about the passage, especially if it is problematic for some present. Here is an example from Rachel's experience when she was studying at a seminary in New York. Every morning she met with two or three others to pray. One morning the text for the day was 1 Timothy 2.11-15:

> Let a woman learn in silence with full submission. I permit no woman to teach or to have authority over a man; she is to keep silent. For Adam was formed first, then Eve; and Adam was not deceived, but the woman was deceived and became a transgressor. Yet she will be saved through childbearing.

The reader then proclaimed, 'This is the word of the LORD'. But the rest of the group withheld the words, 'Thanks be to God'. There was silence and then laughter. As a community of prayer, the group withheld their consent to these words, which they experienced as damaging. They refused to acquiesce to that text.

This is an example of the way we often draw on other sources of knowledge, such as our own faith experience, when we interpret scripture. Readers learn to value insights or revelation in their lives as well as through the lives recorded in the Bible. We will consider how we draw together these different sources of knowledge in Chapter 6.

> **Try it out**
>
> There are a number of vindictive prayers in the psalms which are sometimes omitted from use in church worship. Psalms like Psalms 58 and 83 are omitted from some lectionaries altogether, while others have the offending verses omitted (see Psalms 59.5–8 and 69.9–10 and 22–28). Yet, such psalms are part of the Bible. Kathleen Farmer points out that, 'these prayers describe the way real people in real situations have felt in the past and may still feel today' (Farmer in Farmer 1998, p. 826). Read one or more of these psalms and consider the benefits and risks of reading these psalms, or the omitted sections of the psalms, in the context of public worship.

Interpretation for Christian discipleship: practice criticism

Committed, contextual biblical interpretation is not just for people experiencing social or political oppression. Today, more and more readers of the Bible throughout the world are recognizing that an essential component of biblical interpretation is the step by which they identify what the passage is encouraging them to do – and then to attempt to do it! Gorman calls this method embodiment or actualization. It asks, 'If readers took the message of this text seriously, how would their lives be different?' (Gorman 2001, pp. 131–3, 203).

While interpretation for discipleship may appear simply to be a western term for contextual interpretation, there are differences. The main contexts which affect interpretation here are the church and the canon. The interpreter's location in the life of the church and the text's location within the canon both affect the scope and focus of acts of interpretation. While other contextual factors are not ignored, in practice they often play only a supporting role. Not surprisingly then, interpretation for discipleship often focuses on the spiritual and theological meanings of the text, rather than on its political or social impact.

Some biblical scholars now prepare commentaries aimed at fostering discipleship. That is, with the explicit purpose of doing their interpretative work to help people know and follow God as Christian disciples. Such commentaries aim to bridge the gap between conventional introductions to the New Testament and the real-life questions of people's lives, and to make a 'link between the struggles of our ancestors and our own struggles; between the challenge of discipleship in Jesus' time, and in our own' (Howard-Brook and Ringe 2002, p. ix).

The British New Testament scholar John Vincent has worked with a team of scholars and pastors for some years on a method known as Practice Criticism. This approach interprets the New Testament documents with the primary question: what is this text pointing me to do as a disciple? See *Acts in Practice* (2012) and *Discipleship: The New Testament Mosaic* (forthcoming).

Scholars writing to foster discipleship are usually careful to make their social location, ideological commitments and exegetical purposes explicit. This helps to ground and reveal the limits of their acts of interpretation. They also all make clear that they need the help of others in the believing community to live out their ideological and faith commitments. Refreshingly, for readers used to seeing scholars maintain a safe distance from the life of the church, these scholars even try to identify ways that the church can help them do this. For example, David's chapter on Acts in *Discipleship: The New Testament Mosaic* offers the following guidance for contemporary disciples:

> Be equally focused on the welfare of the church and the world; be attentive and responsive to the leading of the Spirit of God; give and receive hospitality; take decisions and face up to disagreements; see Christian witness as multi-dimensional; have a worldwide commitment to spiritual and social liberation; expect and cope with opposition from those in power; remember that, because Acts teaches by narrative and example, we have to work out what it means to 'do likewise' in our own time and place.

Other biblical books and interpreters may well emphasize other discipleship practices. Responsible interpretation for discipleship obviously requires ongoing conversation with others. There is a strong Christian tradition advocating studying the Bible for discipleship with others.

Interactive Bible studies are one of the ways in which the Bible can be interpreted corporately, relationally and in dialogue with other interests. Such approaches can be quite simple, for example memorizing and retelling Bible narratives or doing *lectio divina* together in a busy town centre. Other approaches can be more complex: exploring biblical themes in contemporary art, writing letters to biblical characters or imagining new incidents in biblical narratives. By pressing participants to draw on memory and imagination to interact with the Bible, such approaches help them to see for themselves that the Bible is a product or memory, experience, imagination and faith. It also often leads to participants transforming personal insights.

The classic resource books for this have been written by Hans-Ruedi Weber, formerly the director for biblical studies at the World Council of Churches and a professor at the Graduate School of Ecumenical Studies at Bossey, near Geneva. These are *The Book that Reads Me* (1995) published in the USA with the title *The Bible Comes Alive* (1996) and *Walking on the Way: Biblical Signposts* (2002). The former offers a rich collection of examples and the latter shows how many of these methods can be used for the study of Luke's gospel.

Scriptural Reasoning

Scriptural Reasoning is a recent movement which invites people of different faiths to reflect on one another's scriptures together. It began with Jews, Christians and Muslims reflecting on the treatment of common subjects or themes in the Hebrew Bible, the New Testament and the Qur'an, and has subsequently spread to include members of many other living faiths.

The process is relatively simple: people of different faiths agree to meet together to reflect on how a topic is covered in the scriptures of each faith. Examples of topics might be fasting, revelation, etc. Scriptural Reasoning groups usually meet regularly so that participants get to know one another well. A group co-led by David in Manchester meets nearly every month and has spent three or four meetings discussing a variety of passages on different topics.

Short texts on an agreed theme are circulated beforehand. When the group meets, the members discuss each text in turn, after each one has been introduced very briefly by someone of the faith from which the text comes. Because the scriptures of each faith have different formation histories, and function differently in each faith, there is no standard approach to all the texts. In the discussion that follows it quickly becomes apparent that the text in the original language is what many think of as 'scripture', with translations being secondary concessions to those who do not know the original language. This raises the bar for Christians, who might be comfortable not attending to the Hebrew, Aramaic and Greek of the Bible.

The discussion of the text also quickly introduces information about how these scriptures are used in the faith in question. Christians are surprised to learn how passages of the Hebrew Bible that might seem of secondary importance to them are of central importance to Jews (and vice versa). One of the most important educational elements of this process is that it defamiliarizes the text. Christians are surprised at what members of other faiths know and do not know about the New Testament (or the Hebrew Bible). As other members of the group ask them questions, they in turn may be humbled to recognize how little they know about their own scriptures and the scriptures that are sacred to others.

Sometimes there is the shock of recognition. Members of the group are surprised to find that the scriptures of other faiths may be very similar to their own and may draw on or distort the teachings of their scriptures. This 'compare and contrast' process, which is one of the ways humans learn, frequently leads to a deeper understanding of their own scriptures and a warmer appreciation for the faith and scriptures of others. Often there will be differences of emphasis and interpretation between members of the same faith as well, and members of other faiths may be able to help clarify these differences and place them in the context of wider discussions, for example a discussion of a text about Mary the mother of Jesus, which is of different importance to Jews, Christians, Muslims and Baha'is, needs explaining to Hindu or Buddhist members of the group, who will have their own comparable traditions of the birth and family life of a prophet or holy person.

This approach to scriptural interpretation has three main benefits. It fosters good relationships between people of faith; it deepens the understanding of the faith traditions and practices of others; and it develops the faith of people of faith. It is a committed interpretation process because it requires participants to share their understanding of their scriptures from the perspectives of being participants in that faith tradition. People talk to one another about their scriptures from within their own lived faith experience. Paradoxically, people without faith recognize the importance of this and are usually encouraged to hear that such conversations are going on and with such constructive results. In David's experience, interpreting the Bible in conversation with people of other faiths and interpreting their sacred texts in the same way, strengthens the social fabric and enables people of faith to work together with integrity in the public realm. This building up of relationships and strengthening of partnerships is of great benefit in the increasingly diverse and globalized world of the twenty-first century.

Try it out

Scriptural Reasoning is easy to try out. Contact a local interfaith group and invite members of different faiths to meet for a taster session. Choose a topic of obvious importance to all, such as: how to educate children, how to care for the natural world, the importance of song for faith. Ask participants to bring along copies of a short text (say five to ten lines) on the topic from their scriptures, with enough copies for each group member.

Give each group member the chance to read their text aloud and say why they have chosen to share this passage. Then let the discussion flow naturally. There will be many questions from members of the other faiths. Just be sure to allow enough time for all the texts to be read and discussed. If you run out of time, plan to do the others at a second meeting.

You may well find that many of the issues raised in this book are relevant to the way these discussions proceed. Does this suggest that the process of Bible interpretation is the same as, similar to, or different from, the process of interpreting the Scriptures of other faiths?

Commitment to scholarship: using commentaries

In the final section of this chapter, we look at the use of commentaries to aid interpretation. There is a reason why this topic has been deferred to now: if consulted too early, commentaries impair our ability to listen to the Bible for ourselves. They can intimidate us by their scholarly language and learning, influence us to view the text with their biases, disappoint us by ignoring what we think is important, drown out the soft voices within the text which are straining to be heard, particularly the voices of those on the social margins, and so on. They also take years to write, while interpretative needs may arise very quickly and need a more rapid response. In a nutshell, commentaries can make us forget the very questions we brought to the text to find answers. We need to remember that commentaries should be used to support, rather than direct, our own interpretative investigation.

> **Try it out**
>
> To see how important it is to remember that we have to begin with our own provisional interpretation of a text, try out this imaginative test:
>
> You are stranded, alone, on a desert island, with just a Bible to read, and you wonder whether this book can help you survive or escape. On your imaginary island, you first need help to meet the basics of life: water, food and shelter. Then you need to take stock of your situation. Where are you? Are you really alone? Are you in danger? Where will you find the inner resources to keep going, while you build a boat, or wait for rescue? Let your imagination run free: what kind of commentary would be useful to you in that situation?

The purpose of the imaginative exercise above is to show you how commentaries written by people living in very different circumstances from yours are unlikely to be as helpful as those written with yours in mind. If there were a series of commentaries written by castaways, they might well be your first choice!

Setting aside our desert island example, and assuming that we do have access to a theological library or bookshop, which commentaries should we consult? Commentaries, like friends, need to be chosen wisely. Our choices will be based on our own changing circumstances and needs. This means that there is no answer to the question, 'What is a good commentary on such and such a book?' without also considering, 'Good for whom?' and 'Good for what purpose?'

Choosing a commentary

When looking for commentaries to consult, we should start by considering our own experience. Have we used commentaries before? If so, what did we use them for, and which ones did we find to be most helpful for that purpose? If we have had commentaries on our bookshelves for many years, but have hardly looked at them, it may be worth asking ourselves why this is and whether they are likely to be much help now. There are so many modern commentaries available that it is usually unnecessary (and unwise for beginners) to struggle with difficult or outdated commentaries. There is a place for classic commentaries from the past, but guidance and experience will be needed to know which these are. When approaching a biblical book or topic for the first time, it is wise to look for those that interact with the scholarly consensus, rather than those that argue for new or untested views.

Some commentaries are more expositions than commentaries, frequently based on a series of sermons or Bible readings given in a particular church context. If the expositor has taken the trouble to be a careful exegete and if the context for which the expositions were prepared is similar to the one we are engaging with, then such interpretations may offer us useful guidance. However, we should use such expositions with caution.

Next we should consider the purpose we have for consulting commentaries on any particular occasion. If we think of the tools introduced in this book, we will be aware that we need commentaries to provide some basic information about the book from which our chosen passage comes, and a very wide range of detailed information. Most commentaries will provide the basic historical and literary information we need to orientate ourselves, such as the genre of the book; where, by whom, when, and for whom it was written; its shape and major subdivisions. However, even on the basics, commentators will differ, so more than one needs to be consulted.

As far as detailed information is concerned, no single commentary, no matter how large, will provide all the information we need. So we need to choose commentaries which focus on our area of interest. We will be guided in our search by knowing as much as possible about the author(s) of the commentary: their age, gender, nationality, ethnicity, vocation, research interests, denominational or religious affiliation, and so on, remembering that all commentaries are products of earlier conversations with other interpreters. We should choose commentaries which seem to engage with a topic or issue that concerns us at the time.

We also need to consider our own current level of technical skills. For example, if we have some knowledge of classical Hebrew or *Koine* Greek, then commentaries that refer to the original languages will be useful. If we don't, we will want to be assured that the author knows the original language of the passage, and is sensitive to the needs of readers who do not know it. Real experts are usually able to explain complex matters simply, and it is usually safe to avoid authors who seem over-complex.

Remember that people's needs differ. Here are some questions we might ask when we consider using a commentary for a particular interpretative task.

- Is it easy for me to use it for this purpose?
- Does the introduction help me see the shape and key theological issues?
- Is it written with reference to the original language(s)?
- Does it make good use of appropriate exegetical tools?
- Does it make connections with issues in contemporary life?
- Does it take a committed approach: political, theological, denominational, etc.? If so, what? If not, what ideological commitments is the author concealing?

Guides to commentaries

Despite the attraction of owning a set of books with matching covers, we should not buy complete sets or series unless we have already found a number of volumes in the series very useful. Commentaries in series are usually written by different authors and so vary in quality. It is worth knowing the general character of particular commentary series, as we will find some series useful and others unhelpful at whatever stage we are at in our work of interpretation.

Soulen and Soulen (2011, pp. 40–2) offer a brief description of some of the major series.

Further help with the choosing of commentaries can be found in larger guides to commentaries. Remember that those who comment on commentaries will have their own agendas and we should be aware of the purposes and orientation of the authors of such guides. Most of those listed below are by evangelical Christians who have relatively conservative views of the inspiration of the Bible. However, they are also written by scholars who understand the complexity of the exegetical and hermeneutical task faced by commentators. Overall, these guides are useful both in describing the character of series as a whole and, especially, in identifying which are particularly good volumes within each series, as well as classics.

The best single volume guide to books which aid the study of the Bible is Bauer's *An Annotated Guide to Biblical Resources for Ministry* (2011). This is particularly useful as it also provides guidance on other important study aids such as concordances, word studies, lexicons, introductions, etc. Tremper Longman III provides a useful guide to Old Testament commentaries in *Old Testament Commentary Survey*, 5th edition (2013) and John Goldingay and Don Carson's *New Testament Commentary Survey*, 7th edition (2013) is equally useful.

Finally, we should not just find and stick to our favourite authors but remember that it is also important to look at commentaries written from different perspectives from our own, and with different commitments. These help us to see where our blind spots or prejudices are and widen our vision. Christians will often find that commentaries written by Jewish scholars are very helpful in their study of the Hebrew Bible and the New Testament. Good starting points are *The Jewish Study Bible* (2014) and *The Jewish Annotated New Testament* (2011). An excellent example of dialogue between Jewish and Christian scholars is *The Gospel of Luke* (2018), co-authored by Amy-Jill Levine and Ben Witherington III, which recognizes, celebrates and grapples with the diversity of perspectives and commitments each author offers.

This chapter brings to an end our discussion of all the different factors that affect our biblical interpretation: our goals, our experience and expectations, ways of looking more closely at the text and ourselves, and the commitments we and others bring to every act of interpretation. In the next chapter we look at ways of using this information to have deeper conversations with the Bible.

6

Enabling Dialogue with the Text

Introduction

When we have a conversation with someone else, there are certain rules we follow. We have to make time available for the conversation, listen carefully to what the other person says so we can respond appropriately and be able to express our own views. We will usually find some common ground as well as some differences of opinion. Good dialogue also requires us to be honest about our views but open to change. And in any conversation, someone has the last word, which either opens up further dialogue or closes it down.

In this chapter, we explore our dialogue with the Bible. How can we accurately hear what the Bible says, particularly when it speaks with several voices? How do we bring our experience into the conversation? And who should have the last word? We have already done much of the preparatory work for this penultimate stage in our interpretive process. In Chapter 3, we explored the tools at our disposal for examining the Bible and taking account of a passage's shape, context and formation. We then thought about how we talk about ourselves and our context honestly (Chapter 4) as well as the impact our commitments make to our reading (Chapter 5). We are now ready to bring all these elements together and consider the various hermeneutical approaches we might use.

For most Christians and Jews, the Bible takes on the role of the primary dialogue partner in the conversation between text and readers. Its authoritative status in these communities means that its contribution to any conversation is regarded as trustworthy and of significance. For such readers, remembering how the Bible has offered guidance and hope in their own lives and the lives of their community of faith in the past, gives them reason to continue to place their trust in the Bible. However, as we saw in Chapter 2, many other readers see the Bible differently. For them, the Bible is just one conversation partner and must take its place alongside their life experience and other knowledge such as scientific theory or ideological criticism.

Whether we intentionally prioritize either the biblical text or our experience, we should note that neither can be relied on to 'keep to the script'. The range of voices, contexts and theological or ideological positions represented across the Bible makes it impossible to fix permanently what the Bible teaches about any theological or ethical issue. Equally, readers who prioritize their lived experience in ethical or theological debates, rather than the experience reflected in the Bible, have to take account of how this too changes over time.

Because of the rich and multi-layered nature of both reader and text, we have already acknowledged that questions about the meaning of a biblical passage can only be answered for a particular time and place. The outcome of the dialogue will change depending on who is involved in the conversation. We should therefore be cautious of any attempts to establish a universally authoritative interpretation of a passage. The Bible always has more to add to the discussion, as do we as readers. Walter Brueggemann (1997b, p. 59) encourages readers to respect the density of the biblical text and its contexts of formation and reception and warns against what he calls 'thin' kinds of scholarship (Brueggemann 1997b, p. 61), interpretations that stay at the surface of the text.

The aim of this chapter is to explore how we can engage in fruitful dialogue with the Bible, whatever our understanding of its inspiration and authority. We can never read the Bible without our reading being influenced in some way by our own life experience and, as we noted in Chapter 4, it is important to acknowledge this so that it enriches our study rather than obstructing it. How then do we hold those insights from our experience and those that emerge from the text in creative tension? What kind of working relationship should we try to create?

Let's explore these introductory observations by looking at a range of approaches to John 10.14 in which the evangelist records Jesus' claim, 'I am the good shepherd'. If we were to read the passage against the background of the whole canon, we would note various connections between this verse and other texts. It recalls the opening line of Psalm 23, 'The Lord is my shepherd; I shall not want', suggesting that the writer of John saw Jesus as acting out God's role on earth. The passage also alludes to the judgement of Ezekiel on certain leaders of Israel who are characterized as careless shepherds who do not care for the flock or search for lost sheep (Ezek. 43). Finally, from the New Testament, the passage in John could be regarded as an enacted version of the parable of the lost sheep (Luke 15.1–7).

If we read from a secular perspective, or as someone of a different faith than Christianity, we will inevitably struggle with biblical claims such as the one Jesus makes about his status in John 10.14, even if we accept the artistic value of a passage, its historical accuracy or its social insights. If we are Christian readers, however, we might find great comfort in this verse, observing how Jesus' bold claim is supported by his ministry of care and guidance recorded in the four gospels. The words and deeds of Jesus would confirm for us that Jesus is a righteous leader who will guide and care for us, keep us from harm and bring us to safety. In this way we would interpret the text by exploring the wider biblical narrative and with reference to our own faith experience.

This kind of devotional interpretation makes a single step from Jesus' claim to the reader's own journey of discipleship, with the reader perhaps thinking: 'Jesus is the good shepherd who promises to provide for his followers, therefore I should follow him.' But, historical criticism teaches us that our access to Jesus is mediated by the evangelists and their communities. Therefore, historical critics would encourage us to take a more cautious approach, first exploring the situation and beliefs of the Johannine community, using historical and sociological tools to understand its struggle with the leaders of the Jewish synagogues and their consequent search for new leadership models. Such an approach to the text would suggest that the focus of the passage is about choosing which leaders to follow and would lead us to consider the competing claims for allegiance we face in our own lives and how we decide who to trust.

Now, what happens to our interpretation of this verse if we introduce our own experience into the conversation? We could reflect on our own role as leaders or followers, thinking about the characteristics we value in a leader and how we develop our own leadership skills. We might also want to explore what kind of leader Jesus was, and consider whether a shepherd who would die for his sheep (John 10.15) is an appropriate role model for leaders today.

Finally, as we have already noted, the lived commitments of some readers will lead them to read the Bible with caution. This verse may therefore cause us to question the notion of a good shepherd. Is the shepherd really good for the sheep? Or is he only good in the eyes of the farmer who profits from the wool and will eventually kill and eat the sheep or their lambs? While noting such cautions, looking at the impact history of this verse, we would note that it has more often functioned as an encouragement to readers who are comforted by the image of the good shepherd and encouraged to follow Jesus, trusting in his promise to provide good things.

> **Try it out**
>
> Read John 10.1–9, the passage before the discussion of the good shepherd. Following the example above, consider how you might interpret the image of the gate: in relation to the wider biblical canon; through your own beliefs and practices, as part of a religious community or otherwise; in connection to barriers, boundaries and gatekeepers today and our own experience of these; and in light of the impact history of this passage over the centuries.

This example illustrates how we can bring together exegetical tools, our experience and social analysis to shape our interpretation of a passage. In the rest of this chapter, we will explore this process in more detail and try to draw together the resources we have built up in previous chapters.

As we have seen throughout this book, the Bible is a complex work with a mixed history of interpretation. As readers, we all have different experiences of the Bible and some of us will wrestle at greater length with our interpretations. Whether we find reading the Bible a positive experience or something with which we struggle, identifying our interpretative method will help us to enjoy the process and do it better.

The relationship between text and interpreters

There are at least two possible relationships between the biblical text and its interpreters.

A direct relationship?

Many readers of the Bible see a direct relationship between the teaching of the Bible and their response, with little need for any kind of interpretation. Certainly, there are some passages within the Bible that seem quite straightforward to us when we read them. These include moral instructions, such as 'You shall not steal' (Ex. 20.15), and encouragement to imitate certain characters, for example, despite their complex and often problematic story in Genesis, Abraham and Sarah are held up as examples of faith (Heb. 11.8–12).

> **Try it out**
>
> Read Luke 2.25–40, the story of Simeon and Anna's encounters with the baby Jesus. Simeon and Anna are remembered within the Church as wise and faithful people whose patience was rewarded. How does the passage portray them? Which of their characteristics would you want to imitate in your own life?

From the earliest times, Christians have been encouraged to become Christ-like, with Paul urging 'Let the same mind be in you that was in Christ Jesus' (Phil. 2.5). Francis of Assisi is perhaps the most famous person who tried to imitate Jesus' life, his dress and even his wounds. One of Francis' followers once had a vision of a grand church procession in which apostles, saints and martyrs were all trying carefully to imitate Christ. At the very back 'came the little shabby figure of Francis, barefoot and brown robed; and he alone was walking easily and steadily in the actual footprints of our Lord' (Moorman 1950, p. 51). Reading the Bible to learn how to follow Jesus is a well-established and valid approach for many Christians. In a modern take on this ancient practice, some Christians wear wrist-straps printed with the letters WWJD that stand for 'What Would Jesus Do?' a reminder to the wearer to act as Jesus would in any situation. The source of the phrase is Charles Sheldon's still relevant story, *In His Steps* (1896). This method of reflection on the Bible extends beyond personal behaviour into social and political engagement, for example, a placard at a London *Stop the War* march in 2003 asked, 'Who Would Jesus Bomb?' But Scott Spencer's study, *What Did Jesus Do? Gospel Profiles of Jesus' Personal Conduct* (2003) reminds us of the historical problem: we have no direct access to Jesus' actions, only what the gospels portray. As with any approach, we need to proceed carefully, using the relevant exegetical tools to ensure our interpretations are accurate and responsible.

Take for example the belief that Jesus encouraged followers to 'turn the other cheek'. This seemingly straightforward command still needs to be interpreted in relation to the religious, social and political context in which it was given.

> **Try it out**
>
> Read Matthew 5.38–42 and think about how Jesus' words might be able to guide his followers to respond to aggression or violence.

Walter Wink's interpretation of Matthew 5.38–42 demonstrates the importance of knowing about Jesus' context as well as his words. While Jesus' command to turn the other cheek has often been understood as encouraging passive acquiescence to evil, Wink suggests Jesus was instead advocating non-violent resistance of the Roman forces. Wink points out that to turn the left cheek towards the social superior who had just slapped the right cheek was a way of resisting the intended humiliation. The superior cannot respond by hitting with the left hand (since it is unclean) but cannot easily give a backward slap onto the left cheek with the right hand either so would only be able to punch the left cheek. But since only people of equal standing punched each other, this would remove the humiliating nature of the act – although not the physical hurt (Wink 1992, pp. 175–84). Thus Ulrich Luz suggests, 'Wink's interpretation offers an impressive third way between violent resistance and resignation' (Luz 2007, p. 274). This example indicates the potential pitfalls of making simple and direct correlations between the Bible and our own situation without understanding the meaning of an action in its original social context.

Like individual readers who apply biblical teaching directly to their own situation, some communities also draw a close correlation between their situation and situations within the Bible. Some of the vernacular approaches that we looked at in Chapter 5 do this. To take a further example, many Rastafarians identify their community's experience of enslavement and deportation, with that of the Israelites' captivity in Babylon (Murrell 2000). In reggae music and other Rastafari cultural expressions, 'Babylon' becomes a way of speaking about America, the Caribbean, or Britain; places to which enslaved Africans were taken by force and where they still suffer racism. There are many biblical allusions in reggae music: Bob Marley's song 'Survival' refers to Daniel 3.24–26 and the survival of Shadrach, Meshach and Abednego who were thrown into the fiery furnace but 'never get burn'. Yet, the way in which biblical language is reworked and shaped to speak to a new context should caution us against over-simplifying such readings (Thompson 2012, p. 331). More accurately, by reading themselves into the biblical text, reggae artists enable it to speak afresh of resistance and liberation.

> ## Try it out
>
> Look for the lyrics of one or two songs from one of the many music genres that frequently refer to the Bible (blues, soul, gospel, country, bluegrass, world, hip hop, etc.). How do they use biblical metaphors, themes, characters or situations? What are the benefits and problems of using biblical vocabulary to talk about current realities? How does such use of the Bible in song lyrics modify your understanding of the original biblical references?

The biblical themes of exodus, exile and redemption that reflect foundational events for the Jewish and Christian community are often used by later readers in this way. They signify significant moments for Jews and Christians but have also gathered new meanings in different contexts. Because of their depth and range, they can be used to explore a wide variety of situations because the relationship between the Bible and interpretive context can also be indirect. Social commentators who make use of these themes tend not to indicate a clear match but rather use them to hint at a relationship of some kind between the two situations and thus highlight aspects of the contemporary experience. One example of the use of both exodus and exile (but little mention of redemption) can be found within the Brexit debate between 2016 and 2019 that included warnings of an 'exodus' of skilled workers and investors from the UK, as well as discussion of the 'self-imposed exile' of the UK from Europe. Here, both terms are used negatively to indicate loss of relationship and connection.

A correspondence of relationships

In Chapter 3 we looked at how interest in the social background of the Bible and the application of social scientific tools has thrown new light on the situation in which different biblical writings arose.

The gap between the worlds described in the Bible and contemporary realities lead the Brazilian theologian Clodovis Boff to challenge the idea that we can read actions or responses appropriate to our own situation direct from the biblical texts. In his book, *Theology and Praxis: Epistemological Foundations* (1987), he described the approach we looked at in the previous section as the 'correspondence of terms', in which the reader sees a direct parallel between the biblical situation and their own context. Boff felt this method draws oversimplistic parallels between biblical contexts such as the exodus and his context of political and economic conflict in Latin America; for example, in a picture of the massacre of the innocents drawn by members of the Solentiname community. Herod's army is replaced with soldiers in the uniform of the Nicaraguan dictator Somoza (Rowland and Corner 1990, p. 55). A further limitation of a seemingly direct comparison is that it does not allow for the fact that there are many contexts embedded in biblical texts and not just one.

Thus Boff prefered to talk about a 'correspondence of relationships'. This approach notes the layered nature of biblical texts and how they reflect the situation from which they emerged as well as the situation they claim to describe. It looks at how biblical writers themselves adapt earlier events and traditions and apply them creatively to their own situation. This provides guidance to post-biblical interpreters. By observing how the biblical texts seek to answer the questions of their own day, later interpreters are enabled to interpret the text in a similarly creative way, and thus offer appropriate guidance to their readers.

> **Try it out**
>
> Read Jeremiah 32.1–15 in which the prophet Jeremiah is ordered by God to take ownership of a plot of land. Think about what buying a piece of land today could signify, for example, a sign of increased wealth, a way of preventing further buildings obscuring the view, space for a large animal such as a horse. Next think about what land signifies in the Hebrew Bible: Who owns the land? What is its relationship to the people? In the final verse of the section, Jeremiah's action is revealed as a sign of hope: 'For thus says the LORD of hosts, the God of Israel: Houses and fields and vineyards shall again be bought in this land.' Buying a piece of land today might not signify hope, but what other actions would be seen as 'hopeful' in your context?

The correspondence of relationships approach encourages a flexible method of engagement with the text. Boff observed:

> We need not, then, look for formulas to 'copy' or techniques to 'apply,' from scripture. What scripture will offer us are rather something like orientations, models, types, directives, principles, inspirations – elements permitting us to acquire, on our own initiative, a 'hermeneutical competence,' and thus the capacity to judge – on our own initiative, in our own right – 'according to the mind of Christ,' or 'according to the Spirit,' the new, unpredictable situations with which we are continually confronted. The Christian writings offer us not a what, but a how – a manner, a style, a spirit. (Boff 1987, p. 149)

Boff's method was based on an ideological commitment to liberation for the poor. It assumes that the Bible advocates liberation as well as entrusting readers to make good judgements about the text and how to apply it to their situation. Boff's encouragement to the reader to make their interpretation according to the mind of Christ relies on an accurate understanding of how Jesus or the early Christians responded to their situation, and as we have seen, this requires close analysis of the social context of the New Testament.

Identifying three broad interpretative approaches

All interpreters use some sort of principle to guide their dialogue with the text. Different hermeneutical approaches offer different ways of resolving the tensions within the Bible, or between disputed interpretations of a passage, or the claims of the text and the reader's own experience. We have already made reference to most of the hermeneutical principles used by readers of the Bible but, at this stage in the book, it may be helpful to review them. They fall into three broad areas.

The first set of approaches is based on the Bible and either seeks to read individual texts or books in conversation with the whole canon; or gives priority to particular sections, which are seen as foundational (such as the Torah, the gospels or Paul's letters). These approaches all emphasize dialogue with the text.

The second set is based on particular doctrines or beliefs, which are considered core beliefs for that community, for example, the Anglican emphasis on the sacraments or the Pentecostal emphasis on baptism in the Spirit. These approaches, while doctrinally different from one another, all emphasize dialogue with particular faith communities and traditions.

The third set uses hermeneutical principles based on the contexts, cultures or commitments of the readers. These approaches all emphasize dialogue between the interests of the text and the concerns of the contexts in which it is being interpreted.

In the next section we see what these look like in more detail.

Hermeneutical approaches based on the biblical text

In Chapter 2, we looked at the formation and authority of the canon. While some interpreters always try to read individual passages in the context of the canon as a whole, others regard certain sections of the Bible as more authoritative than the rest. The primary example of this approach is the priority given to the Torah in the Jewish tradition and the Gospels in the Church. By privileging certain books or themes within the Bible, interpreters are able to judge between diverse teachings.

Holding the canon together

Since the 1970s, there has been an increased interest in the canon as the context for interpretation. Two biblical scholars have focused on the impact of the canon on interpretation, but asking differently. James Saunders focused on the process of canon formation to explore how texts became authoritative to Jewish and Christian communities (see Saunders, *Torah and Canon*, 1972). Some other scholars have approached canonical criticism in this way. Michael Fishbane (for example, in *Biblical Interpretation in Ancient Israel*, 1985) explored how later biblical writers adapted and used earlier material, reinterpreting theological ideas for a new context (Saunders and Gooder 2008, pp. 63–4).

In contrast, Brevard Childs' canonical approach noted in Chapter 2 focuses on the final form of the canon and is interested in how the Bible is read as a text which has authority for the community of faith. His method takes the canon to be the arena in which any individual text is read and interpreted (Callaway 1999, p. 147). Since the canon contains a diversity of voices and perspectives, this results in an ongoing discussion, in which no single voice dominates. Indeed, the plurality of the biblical witness, messy and contradictory as it may be, is essential to its interpretation.

Intertextual readings similarly engage with the breadth of the canon, exploring allusions, citations and shared traditions that link different biblical passages. For example, Timothy Stone (2013) considers how both the book of Jonah, and the story of the calming of the storm in Matthew 8.23–27, draw on imagery from Psalm 107 to explore God's power over land and sea. Intertextual approaches further resist the idea that the meaning of a passage can be limited or fixed, arguing instead that the biblical text is dynamic and fluid.

> **Try it out**
>
> The Bible uses a number of different images and traditions to speak of the creation of the world. Stephen Dawes (2010, pp. 77–8) identifies four of them: majestic order (Gen. 1); messily organic (Gen. 2); mythic conflict (Isa. 51.9–11); playfully creative (Prov. 8.22–31). How do these four portrayals of creation work together? What would be lost if there was only one account of creation in the Bible?

In conclusion, interpretative approaches that look at either the formation or breadth of the canon all tend to result in more complex, nuanced and dynamic readings of the text. While these canonical approaches try to prevent interpreters from excluding other biblical texts as conversation partners, in practice many approaches give more attention to particular parts of the canon, as we shall see in the next section.

A canon within a canon

Beyond the identification of either the Torah or the Gospels as the primary texts within the Bible that happens in most Jewish and Christian contexts, various theological movements throughout history have formed their own 'canon within the canon'. Such selections tend to include teaching that promotes the particular theological or social beliefs of the group. Ernst Käsemann, for example, proposed a 'higher canon' composed of the gospels and certain Pauline letters such as Romans that were believed to highlight the principle of justification by faith. Some feminist scholars develop their own canon, selecting texts that seem to promote women's wellbeing. Of course, any such selective approach to the Bible is a form of Marcionism (named after the second-century CE theologian Marcion whose rejection of the Hebrew Bible we considered in Chapter 2) and, as the following example demonstrates, often fails to resolve interpretive conflict.

Néstor Míguez describes how radical Christian communities in Latin America initially relied on a selection of biblical texts: Exodus; parts of the Deuteronomistic history; prophets such as Amos; the synoptic gospels; the beginning of Acts; James; and Revelation. These texts were believed to speak most directly to the Latin America situation. But soon liberation theologians realized that they couldn't rely on a few helpful passages that clearly spoke of justice and equality, but needed to take a fresh approach to reading the whole Bible. There was a shift in focus: 'from a "liberationist canon" to a "canonical liberation"' (Míguez 2004, p. 9). Only by drawing upon the whole canon were liberation theologians able to respond to their critics.

Here, then, we see the limits of a 'canon within the canon' approach. While we might all have biblical books or passages that are particularly significant for us, the canon is designed to work as a whole, and if only certain parts of it are read, key themes are neglected and important ideas lost. Of course, in synagogues congregations will more frequently hear the Torah, and in churches the gospels are a constant, but other books need to be engaged with also. Jewish faith communities tend to be better at this, but, as Alan Cooper points out, biblical books like Leviticus that are often ignored by Christians as being 'legalistic' have important insights to offer Christian readers, notably the need to live a holy life, in harmony with all creation (Cooper and Scholz 2004).

Themes and movements within the canon

Retaining the whole of the Bible instead of keeping to a narrow selection enables us to read texts together and use them to interpret each other. However, we still have to make a judgement between different texts, often based on an understanding of the central message of the Bible. One common approach is to identify a unifying movement or dominant theme within the scriptural narrative. To some extent, all readers of the Bible do this in an attempt to impose some sort of order on the wide-ranging material before them, although each reader may highlight a different core message or movement within the text. We should note, however, that some readers question the existence of an overall pattern or narrative that unites the canonical material, believing that the diversity of the Bible has inherent value since it keeps open the arena of debate.

As an illustration of this approach, we turn to one scholar's attempt to identify a particular movement running throughout the Bible that can then function as an interpretive key. American feminist Rosemary Radford Ruether suggests the Bible itself contains 'resources for the critique of patriarchy and of the religious sanctification of patriarchy' (Ruether 1983, p. 23). She describes these as 'critical prophetic principles' and claims normative status for them. Ruether outlines four themes of the prophetic-liberating tradition of the Bible:

> (1) God's defense and vindication of the oppressed; (2) the critique of the dominant systems of power and their powerholders; (3) the vision of a new age to come in which the present system of injustice is overcome and God's intended reign of peace and justice is installed in history; and (4) finally, the critique of ideology, or of religion, since ideology in this context is primarily religious. (Ruether 1983, p. 24)

Ruether goes on to illustrate the centrality of these themes in the prophets and the synoptic gospels, for example Amos' critique of cultic worship. She also points out how this prophetic strand acts as an internal critique, 'through which the biblical tradition constantly reevaluates, in new contexts, what is truly the liberating Word of God, over against both the sinful deformations of contemporary society and also the limitations of past biblical traditions' (Ruether 1985, p. 117).

Ruether sees this constant reassessment and search for liberation continuing beyond the Bible into social movements throughout history, suggesting that the biblical principle of prophetic liberation works with the feminist critique to bring about social change. For this reason, the Bible must be read with an eye to the future coming of God's kingdom – or eschatologically, in order that it might offer liberation to groups beyond those liberated by the biblical writers (such as women). In summary, Ruether identifies and promotes a strand of tradition that can be used to judge the whole of the Bible. For Ruether, these liberative teachings always take priority over contrary texts or dissident readings.

We now offer a worked example of this kind of approach, reading Numbers 35 in the light of a wider movement within the Torah that critiques violent interpretations of this passage when read in isolation.

Try it out

Read Numbers 35 and note how violence is presented within the chapter. What forms of violence are recorded and how are they regarded? Who is responsible for the different acts of violence? Is God said to either commend or denounce the violence?

Violence pervades the whole of Numbers 35 and as readers in a still violent world we may question whether the chapter offers us any useable strategies for responding to violence. At first glance, it appears to advocate an eye-for-an-eye method of dealing with murderers which is bound up with notions of moral purity:

> You shall not pollute the land in which you live; for blood pollutes the land, and no expiation can be made for the land, for the blood that is shed in it, except by the blood of the one who shed it. You shall not defile the land in which you live, in which I also dwell; for I the LORD dwell among the Israelites. (Num. 35.33–34)

If we believe that retributive justice is the main theme of the Bible, we would be content to conclude our interpretation at this point, noting the need to take responsibility for our actions and be punished accordingly. However, if we think the Bible's overall thrust is more focused on grace and forgiveness, we would need to set this passage in a wider context and explore other ways of understanding these demands. Where else in the Torah does the land respond to blood being spilt?

> **Try it out**
>
> Now read Genesis 4.8–16, 25–26. How does God respond to the cry of the earth in this passage? How is Abel's death redeemed? Look at both the treatment of Cain and the response of Eve.

By reading Numbers 35 alongside Genesis 4, we discover other methods of responding to bloodshed. Even though Abel's blood pollutes the earth, further blood is not required to restore order, unlike the law outlined in Numbers 35. God does not demand the death of Cain and, although banished, Cain leaves with a mark of protection on him. Moreover, Abel's death is redeemed by the birth of a third child to Eve rather than by another death. Brigitte Kahl notes: 'Eve's naming of Seth takes up the cry of Abel's blood, out of the mouth of the earth. It restores justice . . . purifies and decontaminates what has been the source of curse and paralyzed fertility' (Kahl 2001, pp. 66–7). In this reading love, not vengeance, cries out from the earth.

Thus, reading Numbers as part of the Torah and using a hermeneutical key that identifies the dominant teaching of the Bible as a proclamation of God's grace opens up the possibility of other readings.

Reading from the shadows and silences in the text

Finally, as we have seen when thinking about literary approaches to the Bible, while still looking within the Bible, it is possible to pay close attention to the edges of or the gaps within narratives. Towards the end of Chapter 2, we saw how some readers of the Bible prefer to begin at the margins of a story, or with texts that have tended to be ignored. They do this because they are suspicious of the story as it has traditionally been told and return to the text to discover other sides to the story, perhaps through a conviction that the Bible witnesses to unsettling truths which are not easily grasped.

Such approaches demonstrate the value of searching for what is hidden in the shadows, looking for meaningful clues left in the silences. They may prompt us to look beyond the text for other accounts of the described events that might challenge the biblical writer or editor's interpretation. An example of this would be Rachel's use of Diego Velázquez's painting *The Kitchen Maid with the Supper at Emmaus* (1618) when preaching on Luke 24, to consider how Jesus' story touches briefly on the life of the servant girl who enables the meal at Emmaus to take place but who catches only snatches of the conversation. Rachel reflects on the alternative timeframe of the girl: 'When first one, then the other two men leave suddenly, she will return to the table, carefully gather up the cups and crumbs, smooth the cloth, blow out the candle and – at last – rest.' What new insights are to be gained when Luke's account is seen through the eyes of this girl? How are we helped to pay attention to the whole picture?

Hermeneutical approaches based on theological beliefs

The alternative to hermeneutical approaches that look within the Bible is to look beyond the text for principles to guide our interpretation. Elsewhere, we have looked at a number of examples of how other texts, cultural traditions or ideological commitments are brought into dialogue with the Bible. In this section, we will look at examples of when theological convictions are given priority in the interpretive method.

Selecting an external interpretative principle requires us to be alert to how we might attempt to harmonize the text and external resources, denying the critique they may present to each other. For instance, we noted in Chapter 4 how church doctrines have been used as a lens through which to read the Bible, and how on occasions this has led to Christian theology being imposed on the text rather than emerging from it.

Although there is a wide range of theological readings of the Bible, from both Jewish and Christian communities of faith, in this section we focus on Christ-centred readings of the Bible. Christian theologians such Karl Barth argue that Christ should always be at the centre of any attempt to interpret the Bible. For many Christians, especially those belonging to the Orthodox churches, the incarnation is the central event in history and thus the theological key to understanding everything else. Other Christological readings may focus on Jesus' saving death and resurrection, while still others may focus on his ministry of teaching and healing. Reading the Bible through such lenses enables Christian readers to keep focused on the Gospel.

Christological readings use an internal interpretive key (the New Testament's witness to Christ), but they are dependent nonetheless on the interpretation of the biblical story of Jesus by the Church and therefore rely on this as an external principle. The following paragraphs introduce a variety of Christological approaches to the Bible, which have developed through the history of the Church, some of which are clearly at odds with others.

Some Christians effectively ignore the Hebrew Bible, believing the coming of Christ removed the need for these texts. Although few Christians today formally argue for a truncated canon consisting only of the New Testament, the lack of attention and care paid to the Hebrew Bible (for example, the tendency to preach mainly on New Testament texts in many local churches) indicates how such attitudes are widespread in practice. We noted in Chapter 2 how subverting the Hebrew Bible to the New Testament has damaged Jewish-Christian relationships over the centuries, and prevented Christians from engaging with the depth and range of the biblical witness.

The existence of the canons is a constant reminder that the early Church chose to hold onto the Jewish scriptures, claiming them as the Old Testament and thus setting them in relation to the New Testament witness. Early Christian readers developed a typological approach to the Jewish texts that led them to believe there were hidden meanings in these texts that pointed to the coming of Christ and establishment of the Church. The Hebrew Scriptures were believed to have a double meaning, the primary meaning bound to the context of the passage and a second, Christian, meaning that is regarded as more important. This approach is present in the New Testament itself; for example, Romans 5.14: 'Yet death exercised dominion from Adam to Moses, even over those whose sins were not like the transgression of Adam, who is a type of the one who was to come.'

Typology was popular in the early church and medieval period when many Christians used it to see Christ signified in the Hebrew Bible. For example, early Christians interpreted certain motifs within the Joseph narrative to signify Christ and the church: grain and a wine cup; the tree on which a person is hung; periods of three days; descending into a well or into the depths of prison. One of the benefits of typological approaches was their impact on the visual arts as painters brought into dialogue different scenes and characters from both testaments; for example, the medieval Trier Gospel from Germany includes an image of the baptism of Christ paired with an image of Noah in the ark.

Typological approaches helped keep the Hebrew Bible in the life of the Church and prevented Christians from discarding it in favour of the New Testament. Hans-Ruedi Weber argues that the *Biblia Pauperum* developed by Benedictine monks in the late Middle Ages offered a visual interpretation of the relationship between the Old and New Testaments that is still useful today. Using a fifteenth-century illustration of the descent of the Spirit at Pentecost, he shows that the event is prefigured by the gift of the Torah on Mount Sinai and the fire consuming Elijah's sacrifice on Mount Carmel. Alongside the central panel are pictures recalling prophecies from the Psalms, the Wisdom of Solomon, Ezekiel and Joel (Weber, 2002, pp. 51–9).

While this approach helped to show how a passage might be related to others in the canon, it ran the risk of neglecting earlier 'plain' meanings of a text. In fact, patristic and medieval scholars never regarded typological readings as sufficient in themselves, instead advocating a fourfold method of interpretation (literal, moral, allegorical and ultimate) that recognizes the layers of meaning and significance of the text (Soulen and Soulen 2011, p. 72). Today there is even more caution about the value of allegorical or typological readings. The Vatican's document *The Interpretation of the Bible in the Church* (The Pontifical Biblical Commission 1993), for example, encourages Catholics to seek out the literal sense of the text, with careful reference to the different types of literary genres in the Bible and the different ways they express truths, as well as the original historical context of the text. This meaning should always be held alongside the insights that emerge through a wider faith-related reading. For example, when Christians look at how the coming of Christ might be seen as the fulfillment of prophecies in the Hebrew Bible (as the gospel writers propose in the infancy and passion narratives), they should make such interpretations in continuity with the original literal meaning of the text.

Some Christian scholars advocate a more developed method of interpreting the Hebrew Bible than a typological one. Brevard Childs argues that while Jews read the 'Hebrew Bible', Christians read the 'Old Testament', making it clear that Christians always read both canonical collections together. Childs' approach does not require the reader to reject Jewish understandings but rather he encourages Christians to hold both readings together in a coherent fashion (Brueggemann 1997b, p. 91).

Try it out

Read Isaiah 61.1–3 and Luke 4.16–21. With the aid of resources such as the *Jewish Study Bible* (2014) see how the Isaiah text is read without reference to Jesus' use of it. Ponder the paradox that Jesus is described in Luke as reading it in a standard first-century Jewish context. If you are a Christian reader, think about how your Christian beliefs and the use of this passage in the life of the church affect your understanding of this passage. If you are a secular reader, or have a

> different faith commitment, think about your understanding of this passage. What is the identity of the suffering servant? If possible, talk to another reader who has a different perspective.

Most biblical scholars are rightly cautious of Christological readings of the Hebrew Bible, particularly in light of the anti-Semitic tradition of interpretation within the Church. When Christians read the Hebrew Bible solely through the lens of Christian belief they risk implying that Jewish readers do not have the full story. To avoid neglecting profound Jewish understandings, Christian readers of the Hebrew Bible should resist automatically looking for answers to interpretive questions in the New Testament. The books of the Hebrew Bible should be valued in their own right, as well as part of the wider canon of faith. *The Preaching Without Prejudice* series encourages Christian preachers to be attentive to anti-Semitistic interpretation of the gospels, letters and the Old Testament (Allen and Williamson 2004, 2006 and 2007). Scriptural reasoning also offers a method for Christians to discover afresh Jewish interpretive traditions.

In addition, Christian interpretation of the New Testament should seek to engage with Jewish scholarship on first-century Judaism. Alongside the *Jewish Study Bible* (2014), *The Jewish Annotated New Testament* (2011), edited by Amy-Jill Levine and Marc Zvi Brettler, offers valuable correctives to Christian misunderstandings of Jesus' context and teachings. Amy-Jill Levine's *Short Stories by Jesus: The Enigmatic Parables of a Controversial Rabbi* (2014) locates Jesus within wider Jewish movements and debates.

To conclude this section, we look at an alternative Christ-centred approach to the text that, while focused on the figure of Jesus, does not deny other faithful readings. Tim Gorringe's political liberationist reading of the Bible is based on the consistent call for justice throughout the Bible, particularly for the poor and oppressed, but uses Jesus' actions rather than the Christ event as the starting point for his interpretation.

> This claim would rest on the hermeneutic significance of Jesus' story for the whole biblical narrative, on Jesus' commitment to the marginalized, his teaching about service and greatness, on the fact of his crucifixion by Roman power and the way the theme of service and death is interpreted by Paul in passages

such as 1 Corinthians 1—3, and Philippians 2.5ff. To read the Bible in this way is not to support just one political programme, but it does on the other hand rule out a great many. (Gorringe 1998, p. 78)

Gorringe's approach is similar to those we have already looked at that identify a core strand of teaching or critical movement within the Bible with which to interpret the whole text. He uses it to set out the limits of political interpretation of the Bible, challenging the legitimacy of political readings that do not represent a commitment to social justice and transformation.

Many Christians employ some sort of Christological approach to the Bible because of their understanding of the significance of Jesus' life, death and resurrection. Using a Christological lens can help Christian readers locate a text within the wider arena of their faith. However, it should be used with care and respect for earlier and ongoing meanings of the text.

Hermeneutical approaches based on the interpreter's contexts, cultures and commitments

When marginalized groups discover that dominant accounts of reality do not represent their experience, they often develop their own sources of truth. For example, in the 1980s Chuck D. of hip hop group Public Enemy repeatedly called rap music 'black people's CNN' (Toop 2000, p. 46) because mainstream sources of information were unable (or unwilling) to broadcast what was really happening among black communities. In response to this, hip hop artists became 'self-proclaimed contemporary prophets', offering 'truth-revealing parables and pictures' (Perry 2004, p. 2). Similarly, biblical interpreters from communities who feel their life experiences are not represented truthfully in the Bible have found other sources of knowledge with which to engage it. Oral Thomas (2008) reminds us that much of the biblical narrative is told from the perspective of the elite. In addition, the Bible has historically been interpreted by the powerful. By itself, therefore, its potential for liberation may be limited or hidden. For

Thomas, Caribbean culture, traditions and stories are important other 'texts' alongside which the Bible is interpreted; creating resistant reading from the margins.

We noted earlier how the Bible contains a critical dialogue between various traditions. This debate within the canon encourages contemporary readers to engage in a similar process of dialogue between the Bible and their own life experiences. As we saw in Chapter 5, many committed interpretative approaches prioritize contemporary human experience, even over the witness of the Bible. They argue for the truth-bearing possibilities of contemporary human experience as well as that of the faith experiences recorded in the Bible.

While most contextual interpretations encourage readers to acknowledge and trust insights from their lived experience, liberation readings seek to prioritize the insights of poor and marginalized communities. Christian Aid's *NRSV Bible* (2003) illustrates this interpretive method by putting on the front cover a picture of Asebech Amha, a young Ethiopian girl. This reminds readers to approach the Bible with the needs and hopes of poor and marginalized people such as Asebech in mind. In a similar way, Argentine theologian Nancy Bedford expresses the desire that her commentary on Galatians would be life-giving for her three daughters; the unwritten suggestion being that biblical interpretation has not always served women well (Bedford 2016, p. xvi).

Feminist interpretations often come to the text with questions about how the text has traditionally been understood and, as Chapter 4 noted, regard biblical interpretation as a political act. Elizabeth Schüssler Fiorenza outlines a fourfold hermeneutic that takes suspicion as its necessary starting point (Fiorenza 1984b). She suggests that suspicion of a biblical text, which has been written and interpreted predominantly by men and used throughout history to marginalize women, is a vital starting point for feminist readers. The second step is one of remembrance, as the reader seeks out the lost and hidden stories of women in the Bible. This leads the reader to the third step of proclaiming a new, fuller witness. Finally this process enables 'creative actualization', as readers realize the liberating potential of their imagination once they begin to read between the lines.

> **Try it out**
>
> How do you understand the key terms used by Schüssler Fiorenza: suspicion; remembrance; proclamation; and creative actualization or imagination? Which of these words feel familiar ways of describing the process of biblical interpretation? You may think of the Protestant emphasis on the proclamation of God's word through preaching; or, if from a strongly sacramental tradition, might be drawn to the idea of remembrance, through ritual celebration and discipleship. Perhaps you have experience of reading the Bible with children and therefore are comfortable with the importance of engaging playfully and imaginatively with the text. More surprising, perhaps, is the idea that suspicion might be a helpful part of the process of coming to understand the Bible; although, if you are studying the Bible from a secular perspective, this may be your starting point.

In Chapter 2 we considered how some biblical interpreters challenge the notion of a fixed canon. Elizabeth Schüssler Fiorenza advocates an image of the Bible as a walled garden and encourages readers to makes use of resources within and beyond the wall. She believes canonical authority should not be oppressive and restrictive but should foster 'creativity, strength and freedom' (Schüssler Fiorenza 1994, p. 11). Thus the authority of the Bible is redefined as a starting point for liberative action, encouraging the reader to explore new ideas and approaches, rather than the traditional notion of the canon functioning as a boundary marker. This is especially important in contexts in which the Bible arrived late on the scene, and remains to a certain extent a 'foreign body' which struggles to describe local reality.

Kwok Pui-Lan (1995) believes Christians have to be able to let the Christian story and their own cultural traditions inform each other. This involves imagination as new images are created and ancient stories reinterpreted to help the two traditions connect. She offers the example of C. S. Song's weaving together of the Chinese story of Lady Meng with the passion narrative (Song 1981). A more recent example would be Fan Pu's paper cut *Biblia Pauperum* (2013), in which biblical stories are told through a series of triptychs that weave biblical verses with themes from Confucius' teachings (Hoekema 2014). Such vernacular interpretations enable Christians to read the Bible alongside local folk stories, sacred texts and cultural traditions affirming all as valid for faith exploration. Indeed, R. S. Sugirtharajah argues that: 'Read in Asia, the Christian Bible needs to be illuminated by other textual traditions in order to gain credibility and relevance' (2013, p. 258). Kwok suggests readers should use their 'dialogical imagination', involving active listening and openness to difference, to make real use of the resources their cultural and social context offer as they seek to discover the message of the Bible. This process gives value to different cultures and communities and suggests that just as the Bible can transform culture, so too can culture transform understandings of the Bible.

However, R. S. Sugirtharajah notes two problems with using indigenous stories and symbols in dialogue with the Bible. First, the danger of idealizing traditional culture and ignoring problematic practices such as caste hierarchies. Second, he warns that the symbols and stories used may no longer be relevant or central to the grassroots communities who are struggling to survive (Sugirtharajah 1995, p. 464).

When the Bible is read alongside other 'texts', whether made up of words, movement, sounds, images, or lived experiences, new insights can emerge from the interaction. As we saw in Chapter 5, Scriptural Reasoning is one such process of interpretation which finds new insights through reading sacred texts on the same topic but from different faith traditions alongside each other.

To conclude this section, we should note that most of us create our own unique interpretative lens that represents a mixture of the methods outlined above. For example, we may choose to prioritize the gospels alongside reading with a commitment to a particular political ideology, while at the same time being influenced by creative interpretive methods developed through local art and culture. Finally, we should note that any interpretative lens needs to be reviewed with care to ensure it does not leave us vulnerable to ideological distortion since our own cultural and social alliances often prevent us from recognizing more challenging interpretations.

Interpreting the Bible through storytelling

The common theme of all these interpretive approaches is that they promote dialogue within and/or beyond the Bible. Musa Dube from Botswana looks at how African women use traditional storytelling methods to reread the Bible and apply it to their own context. This method makes use of African ways of depicting life and transmitting values and wisdom. It recognizes that the story is dependent on the teller and the hearers as well as the actual story. 'The teller or writer thus does not own the story or have the last word, but rather the story is never finished: it is a page of the community's fresh and continuous reflection' (Dube 2001, p. 3).

Dube retells Mark 5.24–43, in which a woman is healed by touching Jesus on his way to heal a sick girl, as an allegory of the healing of 'Mama Africa' also suffering from years of bleeding. She concludes:

> Mama Africa is standing up. She is not talking. She is not asking. She is not offering any more money – for none is left. Mama Africa is coming up behind Jesus. She is pushing through a strong human barricade. *Weak and still bleeding but determined, she is stretching out her hand. If only she can touch the garments of Jesus Christ.* (Dube 2001, pp. 59–60, Dube's italics)

The English evangelical scholar Richard Bauckham similarly suggests that rather than seeing the authority of the Bible as a set of rules, its authority should be understood as similar to that conveyed by a story. As readers, we enter into stories and are changed by them. While Bauckham claims that the Bible is the most important story for Christians, he notes that the biblical story does 'hold open space' for other stories (Bauckham 1999, p. 13). Indeed, Bauckham describes the biblical story as unfinished and suggests that as readers we play a role in developing it. However, Bauckham notes that Christians believe they have been shown the conclusion of this 'great story' through the resurrection of Christ which points to the ultimate inauguration of the reign of God in heaven and earth.

For Bauckham (as with Musa Dube's storytelling method) the Bible reveals its authoritative teaching like other stories: gradually, dynamically and in a way that keeps its readers involved (Bauckham 1999, p. 18). All commands and teachings in the Bible have to be understood in the wider context of its overall narrative framework.

In common with the approach adopted in this book, Bauckham argues that the meaning of the Bible does not lie either with the text or the reader but in their interaction, as we have repeatedly observed. The otherness of the text means that readers need to pay it careful attention:

> In summary, this is a hermeneutic which requires the interpreter seriously to listen to the text and to do so as someone who listens, not in abstraction from her own context, but in deliberate awareness of her own context. It is the listening that allows the text to speak with authority and the context that allows the text to speak with relevance. (Bauckham 1999, p. 22)

> **Try it out**
>
> Experiment with retelling to yourself, or someone else, one of the following passages as a story: John 2.1–11; Esther 4.1–17. You might choose to tell them in the first person, as if you were one of the biblical characters involved. What difference does this make to your understanding of the passage? How does this method allow you to enter into the story and explore it through your own experience?

What kind of story do you discover in the text? For some scholars, such as Ericka Shawndricka Dunbar (2018), the book of Esther is a testimony of human trafficking, sexual violence and resistance. What kinds of stories do we allow the Bible to tell?

Can we read the Bible against ourselves?

Given that there are different views of the relationship between the text and reader, how can we ensure that our interpretive principle does not simply reinforce our existing beliefs and remain open to the challenge of the Bible? Here are some suggestions. First, we should always be suspicious of readings that seem to wholly justify our actions. Second, we should challenge readings that domesticate the Bible, making it safe. Victorian interpretations of the infancy narratives transformed the nativity into a scene of middle-class family bliss. The hymn 'Once in Royal David's City' encourages Christian children to be 'mild, obedient, good as he'. Such domestication obscures the poverty and insecurity into which the evangelists suggest Jesus was born, and imports a non-biblical picture of his family life. The only biblical account of Jesus' adolescence describes Jesus causing his parents great anxiety (Luke 2.41–51). And rather than being mild, Jesus is described as strong and wise (Luke 2.40, 52).

Third, as readers and interpreters we must be willing to be questioned by the Bible as well as questioning it. Dietrich Bonhoeffer criticized Christians in Germany who, 'only read the Bible for themselves, discarding what they didn't want . . . the call is also to read Scripture *over-against* ourselves, allowing Scripture to question our lives' (Fowl and Jones 1991, p. 145). In a lecture entitled 'The Church is Dead', delivered at a conference in Switzerland in 1932, Bonhoeffer asked:

> has it not become terrifyingly clear again and again, in everything that we have said here to one another, that we are no longer obedient to the Bible? We are more fond of our own thoughts than of the thoughts of the Bible. We no longer read the Bible seriously, we no longer read it against ourselves, but for ourselves. If the whole of our conference here is to have any great significance, it may be perhaps that of showing us that we must read the Bible in quite a different way, until we find ourselves again. (Bonhoeffer 1965, pp. 185–6)

Here is an example of how we may read the Bible against ourselves, for those of us who are located at the centres of global power, drawing on insights from postcolonial criticism, which as we saw in Chapter 5, interprets the Bible through the lens of colonialism.

Try it out

Read Mark 5.1–20. What do you think this story is about? Write down a few ideas before reading the section below.

For a long time western readers have been blinded to the anti-imperial teaching of Mark's Gospel because they have been conditioned to accept the Roman Empire as a positive model of governance and learning. Richard Horsley notes:

> In theological schools as well as Sunday schools we learn that in many ways, by establishing order and an elaborate network of roads, the Roman Empire made possible the spread of the Gospel by apostles such as Peter and Paul. But by and large we have little idea of the extent to which Roman imperialism created the conditions from which the mission of Jesus and the Jesus movements arose. (Horsley 2003, p. 17)

Jesus' brief yet dramatic visit across the Sea of Galilee during which he heals a demoniac is often regarded as the inauguration of a mission to the Gentiles. Passages such as this offered Christian missionaries a mandate to take the gospel to the far corners of the world. But if we pay attention to Jesus' and later Mark's context, we discover that this story is not a mandate for Christian expansion and empire building. Indeed, the historical connections between Christian mission activity and western colonialism should make readers highly suspicious of any such interpretation. The social context for Jesus' mission was the Roman occupation of Palestine and the repression that accompanied it. Interpreters such as Horsley and Ched Myers (1990) suggest Mark 5.1–20 is a coded challenge to the Roman legion stationed nearby. If then, Mark's account is read as a highly political comment on the Roman Empire, what might it have to say to those readers living in the 'new empire' of today?

Bonhoeffer's warning against a cosy relationship with the Bible is still relevant. If our interpretations do not challenge us, we should investigate our assumptions more deeply to ensure we are not letting ourselves off the hook.

Can we read against the Bible?

In contrast to the previous section, some biblical interpreters believe that there are parts of the Bible that are difficult to interpret positively and therefore advocate resistance to the text, warning us to be prepared to struggle against the text when all we can see in it are perspectives or beliefs that violate us. Renita Weems argues that biblical interpretation should be a process of:

empowering readers to judge biblical texts, to not hesitate to read against the grain of a text if needed, and to be ready to take a stand against those texts whose worldview runs counter to one's own vision of God's liberation activity in the world. (Weems 2003, p. 31)

There are some texts where violence and injustice are clearly visible, and we will explore possible strategies of resistance to these in a moment. Yet, to begin with, let us take a less obvious example of a text we might be wise to resist: the Ten Commandments.

> **Try it out**
>
> Read Exodus 20.1–17. Imagine you are a married woman, a poor rural labourer, or a foreigner who has been sold into slavery. How do these laws impact on your everyday life? Are there any of the commandments that seem difficult or irrelevant?

Challenging the claims of the text itself, David Clines (1995) argues that the Ten Commandments are not neutral universal laws, but rather emerge from a specific social context and work for the benefit of certain groups within that context, namely, older men who own property. Thus, the prohibition against stealing protects those who have property rather than those who do not; and the prohibition against adultery reflects concerns over inheritance. Even the Sabbath law, often seen as ensuring a day of rest for all members of society, does not take account of the situation of many rural poor who would have to continue to feed animals and work the land; and of others who lived hand to mouth.

In more recent times, we have become more aware of the vulnerability of children in the home, church and society, and therefore the need to challenge teachings which assume that it is always right for a child to honour their parent, without reference to the value of the child's wellbeing. Thus, our own individual or collective experience of suffering and struggle, and our changing understandings of justice and right relationships, may provoke new questions of the Bible.

In the search for liberative readings of the Bible, we need to distinguish between parts of the Bible that offer life and those that describe death. There are some biblical stories that serve only as a terrible record of the wrong humans can do.

A clear example of resisting such texts is Phyllis Trible's approach, outlined in *Texts of Terror* (1984), which responds to problematic texts from the Hebrew Scriptures by denouncing their moral authority. She studied stories of rape, abuse and murder and considered how these stories of abused women bear witness to ongoing patriarchal violence. By reading against these texts, Trible suggests readers can respond to the violated women of the story through a renewed commitment to justice and equality.

In Judges 11, Jephthah makes a vow to Yahweh that should he be victorious over the Ammonites, he will sacrifice 'whoever comes out of the doors to meet me' (Judg. 11.31). But in a horrific turn of events, it is his only daughter who comes dancing out to greet him on his return. Trible suggests our response should be this:

> Like the daughters of Israel, we remember and mourn the daughter of Jephthah the Gileadite. In her death we are all diminished; by our memory she is forever hallowed. Though not a 'survivor,' she becomes an unmistakable symbol for all the courageous daughters of faithless fathers.... surely words of lament are a seemly offering, for did not the daughters of Israel mourn the daughter of Jephthah every year? (Trible 1984, p. 108)

So Trible argues that we must tell such sad stories but always against any interpretation that justifies violence. She cautions us against attempting to smooth over our discomfort by suggesting that there is any redemptive element to such innocent suffering. Rather we must employ a critical reading that, 'interprets stories of outrage on behalf of their female victims in order to recover a neglected history, to remember a past that the present embodies, and to pray that these terrors shall not come to pass again' (Trible 1984, p. 3).

As interpreters of the whole Bible, we cannot simply choose to ignore these difficult passages. They are part of the canon and so it is vital that we continue to engage questioningly with them. Ignoring such texts leaves them open to continued misinterpretation. It is only through intentional and ongoing reflection on them, in dialogue with others, that we can challenge the violence of such texts and their problematic interpretive history.

Paying attention to the minor characters or nameless victims that haunt the Bible is one important way to avoid repeating the violence generated by many traditional interpretations. Looking away from the violence done to small, seemingly insignificant figures in a biblical story encourages us to look away from similar acts of violence and unknown victims in our own world.

Gina Hens-Piazza offers the following strategy for reading violent texts. First, make use of social scientific research to ensure we understand as accurately as possible the reality of the context from which the text emerged and which it reflects. This should prevent us from making inaccurate judgements about the action of characters in the text. Second, read stories of violence in memory of the victims within the text and beyond it. Next, resist the promptings of the narrator or our own instincts when they lead us to justify the violence of the text or identify with the characters who are painted in the most positive light. And finally, search out counter-texts that offer alternative ways of responding to violence (Hens-Piazza 2003, pp. 119–22).

Hens-Piazza makes use of this approach in her commentary on *Lamentations* (2017), which is significant for being one of only a few commentaries on this text written by female scholars (Hens-Piazza mentions earlier works by Kathleen O'Connor and Adele Berlin as significant, p. xi). She recognizes that some feminist scholars have argued that the violence against women and their silencing in *Lamentations* is so problematic that it should be removed from the biblical tradition (p. xlii). Yet for her, the value of the text is its ability to make visible such violence, and, through committed interpretation, draw out courageous resistance and voices (p. xliii). As part of the *Wisdom Commentary* series, the discussion incorporates a number of voices alongside that of the central author. These reflections on the experience of sexual violence, poverty and war, serve as the alternative accounts which Hens-Piazza draws on in her efforts to resist the violence of the text and its theology. In her conclusions, Hens-Piazza notes how the character of Woman Zion resists her suffering and challenges the theology which suggests such suffering is appropriate punishment. In so doing:

> She gives voice not only to her own emancipation from the clutches of self-blame and victimhood; she also occasions a prayer space for other women to express their anger and their pain. And in the process, women can move forward in an embrace of the full value of their lives as women and begin to recognize the real Holy Presence within their midst. (Hens-Piazza 2017, p. 99)

> **Try it out**
>
> Read Luke 23.39–43, a familiar part of the Passion narrative. Using the four-step process outlined above, explore how violence is manifest in this passage and how it might be read in a way that counters violence.

Despite the importance of attending to these difficult texts, we should not restrict our attention to them. Frequently, for our own well-being, we need to hear words of comfort rather than oppression. African American writer Howard Thurman tells the following story about his grandmother:

> My regular chore was to do all of the reading for my grandmother – she could neither read nor write ... With a feeling of great temerity I asked her one day why it was that she would not let me read any of the Pauline letters. What she told me I shall never forget. 'During the days of slavery,' she said, 'the master's minister would occasionally hold services for the slaves ...' Always the white minister used as his text something from Paul. At least three or four times a year he used as a text: 'Slaves be obedient to them that are your masters ..., as unto Christ.' Then he would go on to show how, if we were good and happy slaves, God would bless us. I promised my Maker that if I ever learned to read and if freedom ever came, I would not read that part of the Bible. (Thurman 1949, pp. 30–1)

We must seek liberation from the text: both from the potential violence of the text and by finding liberation in the text. This search for liberation is our final step in the process.

7

Our Goal: Life-Affirming Interpretations

Revisiting our start point

At the end of any process of interpretation, we need to assess how far we have come towards the goal we began with. What task, question or situation brought us to the Bible and have we arrived at a satisfactory interpretation for this purpose? As we began Chapter 1 by noting the importance of defining the purpose of each act of biblical interpretation, so we now consider how to assess whether our goal or goals have been met.

> **Try it out**
>
> How much closer are you to understanding one of the questions you brought to the text at the start? In what ways has your question been refined by the interpretative process?

Chapter 1 noted there are many different reasons for reading the Bible. These may be grouped into public purposes and faith-based purposes. However, many public interpreters (including academic interpreters) work from an implicit or explicit faith perspective (or other commitments that affect their reading). Similarly, many Jewish and Christian readers, and particularly those in leadership positions, use academic scholarship to inform and enrich their interpretations.

OUR GOAL: LIFE-AFFIRMING INTERPRETATIONS

That said, it is important to be aware on any occasion whether the Bible is being interpreted in the context of religious faith, or in an academic or other public context, because the reasons for the interpretative work and the expected outcomes are different.

Randy Litchfield suggests that Bible study in local church groups has a number of purposes, all with the aim of helping Christians to develop in various ways. These include growing in discipleship, experiencing God through the Scriptures, developing their understanding of the Scriptures, seeking guidance for their lives, forming and transforming themselves and their communities, being responsible stewards of the Christian tradition and developing their ethical responsibility (Litchfield 2004, p. 228).

Academic and public study of the Bible is also carried out for a wide variety of purposes. In Chapter 3 we looked at some of the literary, historical and impact historical questions that need to be investigated. In Chapter 5 we looked at the ways interpreters around the world aim to bring the Bible into dialogue with pressing contemporary social, political, cultural, theological and ethical issues. We also saw these two broad areas of enquiry are no longer kept separate and that committed readings are now established as a valid and exciting area of academic research. Interpreters are very aware that biblical interpretations have an impact on public life and so research into the impact history of the Bible has become one of the most important areas of development in the field of biblical studies today. The early twenty-first century has also seen a rise in global conflicts, which some people see as foreign aggression or terrorism and others consider appropriate interventions for the sake of peace and security. These conflicts are rooted, at least partly, in clashes of religious and cultural perspective. Against all the predictions of the mid-twentieth century, religion and the Bible are very much back on the agenda today. For this reason, learning to interpret the Bible is an important skill for all who wish to participate in public life. It is also a transferable skill which can help us to read the sacred texts of other religious faiths more sensitively.

Try it out

If you approach the Bible primarily from a faith perspective, think about which of the goals of academic study you also want to pursue,

> and vice versa. How might you encourage dialogue across the boundaries of academic and faith communities? What opportunities do you have to read the Bible with people with different intentions or expectations from your own?

Seeking healing, transformation and liberation

Whether the Bible is studied from an academic or public perspective or from a faith commitment, or a combination of both, the process outlined in this book suggests that all readers can share a common goal: to discover good news through dialogue with the text which can be lived out. The notion of good news may seem limited to Christian readers (after all, the word 'gospel' means 'good news') but news that is genuinely good can take any number of forms. It can apply to a range of goals, private or communal, academic or devotional, and can alert readers to difficult truths as well as positive insights. It can offer validation of the reader's experience, with associated comfort, reassurance and healing, or challenge to ourselves or others, or even forthright condemnation of oppression, whether recorded in the Bible or perpetuated today.

The process we offer in this book argues that good news for the reader, and for others affected by their reading, is the proper goal of biblical interpretation, whether such good news is focused on advancing our historical understanding of a particular period in the formation of the Bible, or on offering the reassurance of God's peace to those wanting to grow in faith.

Yet good news for some can mean bad news for others. How are we to adjudicate between these competing goals? We believe that one important criterion is: Does our interpretation help the poor, powerless or marginalized? This value derives from the Bible itself, which repeatedly highlights God's concern for the oppressed, aliens, widows and orphans. By giving priority to the questions and needs of the most vulnerable, interpreters can be more confident that their readings are life affirming for all. Thus the aim of our biblical interpretation should be to engage in conversation between text and context to find, and realize, good news that nurtures life for all, and especially for those who need help the most.

OUR GOAL: LIFE-AFFIRMING INTERPRETATIONS

Much of the Bible is about people's encounters with a God who is presented as good and as caring for the whole natural order, and so there are many passages in it which might offer good news to all readers. Most theological readings of the Bible begin with the principle that God is good, that God's world is good, and that God's purposes for all of it are good. But such readings should also recognize that this is not always evident in human experience. Indeed, people sometimes experience God and the world as sources of suffering and evil instead. Moreover, as we have seen, human liberation can sometimes be hard to find in some of the more difficult passages in the Bible, and in light of the bad consequences of irresponsible biblical interpretations. The figure of Jacob wrestling with a mysterious figure (an angel or demon, or even God?) until the break of day in Genesis 32, can serve as a model for us as we sometimes struggle to extract a blessing from the Bible.

Filipina theologian Muriel Orevillo-Montenegro recalls how following her rejection of a god who inflicted suffering, she 'searched diligently' for the true God of love (unpublished paper, 1998). Her experience of communal struggle encouraged her to look for a liberating word for the oppressed within the biblical narrative. In a similar way, William Abraham's notion of the canon as a space for formation leads him to see how 'Scripture functions to bring one to faith, to make one wise unto salvation, to force one to wrestle with awkward questions about violence and the poor, to comfort those in sorrow, and to nourish hope for the redemption of the world' (Abraham 1998, pp. 6–7).

Some interpreters argue that the Bible itself advocates methods of reading that promote peace, justice and love. Ulrich Luz recommends using Jesus' radical love as 'a criterion of truth' for biblical interpretation and application (Luz 1994, p. 96). This should lead us to reject interpretations that do not promote more loving ways of living in the world. Néstor Míguez brings together the criterion of love and justice, recognizing that biblical interpretation has an impact beyond the reader. He argues, 'interpretation is not only an intellectual exercise; it is also a liberating experience of overcoming injustice, a living experience of loving others' (Míguez 2004, p. 10).

Although it has at times failed to do so, the institutional Church is committed to reading and following the Bible in ways that enable the flourishing of life. This has led individual church leaders and public gatherings of leaders to challenge interpretations of the Bible that cause social harm. The Vatican warns against 'every attempt at actualization set in a direction contrary to evangelical justice and charity, such as, for example, the use of the Bible to justify racial segregation, anti-Semitism or sexism' (The Pontifical Biblical Commission 1993, cited in Houlden 1995, p. 85). We are aware that the churches have not always lived up to this goal, but this is still something which the churches expect of themselves and which society at large expects of them.

> **Try it out**
>
> Look at a church newspaper or listen to a religious programme such as *Thought for the Day* on BBC Radio 4, to identify how people seek to offer socially constructive interpretations of the Bible in relation to a current issue. Do you support their views?

In Chapter 1, we proposed that we should aim for 'provisional yet responsible' interpretations of the Bible. Provisional readings acknowledge that though our context as readers is always changing, we can still offer responsible interpretations of the Bible each time we engage with it. As we have seen, being responsible interpreters requires us to work with integrity, paying close attention to ourselves and to the text before us. This requires us to be both consistent and dynamic in our interaction with the Bible.

Be consistent

To be consistent in our handling of the text, we should always come to the text aware of where we are and aware of the wider situation we are reading from. In Chapter 2 we noted that we need to be aware of how we view the Bible and why we see it in that way. We should also be attentive to the actual text in front of us and diligent in our attempts to understand what it actually says, rather than what we think it says. As we noted in Chapter 3, there are a range of exegetical tools at our disposal to help us do this. As responsible interpreters we should always try to use the tools best suited to the task and passage we are working on, and be willing to try out new methods where necessary. If we have a commitment to reading as part of a particular community (the church, a social or ethnic group, as a New Testament scholar, etc.) we should be upfront about that and how it informs our reading. Furthermore, we should take account of the work done by other readers, both in the academy and at a popular and devotional level.

Being consistent should prevent us from letting the text or ourselves off the hook by applying a different interpretative strategy to difficult or challenging texts. It requires us to remain open both to the text and to who we are, and to recognize when this dialogue invites new definitions of ourselves, the world or our beliefs. That is, we should expect our consistent encounter with the text to change us for the better.

Be dynamic

Seeking out life-affirming interpretations should also encourage us to be dynamic in our relationship with the Bible. The open-ended and dialogical nature of the text encourages us to go beyond surface readings, noticing divergence and movement, and being alert to the range of meanings that the text contains.

Moreover, as we noted in the previous chapter, from a Christian perspective the Bible is perceived to tell an unfinished story which will only be completed with the coming of God's kingdom. This openness suggests the reader has a role in shaping the ongoing story of the Bible's interaction with the world. Richard Bauckham notes:

> The *unfinished* nature of the biblical story – or, more positively, the eschatological hope as the ultimate future God will give to his world – is what creates the space for finding ourselves and our contemporary world in the biblical story. It is what enables and requires the hermeneutic of listening in context that we have briefly suggested. It is what resists the premature closure that would stifle the freedom of obedient Christian living in the contemporary world. (Bauckham 1999, p. 23)

Such an understanding of the process of reading gives us responsibility for developing the story. The World Council of Churches notes the responsibility of the church to anticipate the coming kingdom of justice and peace in its response to the Bible:

Just as Scripture constantly looks forward in hope to God's future, the interpreting activity of the Church is also an anticipatory projection of the reality of the reign of God, which is both already present and yet to come. Reading 'the signs of the times', both in the history of the past and in the events of the present, is to be done in the context of the announcement of 'the new things to come'; this orientation to the future is part of the reality of the Church as an hermeneutical community. Therefore the struggle for peace, justice and the integrity of creation, the renewed sense of mission in witness and service, the liturgy in which the Church proclaims and celebrates the promise of God's reign and its coming in the praxis of faith, are all integral parts of the constant interpretative task of the Church. (World Council of Churches 1998, pp. 19–20)

In Chapter 4 we explored the nature of our identity as readers. These are both specific to any one moment and context, and yet changing as we move through life: having new experiences, moving to new places and taking up new roles. Awareness of our changing life situation and attitude towards the Bible should stop us being over-confident that we hold the definitive interpretation of any text. What we need is a working interpretation that equips us for action. We can later reassess our earlier readings and modify them based on the experience of testing them out in practice.

This process of action and reflection is known as the hermeneutical circle. This is not a new concept. The idea of a dynamic circle that keeps open the conversation between our context and the text was developed by the philosopher Martin Heidegger, though the theologian Friedrich Schleiermacher had already noted that words, texts and contexts interact in a mutually revising way (Soulen and Soulen, 2011, pp. 82–3). Rudolph Bultmann in turn pointed out that the quality of the life questions put to the text at the start of the process determines the quality of the answers the hermeneutical circle produces, because prior understanding is needed to hear a text well (Bultmann 1950, p. 90).

In more recent times the hermeneutical circle has been adopted by liberation theologians, particularly those working in Latin America. These theologians begin all interpretation from their lived experience. Practical action is the first stage and precedes reflection on the Bible and the situation of the interpreter. With action as the driving force, this approach forces us to keep open the dialogue between text and context. Reflection can lead to action, but by starting with action we are provoked to more specific and rigorous reflection on what we are doing because we know that we shall be using the result of our reflection to guide the next stage of our action. Thus, action helps to ground and focus our reflection on and interpretation of the Bible. Juan Luis Segundo argues, 'each new reality obliges us to interpret the word of God afresh, to change reality accordingly, and then to go back and reinterpret the word of God again, and so on' (Segundo 1976, p. 8).

Notice that the hermeneutical circle is actually a spiral, as each rotation of the circle leads interpreters to higher or deeper understandings of the text and its context. This explains why we can never complete our study of any biblical passage. We come to the text each time at a different stage in our lives, bearing particular concerns, and so we always approach it afresh.

Biblical texts not only repay rereading because of the changing circumstances of our lives, but also because of the long processes involved in their formation and their reception. Each passage echoes the voices and perspectives that affected its development and resonates with other stories within and beyond the biblical canon.

Reading the same text repeatedly helps us distinguish between what remains the same and what changes. The words in the text remain the same, though even these have been subject to some changes during their development, transmission and translation. Because our own perspectives and judgements, and the culture we live in, are all subject to change, we recognize that our interpretations of the text are likely to change in the future.

Try it out

Rachel once spent an academic term studying the story of Cain and Abel (Genesis 4.1–16) and with each new reading discovered something new. As the term progressed, the events of the world, the church calendar, and her changing circumstances all created new questions with which to approach the text. Try this for yourself. Choose one Bible passage to live with for a few months, to see how your changing life affects your interaction with it.

Brian Blount points out that change is a consequence of being alive and attentive:

> Since we're always changing, and our contexts are always changing, the words that interpret the whisper of God's Spirit in our time must necessarily be changing as well. God, you remember Jesus saying, is a God of the living, not of the dead. But a last word is necessarily a dead word. It stops listening. It stops learning. It stops living! . . . *Nothing that is living is ever lasting.* A living word is always a beginning word. (Blount 2002, pp. 56–7, Blount's italics)

To take another image: we trace our provisional readings of the Bible in the swirling dance between text and context. Through disciplined yet lively activity, we explore what we, and those who are still strangers to us, need to know here and now. This reflects a Jewish and Christian understanding of God's activity as a loving dance of creation, restoration and constant renewal.

> ### Try it out
>
> Helder Camera encouraged readers of the Bible to 'Honor the word eternal/ And speak to make a new world possible' (Camera cited in Morley 1992, p. 158). Read 1 Thessalonians 5.12–28. How might your interpretation of this passage open up new possibilities and ways of acting well in the world, while honouring the 'word eternal'?

In his book, *Defenseless Flower*, Carlos Mesters notes of poor communities in Latin America:

> The people's main interest is not to interpret the Bible, but to interpret life with the help of the Bible. They try to be faithful, not primarily to the meaning the text has in itself (the historical and literal meaning), but to the meaning they discover in the text for their own lives. . . . The Bible of life was their lives, in which they tried to put into practice and incarnate the word of God. And it was even more: life itself is for them the place where God speaks. (Mesters 1989, p. 9)

OUR GOAL: LIFE-AFFIRMING INTERPRETATIONS

The ultimate purpose of biblical interpretation is not understanding, but healing, transformation and liberation. It is to enable people to live and flourish. Therefore we end as we began, committed to an ongoing quest for life-affirming interpretations of the Bible, open to the faith perspectives of these ancient texts, even if we do not share these ourselves. The Bible is about humans seeking to encounter God. When we interpret the Bible we participate in the ongoing exploration of the many different ways in which God's liberating and transforming love might be revealed to humanity.

Summary of the Interpretative Process

Chapter 1: Where do we want to go?

This step in the interpretative process asks you to:

- identify your overall reason for studying the Bible;
- identify your interpretative focus in studying a particular passage, and understand how that focus affects your reading of the passage;
- be clear about the questions you begin with, even if these are different to the ones you end up with;
- work towards a provisional and responsible interpretation of a passage.

Chapter 2: Past experience and present expectations

This step in the interpretative process asks you to:

- take account of the Bible's social, cultural and political influence in your own and other contexts;
- take account of the unfamiliar nature of the Bible, both as an ancient Near Eastern text and as a text that is regarded by some as divine;

- identify your own understanding of the Bible's authority and witness;
- read the Bible as a whole, and make use of intertextual methods of interpretation;
- identify your own extended canon and make appropriate use of it;
- note how the use of a lectionary shapes a faith community's interaction with the Bible;
- recognize the value of central and marginal texts;
- consider how you resolve tensions and differences within the Bible.

Chapter 3: Tools for exegesis

This step in the interpretative process asks you to:

- become familiar with a text through a range of methods including copying out and memorizing;
- use discourse analysis to analyse the structure and composition of a text in detail;
- use narrative criticism to identify and explore narrative features such as events, characters and narrative strategies;
- read a text in the original language or make use of a range of translations;
- make use of the insights of textual criticism;
- recognize how words develop over time and the need to explore the historical meaning of a word or phrase in a text;
- use form criticism to identify earlier oral use of a text and its genre;
- use source criticism to identify earlier written sources of a multiple source text;
- use tradition criticism to locate the text within wider cycles of narrative and traditions;
- use redaction criticism to consider the theological beliefs of the final author or editor of a text;
- make use of methods that explore the wider social, political and religious background of a text;
- use impact history methods to explore how a text has been received and its influence over time.

Chapter 4: Our reality

This step in the interpretative process asks you to:

- recognize the role of the reader in creating the meaning of a text;
- describe your own identity and begin to consider how different aspects affect your interpretation, including: gender and sexuality; ethnicity and colour identity; age, ability and wellbeing; socio-economic status and political affiliation; denominational, spiritual and theological traditions;
- undertake social analysis of your context, through careful observation and the use of an appropriate method of analysis;
- consider the communities to which you belong and how you read the Bible as part of them.

Chapter 5: Committed readings

This step in the interpretative process asks you to:

- recognize how your commitments affect your reading;
- take account of global readings, including postcolonial criticism and vernacular readings;
- identify your own ideological commitments, those of the text and those of other methods;
- recognize how reading from a faith perspective influences interpretation, including noting the effect of spiritual reading methods, hearing the Bible in a context of worship, and readings that nurture discipleship;
- explore reading the Bible alongside other sacred texts;
- make good use of commentaries.

Chapter 6: Enabling dialogue with the text

This step in the interpretative process asks you to:

- see interpretation as a form of dialogue;
- consider how the context of a text and the context of interpretation relate to each other;
- identify your hermeneutical key(s) from the Bible, a faith perspective or your context and commitments;
- practise reading the Bible as story and note how this opens up space for dialogue between a text and your context;
- allow space for the Bible to critique your interpretation;
- resist violent or other harmful interpretations of the Bible.

Chapter 7: Our goal – life-affirming interpretations

This step in the interpretative process asks you to:

- revisit your starting point in the interpretive process;
- consider the different academic and faith-based reasons for studying the Bible and how there can be dialogue between them;
- be consistent and yet dynamic in your interpretation;
- commit to life-affirming interpretations of the Bible.

References and Further Reading

Abraham, W. J. (1998), *Canon and Criterion in Christian Theology*, Oxford: Oxford University Press.

Adamo, D. T. (2006) *Biblical Interpretation in African Perspective*, Lanham MD: University Press of América.

Aharoni, Y, and Hav-Yonah, M. (1968), *The Macmillan Bible Atlas*, New York and London: Macmillan.

Allen, R. J. (1987), *Contemporary Biblical Interpretation for Preaching*, Valley Forge, PA: Judson Press.

Allen, R. J. and Williamson, C. M. (2006), *Preaching the Letters Without Dismissing the Law: A Lectionary Commentary. Preaching Without Prejudice, v. 2*, Louisville, KY: Westminster John Knox.

Allen, R. J. and Williamson, C. M. (2007), *Preaching the Old Testament: A Lectionary Commentary. Preaching Without Prejudice, v. 3*, Louisville, KY: Westminster John Knox.

Anglican Consultative Council (2012), *Deep Engagement, Fresh Discovery: Report of The Anglican Communion 'Bible in The Life of The Church' Project*.

Archer, K. J. (2009), *A Pentecostal Hermeneutic: Spirit, Scripture, and Community*, Cleveland, OH: CPT Press.

Augustine (397, 426), *On Christian Doctrine*.

Aune, D. (1997–8), *Revelation*, 3 vols, Word Biblical Commentary, Dallas, TX: Word.

Avalos, H., Melcher, S. J. and Schipper, J. (eds) (2007), *This Abled Body: Rethinking Disabilities in Biblical Studies. Semeia Studies 55*, Atlanta, GA: Society of Biblical Literature.

Aymer, M. (2016), 'Outrageous, Audacious, Courageous, Willful: Reading The Enslaved Girl of Acts 12', in G. L. Byron and V. Lovelace (eds), *Womanist Interpretations of the Bible: Expanding the Discourse. Semeia Studies 85*, Atlanta, GA: Society of Biblical Literature Press, 265–90.

Bailey, R. C. (1990), *David in Love and War: The Pursuit of Power in 2 Samuel 10–12. JSOT Supplement Series 75*, Sheffield: JSOT.

REFERENCES AND FURTHER READING

Bailey, R. C. (1998), 'The Danger of Ignoring One's Own Cultural Bias in Interpreting the Text', in R. S. Sugirtharajah (ed.), *The Postcolonial Bible*, Sheffield: Sheffield Academic Press, 66–90.

Bailey, R. C., Liew, T. B. and Segovia, F. F. (2009), *They Were All Together in One Place: Toward Minority Biblical Criticism*, Leiden: Brill.

Barton, J. (2002), *The Biblical World*, 2 vols, London: Routledge.

Barton, J. (ed.) (1998), *The Cambridge Companion to Biblical Interpretation*, Cambridge: Cambridge University Press.

Barton, M. (2004), 'I Am Black and Beautiful', *Black Theology* 2, No. 2 (July), 167–87.

Barton, S. C. (1995), 'Historical Criticism and Social Scientific Perspectives in New Testament Study', in J. B. Green (ed.), *Hearing the New Testament: Strategies for Interpretation*, Grand Rapids, MI and Carlisle: Eerdmans and Paternoster, 61–89.

Bauckham, R. (1983), *Jude, 2 Peter*, Word Biblical Commentary 50, Waco, TX: Word Books.

Bauckham, R. (1999), *Scripture and Authority Today*, Cambridge: Grove.

Bauer, D. R. (2003), *An Annotated Guide to Biblical Resources for Ministry*, Peabody, MA: Hendrickson.

Bauer, D. R. (2011), *An Annotated Guide to Biblical Resources For Ministry*, Eugene, OR: Wipf and Stock.

Bechdel, A. (1985), 'The Rule', *Dykes to Watch Out For*.

Beckford, R. (2001), *God of the Rahtid: Redeeming Rage,* London: Darton Longman and Todd.

Beckford, R. and Bean, T. (2017), *Jamaican Bible Remix (audio)*.

Bedford, N. E. (2016), *Galatians: A Theological Commentary On The Bible*, Louisville, KY: Westminster John Knox Press.

Behar, R. (1997), 'Sarah & Hagar: The Heelprints Upon Their Faces', in G. T. Reimer and J. A. Kates (eds), *Beginning Anew: A Woman's Companion to The High Holy Days*, New York: Simon and Schuster, 35–43.

Berger, K. (1999), 'Form Criticism, New Testament', in J. H. Hayes (ed.), *Dictionary of Biblical Interpretation*, vol 1, Nashville, TN: Abingdon, 413–17.

Berlin, A. and Brettler, M. Z. (eds) (2014), *The Jewish Study Bible*. 2nd Ed. Oxford: Oxford University Press.

Berry, L. (2014), *Black Country*, London: Chatto & Windus.

Betcher, S. V. (2007), *Spirit and The Politics of Disablement*, Minneapolis, MN: Fortress Press.

Betsworth, S. (2016), *Children in Early Christian Narratives. Library of New Testament Studies*, London: Bloomsbury.

Birch, B. C. and Rasmussen, L. L. (1989), *Bible and Ethics in the Christian Life*, Minneapolis, MN: Augsburg.

Block, J. W. (2002), *Copious Hosting: A Theology of Access for People with Disabilities*, New York: Continuum.

Blount, B. K. (ed.) (2007), *True to Our Native Land: An African American New Testament Commentary*, Minneapolis, MN: Fortress Press.

Boase, E. and Frechette, C. G. (2016), *Bible Through The Lens of Trauma, Semeia Studies* 86, Atlanta, GA: Society of Biblical Literature.

Bockmuehl, M. (1998), 'To Be or Not to Be: The Possible Futures of New Testament Scholarship', *Scottish Journal of Theology*, 51(3), 271–306.

Boer, R. and Segovia, F. F. (eds) (2012), *The Future of The Biblical Past: Envisioning Biblical Studies on a Global Key. Semeia Studies 66*, Atlanta, GA: Society of Biblical Literature.

Boff, C. (1987), *Theology and Praxis: Epistemological Foundations*, Maryknoll, NY: Orbis.

Bonhoeffer, D. (1965), *No Rusty Swords: Letters, Lectures and Notes 1928–1936 from the Collected Works of Dietrich Bonhoeffer Vol. 1* (trans. Edwin H. Robertson and John Bowden, ed. Edwin H. Robertson), London: Collins.

Bowe, B., Hughes K., Karam, S. and Osiek, C. (1992), *Silent Voices, Sacred Lives: Women's Readings For The Liturgical Year*, New York: Paulist Press.

Bradshaw, R. (2013), 'Pentecostal Hermeneutics', in P. Thompson (ed.), *Challenges of Black Pentecostal Leadership in The Twenty-First Century*, London: SPCK, 52–67.

Brettler, M. Z. (2007), 'Biblical Authority: A Jewish Pluralistic View', in W. P. Brown (ed.), *Engaging Biblical Authority: Perspectives On The Bible As Scripture*, Louisville, KY: Westminster John Knox Press, 1–9.

Brotzman, E. R. (1994), *Old Testament Textual Criticism: A Practical Introduction*, Grand Rapids, MI: Baker.

Brown, W. P. (2007), 'Introduction', in W. P. Brown (ed.), *Engaging Biblical Authority: Perspectives On The Bible As Scripture*, Louisville, KY: Westminster John Knox Press, ix–xvi.

Brueggemann, W. (1997a), *Cadences of Home: Preaching among Exiles*, Louisville, KY: Westminster John Knox Press.

Brueggemann, W. (1997b), *Theology of the Old Testament: Testimony, Advocacy*, Minneapolis, MN: Fortress Press.

Brueggemann, W., Placher, W. C. and Blount, B. K. (2002), *Struggling with Scripture*, Louisville, KY: Westminster John Knox Press.

Bultmann, R. (1950), 'The Problem of Hermeneutics', in *New Testament and Mythology and Other Basic Writings*, ed. and trans. S. M. Ogden (1984), Philadelphia, PA: Fortress Press, 69–93.

Bunge, M. J., Fretheim, T. E. and Gaventa, B. R. (eds) (2008), *The Child in The Bible*, Grand Rapids, MI: W. B. Eerdmans.

Byron, G. L. and Lovelace, V. (2016), 'Introduction', in G. L. Byron and V. Lovelace (eds), *Womanist Interpretations of The Bible: Expanding The Discourse. Semeia Studies 85*, Atlanta, GA: Society of Biblical Literature Press, 1–18.

Callaway, M. C. (1999), 'Canonical Criticism', in S. L. McKenzie and S. R. Haynes (eds), *To Each its Own Meaning: An Introduction to Biblical Criticisms and Their Applications. Revised and Expanded Edition.* Louisville, KY: Westminster John Knox Press, 141–155.

Cameron, H., Richter, P., Davies, D. and Ward, F. (eds) (2005), *Studying Local Churches: A Handbook*, London: SCM Press.

Cannon, K. (1995), *Katie's Canon*, New York: Continuum.

Cardenal, E. (1982), *The Gospel in Solentiname Volume IV*, D. D. Walsh (trans.), Maryknoll, NY: Orbis.

Carson, D. A. (1993), *New Testament Commentary Survey*, 4th ed., Leicester: IVP.

Cave, N. (1998), *Introduction to Mark*, Edinburgh: Canongate Books.

Childs, B. (1979), *Introduction to the Old Testament as Scripture*, Philadelphia, PA: Fortress.

Childs, B. (1985a), *Old Testament Theology in a Canonical Context*, Philadelphia, PA: Fortress.

Childs, B. (1985b), *The New Testament as Canon: An Introduction*, Philadelphia, PA: Fortress.

REFERENCES AND FURTHER READING

Christian Aid (2004), *Trade Justice*, London: Church House Publishing.

Cimperman, M. (2015), *Social Analysis For The 21st Century: How Faith Becomes Action*, Maryknoll, NY: Orbis Books.

Clines, D. J. A. (1995), 'David The Man: The Construction of Masculinity in The Hebrew Bible', in D. J. A. Clines, *Interested Parties. The Ideology of Writers and Readers of The Hebrew Bible*, Sheffield: Sheffield Phoenix Press, 212–41.

Clines, D. J. A. (1995), 'The Ten Commandments, Reading From Left to Right', in D. J. A. Clines, *Interested Parties. The Ideology of Writers and Readers of The Hebrew Bible*, Sheffield: Sheffield Phoenix Press, 26–45.

CMS/USPG/The Methodist Church (2004), *The Christ We Share*, CMS/USPG/The Methodist Church.

Coggins, R. J. and Houlden, J. L. (eds) (1990), *A Dictionary of Biblical Interpretation*, London: SCM Press.

Collins, M. A. (2019), 'On The Trail of A Biblical Serial Killer: Sherlock Holmes and the Book of Tobit', in C. Blyth and A. Jack (eds), *The Bible in Crime Fiction and Drama: Murderous Texts*, London: T & T Clark, 9–28.

Cooper, A. and Scholz, S. (2004), 'Leviticus', in D. Patte, *The Global Bible Commentary*, Nashville, TN: Abingdon Press, 30–42.

Creanga, O. (ed.) (2010), *Men and Masculinity in The Hebrew Bible and Beyond. Bible in The Modern World 33*, Sheffield: Sheffield Phoenix Press.

Crenshaw, K. (1989), 'Demarginalizing The Intersection of Race and Sex: A Black Feminist Critique of Antidiscrimination Doctrine, Feminist Theory and Antiracist Politics', *University of Chicago Legal Forum, Special Issue: Feminism in The Law: Theory, Practice and Criticism*. Chicago, IL: University of Chicago Law School, 139–68.

Dalton, R. W. (2007), 'Perfect Prophets, Helpful Hippos, and Happy Endings: Noah and Jonah in Children's Bible Storybooks in The United States', *Religious Education* 102, No. 3 (Summer), 298–313.

Davies, A. (2009), 'What Does It Mean to Read The Bible As A Pentecostal?' *Journal of Pentecostal Theology* 18, No. 2, 216–29.

Davis, C. W. (1999), *Oral Biblical Criticism: The influence of The Principles of Orality on the Literary Structure of Paul's Epistle to the Philippians. Library of New Testament Studies 172*, Sheffield Academic Press, Continuum.

Dawes, S. (2004), 'Revelation in Methodism', in C. Marsh, B. Beck, A. Shier-Jones and H. Wareing (eds) *Unmasking Methodist Theology*, London: Continuum, 109–17.

Dawes, S. B. (2010), *SCM Studyguide to the Psalms*, London: SCM Press.

Defranza, M. K. (2014), 'Virtuous Eunuchs: Troubling Conservative and Queer Readings of Intersex and the Bible', in S. Cornwall (ed.), *Intersex, Theology, and the Bible: Troubling Bodies in Church, Text, and Society*, Basingstoke: Macmillan, 55–77.

Di Jamaikan Nyuu Testament (2012), Bible Society of the West Indies.

Dietrich, W. and Luz, U. (2002), *The Bible in a World Context: An Experiment in Cultural Hermeneutics*, Grand Rapids, MI and Cambridge: Eerdmans.

Divarkar S.J., P. (ed.) and Malatesta S.J., E. J. (1991), *Ignatius of Loyola: Spiritual Exercises and Selected Works ('The Classics of Western Spirituality' series)*, Mahwah, NJ: Paulist Press.

Dube, M. W. (2003), 'Jumping the Fire with Judith: Postcolonial Feminist Hermeneutics of Liberation', in Silvia Schroer and Sophia Bietenhard (eds) *Feminist Interpretation of the Bible and the Hermeneutic of Liberation*, London: Sheffield Academic Press, 60–76.

Dube, M. W. (2010), 'Go Tla Siama. O Tla Fola: Doing Biblical Studies in an HIV and Aids Context', *Black Theology* 8(2), 212–41.

Dube, M. W. (ed.) (2001), *Other Ways of Reading: African Women and the Bible*, Atlanta, GA: SBL/Geneva: WCC.

Dube, M. W. (ed.) (2003), *HIV/Aids and the Curriculum: Methods of integrating HIV/Aids in Theological Programmes*, Geneva: WCC Publications.

Dunbar, E. S. (2018), 'For Such A Time As This? #Ustoo: Representations of Sexual Trafficking, Collective Trauma and Horror in The Book of Esther', paper presented at The Shiloh Project's Religion and Rape Culture Conference, Sheffield.

Dyer, R. (1997), *White*, London: Routledge.

Elliger, K. and Rudolph, W. (eds) (1977), *Biblia Hebraica Stuttgartensia*, 2nd edition, edited by W. Rudolph and H. P. Rüger, Stuttgart: Deutsche Bibelgesellschaft.

Elliot, J. K. (2000), 'Christian Apocrypha', in Adrian Hastings, Alistair Mason and Hugh Pyper (eds) *The Oxford Companion to Christian Thought*, Oxford: Oxford University Press, 30–31.

Elvey, A. (2010), 'Review of *Exploring Ecological Hermeneutics*, edited by Norman C. Habel and Peter Trudinger', *Biblical Interpretation* 18, 418–527.

Erbele-Kuster, D. (2004), 'Rereading the Bible: A Dialogue with Women Theologians from Latin America, Africa and Asia', in *Voices from the Third World* Volume XXVII(1) June 2004, 53–67.

Evangelical Alliance (2017), *What Kind of Society? Vision and Voice For the UK Church*, London: Evangelical Alliance.

Fabella, V. and Sugirtharajah, R. S. (eds) (2000), *Dictionary of Third World Theologies*, Maryknoll, NY: Orbis.

Farmer, K. (1998), 'Psalms 42–89', in W. R. Farmer, A. Levoratti, D. L. Duggan and A. LaCocque (eds) *The International Bible Commentary: A Catholic and Ecumenical Commentary for the Twenty-First Century*, Collegeville, PA: The Liturgical Press, 823–40.

Farmer, W. R., McEvenue, S., Levoratti, Armando J. and Dungan, D. L. (eds) (1998), *The International Bible Commentary: A Catholic and Ecumenical Commentary for the Twenty-First Century*, Collegeville, PA: The Liturgical Press.

Fishbane, M. (1985), *Biblical Interpretation in Ancient Israel*, Oxford: Clarendon.

Foster, R. J. (1999), *Streams of Living Water: Celebrating The Great Traditions of Christian Faith*, London: Fount.

Fowl, S. E. and Jones, L. G. (1991), *Reading in Communion: Scripture and Ethics in Christian Life*, London: SPCK.

Fowler, R. M., Blumhofer, E. and Segovia, F. F. (eds) (2004), *New Paradigms for Bible Study: The Bible in the Third Millennium*, New York: T & T Clark.

Freire, P. [1973] (1993), *Pedagogy of the Oppressed*, London: Penguin.

Gafney, W. C. (2017), *Womanist Midrash: A Reintroduction to the Women of the Torah and the Throne*, Louisville, KY: Westminster John Knox Press.

General Synod of The Church of England (2009), *GS 1748b: The View of Scripture Taken by The Church of England and The Anglican Communion*.

REFERENCES AND FURTHER READING

Gillingham, S. E. (1998), *One Bible Many Voices: Different Approaches to Biblical Studies*, London: SPCK.

Gnuse, R. (1985), *The Authority of the Bible: Theories of Inspiration, Revelation and the Canon of Scripture*, Mahwah, NJ: Paulist Press.

Gnuse, R., (1999), 'Tradition History', in Hayes, J. H. (eds.) *Dictionary of Biblical Interpretation*, vol 2, Nashville, TN: Abingdon, 127–32.

Goldingay, J. and Carson, D. (2013), *New Testament Commentary Survey*, 7th edition, Grand Rapids, MI: Baker Academic.

Gorman, M. (2001), *Elements of Biblical Exegesis: A Basic Guide for Students and Ministers*, Peabody, MA: Hendrikson.

Gorman, M. (ed.) (2017), *Scripture and its Interpretation: A Global, Ecumenical Introduction to the Bible*, Grand Rapids, MI: Baker Academic.

Gorringe, T. (1998), 'Political readings of Scripture', in Barton, J. (ed.), *The Cambridge Companion to Biblical Interpretation*, Cambridge: Cambridge University Press, 67–80.

Goss, R. E. and West, M. (eds) (2000), *Take Back the Word: A Queer Reading of the Bible*, Cleveland, OH: The Pilgrim Press

Grabbe, L. L. (2017), *Ancient Israel: What Do We Know and How Do We Know It?*, London: T & T Clark.

Green, D. and Melamed, C. (2000), *A Human Development Approach to Globalisation*, London: Christian Aid/ CAFOD.

Greggs, T. (2016), 'Sola Scriptura, The Community of The Church and A Pluralist Age: A Methodist Theologian Seeking to Read Scripture in and For The World', in A. Paddison (ed.), *Theologians on Scripture*, London: Bloomsbury T&T Clark, 79–92.

Grieb, A. K. (2002), 'Deutero-Pauline Letters', in W. Howard-Brook and S. Ringe (eds) *The New Testament: Introducing the Way of Discipleship*, Maryknoll, NY: Orbis, 148–67.

Guest, D. (2006), 'Deuteronomy', in D. Guest (ed.), *The Queer Bible Commentary*, London: SCM Press, 121–43.

Guest, D. (ed.) (2006), *The Queer Bible Commentary*, London: SCM Press.

Gunn, D. M. (1999), 'Narrative Criticism', in S. L. McKenzie and S. R. Haynes (eds) *To Each Its Own Meaning: An Introduction to Biblical Criticisms and Their Application*, revised and expanded 3rd edition, Louisville, KY: Westminster John Knox Press, 201–29.

Habel, N. C. (2008), 'Introducing Ecological Hermeneutics', in N. C. Habel and P. Trudinger, *Exploring Ecological Hermeneutics. Society of Biblical Literature Symposium Series 46*, Atlanta, GA: SBL Press.

Hammer, R. (Trans., Intro., and Comm.) and Goldin, J. (Preface) (1995), *The Classic Midrash, Tannaitic Commentaries on the Bible ('The Classics of Western Spirituality' series)*, Mahwah, NJ: Paulist Press.

Haney, E. H. (1998), *The Great Commandment*, Cleveland, OH: The Pilgrim Press.

Hayes, J. H. (ed.) (1999), *Dictionary of Biblical Interpretation*, 2 vols, Nashville, TN: Abingdon.

Hens-Piazza, G. (2003), *Nameless, Blameless and Without Shame: Two Cannibal Mothers Before a King*, Collegeville, PA: Liturgical Press.

Hens-Piazza, G. (2017), *Lamentations. Wisdom Commentary Series* v. 30, Collegeville, PA: Liturgical Press.

Hoekema, A. G. (2014), 'Fan Pu (China): The Bible interpreted Through The Art of Paper Cutting', *Exchange* 43, 379–89.

Holgate, D. A. (1999) *Prodigality, Liberality and Meanness: The Prodigal Son in Greco-Roman Perspective*, JSNTS Sup 187, Sheffield: Sheffield Academic Press.

Holland, J. and Henriot, S. J. P. (1983), *Social Analysis Linking Faith and Justice*, Maryknoll, NY: Orbis.

Holloway, R. (2002), *Doubts and Love: What is Left of Christianity*, Edinburgh: Canongate.

Horrell, D. G. (2017), 'Paul, Inclusion and Whiteness: Particularizing Interpretation', *Journal For The Study of The New Testament* 40(2), 123–47.

Horsley, R. A. (2002), *Jesus and Empire: The Kingdom of God and the New World Disorder*, Minneapolis, MN: Augsburg.

Houlden, J. L. (ed.) (1995), *The Interpretation of the Bible in the Church*, London: SCM Press.

Howard-Brook W. and Ringe, S. (eds) (2002), *The New Testament: Introducing the Way of Discipleship*, Maryknoll, NY: Orbis.

Hull, J. M. (2001a), *In the Beginning There Was Darkness: A Blind Person's Conversations With The Bible*, London: SCM Press.

Hull, J. M. (2001b), 'Open Letter from a Blind Disciple to a Sighted Saviour: Text and Discussion', in M. O' Kane (ed.) *Borders, Boundaries and The Bible*, Sheffield: Sheffield Academic Press, 154–77.

James, R. (2012), 'Doing It Differently: The Bible in Fundamentalism and in African Christianity', *Horizons in Biblical Theology* 34, No. 1, 35–58.

Jansson, T. (2003), *The Summer Book*, London: Sort of Books.

Jennings, W. J. (2017), *Acts. Belief: A Theological Commentary On The Bible*, Louisville, KY: Westminster John Knox Press.

Johns, C. B. (1998), *Pentecostal Formation: A Pedagogy Among the Oppressed. Journal of Pentecostal Theology Supplement Series, 2*, Sheffield: Sheffield Academic Press.

Joint Public Issues Team (2017), *A Place to Call Home?*

Joy, C. I. D. (2001), *Revelation: A Post Colonial Viewpoint*, Delhi: Indian Society for Promoting Christian Knowledge.

Kahl, B. (2001), 'Fratricide and Ecocide: Re-reading Gen. 2–4', in D. Hessel and L. Rasmussen (eds), *Earth Habitat. Eco-Justice and the Church's Response*, Minneapolis, MN: Fortress Press, 53–68.

Katusno-Ishii, L. and Orteza, E. J., (eds) (2000), *Of Rolling Waters and Roaring Wind*, Geneva: WCC.

Keener, C. S. and Carroll R., M. D. (eds) (2013), *Global Voices: Reading The Bible in The Majority World*, Peabody, MA: Hendrickson.

Kille, D. A. and Rollins, W. G. (2007) *Psychological Insight into the Bible: Texts and Readings*, Grand Rapids, MI: Eerdmans.

Kovacs, J., Rowland, C. and Callow, R. (2004), *Revelation*, Blackwell Bible Commentaries, Oxford: Blackwells.

Kwok Pui-lan (1995), 'Discovering the Bible in the Non-Biblical World', in R. S. Sugirtharajah, *Voices from the Margins: Interpreting the Bible in the Third World*, London: SPCK, 289–306.

Kwok Pui-lan (2005), *Postcolonial Imagination and Feminist Theology*, London: SCM-Canterbury Press.

REFERENCES AND FURTHER READING

Lamb, W. (2013), *Scripture. A Guide For The Perplexed*, London: Bloomsbury.
Lambeth Commission On Communion (2004), *The Windsor Report*, London: Anglican Communion Office.
Lawrence, L. J. (2018), *Bible and Bedlam: Madness, Sanism, and New Testament Interpretation. The Library of New Testament Studies Book 594*, Edinburgh: T&T Clark.
Levine, A. (2014), *Short Stories by Jesus: The Enigmatic Parables of A Controversial Rabbi*, San Francisco, CA: Harperone.
Levine, A. and Witherington, B. (2018), *The Gospel of Luke. New Cambridge Bible Commentary*, Cambridge: Cambridge University Press.
Levine, A. and Brettler, M. Z. (eds) (2011), *The Jewish Annotated New Testament: New Revised Standard Version Bible Translation*, Oxford: Oxford University Press.
Levison, J. R. and Pope-Levison, P. (eds) (1999), *Return to Babel: Global Perspectives on the Bible*, Louisville, KY: Westminster John Knox.
Liew, T. B. (2017), 'Black Scholarship Matters', *Journal of Biblical Literature* 136(1), 237–44.
Litchfield, R. G. (2004), 'Rethinking Local Bible Study in a Postmodern Era', in R. M. Fowler, E. Blumhofer and F. F. Segovia (eds), *New Paradigms for Bible Study: The Bible in the Third Millennium*, New York: T & T Clark, 227–250.
Longman III, T. (2013), *Old Testament Commentary Survey*, 5th Edition, Grand Rapids, MI: Baker Academic.
Luz, U. (1989), *Matthew 1–7: A Commentary*, trans. W. C. Linss, Edinburgh: T & T Clark.
Luz, U. (1994), *Matthew In History: Interpretation Influence, and Effects*, Minneapolis, MN: Fortress Press.
Luz, U. (2007, 2001, 2005), *Matthew 1—7*, *Matthew 8—20*, and *Matthew 21—28*, Minneapolis, MN: Fortress Press.
MacDonald, M. Y. (1988), *The Pauline Churches*, SNTSMS 60, Cambridge: Cambridge University Press.
Maduro, O. (2000), 'Social Analysis', in V. Fabella, M. M. and R. S. Sugirtharajah (eds) *Dictionary of Third World Theologies*, Maryknoll, NY: Orbis, 185–87.
Maier, P. L. (2000), 'Oberammergau Overhaul: Changes Make The Passion Play More Sensitive to Jews and More Faithful to Scripture', *Christianity Today* 44, No. 9 (August 7), 74–5.
Mainwaring, S. (2014), *Mark, Mutuality, and Mental Health: Encounters With Jesus. Semeia Studies 79*, SBL Press.
Malherbe, A. J. (1987), *Paul and the Thessalonians*, Philadelphia, PA: Fortress Press.
Malherbe, A. J. (2000), *The Letters to the Thessalonians*, Anchor Bible Vol 32B, New York: Doubleday.
Marx, S. (2000), *Shakespeare and the Bible*, Oxford: Oxford University Press.
McDonald, L. M. (2012), *Formation of The Bible. The Story of The Church's Canon*, Peabody, MA: Hendrickson.
McGowan, A. T. B. (2007), *The Divine Spiration of Scripture: Challenging Evangelical Perspectives*, Nottingham: Apollos.
McKenzie S. L. and S. R. Haynes (eds) (1999), *To Each Its Own Meaning: An Introduction to Biblical Criticisms and Their Application*, revised and expanded 3rd edition, Louisville, KY, London and Leiden: Westminster John Knox.
Mead, J. (2002), *A Telling Place*, Glasgow: Wild Goose Publications.

Melcher, S. J. (2017), 'Introduction', in S. J. Melcher, M. C. Parsons and A. Yong (eds), *The Bible and Disability: A Commentary. Studies in Religion, Theology, and Disability*, Waco, TX: Baylor University Press, 1–27.

Mesters, C. (1989), *Defenseless Flower: A New Reading of the Bible*, Maryknoll, NY: Orbis.

Methodist Church (2004) *What is a Deacon?* London: The Methodist Church.

Metzger, B. (1994), *A Textual Commentary on the Greek New Testament*, 2nd ed., Stuttgart: United Bible Societies.

Míguez, N. O. (2004), 'Latin American reading of the Bible. Experiences, Challenges and its Practice', *Journal of Latin American Hermeneutics*, Year 2004/1 Instituto Universitario ISEDET online version.

Miller-McLemore, B. J. (ed.) (2012), *The Wiley-Blackwell Companion to Practical Theology. Wiley-Blackwell Companions to Religion*, Oxford: Wiley-Blackwell.

Moore, S. D. (1996), *God's Gym: Divine Male Bodies of the Bible*, London: Routledge.

Moore, S. D. (2001), *God's Beauty Parlor and Other Queer Spaces in and Around The Bible*, Stanford, CA: Stanford University Press.

Moore, S. D. (2014), 'Masculinity Studies and the Bible', in J. O'Brien et al. (eds), *The Oxford Encyclopedia of The Bible and Gender Studies. Volume 1*, Oxford: Oxford University Press, 540–7.

Moore, S. D. and Anderson, J. C. (2003), *New Testament Masculinities. Semeia Studies 45.* Atlanta, GA: Society of Biblical Literature.

Moore, S. D. and Sherwood, Y. (eds) (2011), *The Invention of the Biblical Scholar: A Critical Manifesto*, Minneapolis, MN: Fortress Press.

Moorman, J. R. H. (1950), *Saint Francis of Assisi*, London: SCM Press.

Mork, G. R. (2005), 'Oberammergau: The Troubling Story of The World's Most Famous Passion Play', *Shofar: An Interdisciplinary Journal of Jewish Studies* 23, No. 2 (Winter), 140–2.

Morley, J. (1992), *Bread of Tomorrow*, London: SPCK.

Mosala, I. (1989), *Biblical Hermeneutics and Black Theology in South Africa*, Grand Rapids, MI: Eerdmans.

Moschella, M. C. (2008), *Ethnography As A Pastoral Practice: An Introduction*, Cleveland, OH: Pilgrim.

Muddiman, J. (1990), 'Form Criticism', in Coggins, R. J. and Houlden, J. L. (eds) (1990) *A Dictionary of Biblical Interpretation*, London: SCM Press, 240–3.

Murrell, N. S. (2000), 'Tuning Hebrew Psalms to Reggae Rhythms: Rastas' Revolutionary Lamentations For Social Change', *Cross Currents* 50(4) (Winter), 525–40.

Myers, C. (1990), *Binding the Strong Man: Political Reading of Mark's Story of Jesus*, Maryknoll, NY: Orbis.

Naegeli, V., Ngalula, J., Praetorius I. and Rabarijaona B. (eds) (2015), *There Is Something We Long For – Nous Avons Un Désir*, Kinshasa: Edition Tsena Malalaka.

Najman, H. (2012), 'The Vitality of Scripture Within and Beyond The "Canon"', *Journal For The Study of Judaism in The Persian, Hellenistic and Roman Period* 43(4–5), 497–518.

Nestle, E., Aland, K. and Aland, B. et al. (eds) (1998), *The Greek New Testament*, 4th edition, New York: United Bible Societies.

Nestle, E., Aland, K., Aland, B., Karavidopoulos, J., Martini, C. M. and Metzger, B. M. (eds) (1993) *Novum Testamentum Graece*, 27th edition, Stuttgart: Deutsche Bibelgesellschaft.

REFERENCES AND FURTHER READING

Newheart, M. W. (2004), *'My Name Is Legion': The Story and Soul of the Gerasene Demoniac*, Collegeville, PA: Liturgical Press.

Newsom, C. A., Ringe, S. H. and Lapsley, J. E. (eds) (2014), *Women's Bible Commentary. Revised and Expanded Edition*, London: SPCK.

Newsom, C. and Ringe, S. H. (eds) (1998), *Women's Bible Commentary*, expanded edition, Louisville, KY: Westminster John Knox.

Neyrey, J. (1988), 'Bewitched in Galatia: Paul in Social Science Perspective', *Catholic Biblical Quarterly* 50, 72–100.

Norris, K. (2000), *Amazing Grace: A Vocabulary of Faith*, Oxford: Lion.

Norris, K. (2000), *Cloister Walk*, Oxford: Lion.

Norris, K. (2002), *Dakota: A Spiritual Geography*, Boston, MA: Houghton Mifflin (Trade).

Nouwen, H. J. M. (1994), *The Return of the Prodigal Son: A Story of Homecoming*, London: Darton Longman and Todd.

O' Donnell O.P., G. (1990), 'Reading for Holiness: *Lectio Divina*', in R. Maas, R. and G. O' Donnell O.P. (1990) *Spiritual Traditions for the Contemporary Church*, Nashville, TN: Abingdon Press, 45–54.

Oakley, Mark (2016), *The Splash of Words: Believing in Poetry*, Norwich: Canterbury Press.

Oduyoye, M. A. (1990), 'The Empowering Spirit', in S. B. Thistlethwaite and M. P. Engel (eds) *Lift Every Voice: Constructing Christian Theologies from the Underside*, San Francisco, CA: Harper and Row, 245–58.

Økland, J. (2002), 'The Excluded Gospels and their Readers, or: How to Tell when a Kiss is just a Kiss', in *The Many Voices of the Bible* Concilium 2002/1 London: SCM, 68–76.

Orevillo-Montenegro, M. (1998), unpublished paper.

Page, H. R. (ed.) (2009), *The Africana Bible: Reading Israel's Scriptures From Africa and The African Diaspora*. Minneapolis, MN: Fortress Press.

Paterson, G. (2001), *AIDS and the African Churches: Exploring the Challenges*, London: Christian Aid.

Patte, D. et al. (eds) (2004), *Global Bible Commentary*, Nashville, TN: Abingdon Press.

Perdue, L. G. and Carter, W. (2015), *Israel and Empire: A Postcolonial History of Israel and Early Judaism*, London: Bloomsbury.

Pereira, N. C. (2003), 'Changing Season: About the Bible and Other Sacred Texts in Latin America', in S. Schroer and S. Bietenhard (eds) *Feminist Interpretation of the Bible and the Hermeneutic of Liberation*, London: Sheffield Academic Press, 48–58.

Perry, I. (2004), *Prophets of the Hood: Politics and Poetics in Hip Hop*, Durham, NC and London: Duke University Press.

Pervo, R. I. (1987), *Profit with Delight: The Literary Genre of the Acts of the Apostles*, Philadelphia, PA: Fortress Press.

Placher, W. C. (2002), 'Struggling With Scripture', in W. Brueggemann, W. C. Placher and B. K. Blount *Struggling with Scripture*, Louisville, KY: Westminster John Knox Press, 32–50.

Pontifical Biblical Commission (1993) *The Interpretation of the Bible in the Church*, The Vatican: Libreria Editrice Vaticana.

Pontifical Biblical Commission (2014) *The Inspiration and Truth of Sacred Scripture: The Word that Comes from God and Speaks of God for the Salvation of the World*, Collegeville, PA: The Liturgical Press.

Porter, J. R. (2001), *The Lost Bible*, London: Duncan Baird Publishers.

Powell, M. A. (1999), 'Narrative Criticism', in J. B. Green (ed.), *Hearing the New Testament: Strategies for Interpretation*, Grand Rapids, MI and Carlisle: Eerdmans and Paternoster, 239–55.

Pressler, C. J. (1996), 'Biblical Criticism', in *Dictionary of Feminist Theologies*, (eds) L. M. Russell and J. Shannon Clarkson, London: Mowbray, 25–7.

Pressler, C. J. (1998), 'To Heal and Transform: Women's Biblical Studies', in Farmer, W. R., et al. (eds) *The International Bible Commentary: A Catholic and Ecumenical Commentary for the Twenty-First Century*, Collegeville, PA: The Liturgical Press.

Prior, M. (1997), *The Bible and Colonialism: A Moral Critique*, Sheffield: Sheffield Academic Press.

Pyper, H. (2000), 'Jewish Apocrypha', in Adrian Hastings, Alistair Mason and Hugh Pyper (eds) *The Oxford Companion to Christian Thought*, Oxford: Oxford University Press, 31.

Raheb, M. (2014), *Faith in The Face of Empire: The Bible Through Palestinian Eyes*, Maryknoll, NY: Orbis.

Raphael, R. (2014), 'The Power of Bodies: Contextual Readings by Women With Disabilities', in S. Scholz (ed.), *Feminist Interpretation of The Hebrew Bible in Retrospect. Volume II: Social Locations*, Sheffield: Sheffield Phoenix Press, 205–19.

Raymer, V. (2018), *The Bible in Worship: Proclamation, Encounter and Response*, London: SCM Press.

Reardon, B. P. (1989), *Collected Ancient Greek Novels*, Berkeley, CA: University of California Press.

Reaves, J. R. (2018), 'Sarah As Victim & Perpetrator: Whiteness, Power & Memory in The Matriarchal Narrative', *Review & Expositor*, 115(4), 483–99.

Reddie, A. G. (2015), 'Telling The Truth and Shaming The Devil: Using Caribbean Proverbial Wisdom For Raising The Critical Consciousness of African Caribbean People in Postcolonial Britain', *Black Theology: An International Journal* 13(1) (April), 41–58.

Reddie, A. G. (2016), 'Explorations in Front of the Text: A Black Liberationist Reader-Response Approach to Reading the Bible', in A. Paddison (ed.), *Theologians On Scripture*, London: Bloomsbury T & T Clark, 147–59.

Rhoads, D. (ed.) (2005), *From Every People and Nation: The Book of Revelation in Intercultural Perspective*, Minneapolis, MN: Fortress Press.

Rhoads, D., Dewey, J. and Michie, D. (1999), *Mark as Story: An Introduction to the Narrative of a Gospel*, 2nd ed. Minneapolis, MN: Fortress.

Richard, P. (1990), '1492: The Violence of God and the Future of Christianity', *Concilium* 1990/6 *1492–1992: The Voice of the Victims*, 56–67.

Riches, J. (2004), 'Ephesians', in Patte, D. et al. (eds) *Global Bible Commentary*, Nashville, TN: Abingdon Press, 473–81.

Ringe, S. (1998), 'When Women Interpret the Bible', in Newsom, C. and Ringe, S. H. (eds) *Women's Bible Commentary*, expanded edition, Louisville, KY: Westminster John Knox, 1–9.

Rogerson, J. W. and Davies, P. (2005), *The Old Testament World*, 2nd revised and expanded edition, London and New York: Continuum.

Rohr, R. (2012), *Falling Upward: A Spirituality For The Two Halves of Life*, London: SPCK.

Rollins, W. G. and Killie, D. A. (eds) (2007), *Psychological Insight into The Bible: Texts and Readings*, Grand Rapids, MI and Cambridge: Eerdmans.

Rowland, C. (1998), 'The Book of Revelation', in *New Interpreter's Bible* xii, Nashville, TN: Abingdon, 501–743.

Rowland, C. (2005), 'Imaging the Apocalypse', *New Testament Studies* 51(3), 303–27.

Rowland, C. and Corner, M. (1990), *Liberating Exegesis: The Challenge of Liberation Theology to Biblical Studies*, London: SPCK.

Ruether, R. R. (1983), *Sexism and God-talk*, London: SCM Press.

Ruether, R. R. (1985), 'Feminist Interpretation: A Method of Correlation', in Letty M. Russell (ed.) *Feminist Interpretations of the Bible*, New York: Blackwell, 111–24.

Ruether, R. R. (1985b), *Womanguides Readings Towards a Feminist Theology*, Boston, MA: Beacon Press.

Saunders, J. A. (1972), *Torah and Canon*, Philadelphia, PA: Fortress Press.

Saunders, J. A. and Gooder, P. (2008), 'Canonical Criticism', in P. Gooder (ed.), *Searching for Meaning: An Introduction to Interpreting the New Testament*, London: SPCK, 63–70.

Sawyer, D. F. (2005), 'Biblical Gender Strategies: The Case of Abraham's Masculinity', in U. King and T. Beattie (eds), *Gender, Religion and Diversity: Cross-Cultural Perspectives*, London: Continuum, 162–71.

Schell, E. L. (1998), *Quilting Anthology: Scraps*, New York: unpublished.

Schipper, J. (2006), *Disability Studies and the Hebrew Bible: Figuring Mephibosheth in the David Story*, New York: T & T Clark.

Schipper, J. (2011), *Disability and Isaiah's Suffering Servant. Biblical Refigurations*, Oxford: Oxford University Press.

Schneiders, S. (1997), *Interpreting the Bible: The Right and the Responsibility*, Scripture from Scratch, online.

Schottroff, L., Wacker, M.-T. and Rumscheidt, M. (eds) (2012), *Feminist Biblical Interpretation: A Compendium of Critical Commentary On The Books of The Bible and Related Literature*, Grand Rapids, MI: Eerdmans.

Schroer, S. (2003), 'We Will Know Each Other by Our Fruits', in S. Schroer and S. Bietenhard (eds) *Feminist Interpretation of the Bible and the Hermeneutic of Liberation*, London: Sheffield Academic Press, 1–16.

Schüssler Fiorenza, E. (1983), *In Memory of Her. A Feminist Theological Reconstruction of Christian Origins*, New York: Crossroads.

Schüssler Fiorenza, E. (1984a), 'Emerging Issues in Feminist Biblical Interpretation', in J. L. Weidman (ed.) *Christian Feminism: Visions of a New Humanity*, San Francisco, CA: Harper and Row, 33–54.

Schüssler Fiorenza, E. (1984b), 'Women-Church: The Hermeneutical Center of Feminist Biblical Interpretation', chapter in *Bread Not Stone: The Challenge of Feminist Biblical Interpretation*, edited by E. Schüssler Fiorenza, Boston, MA: Beacon Press, 1–22.

Schüssler Fiorenza, E. (1994), 'Introduction: Transgressing Canonical Boundaries', in E. Schüssler Fiorenza (ed.) *Searching the Scriptures vol ii: A Feminist Commentary*, New York: Crossroads, 1–14.

Schüssler Fiorenza, E. (ed.) (1993), *Searching The Scriptures*, New York: Crossroads.

Segovia, F. F. (2000), 'Deconstruction', in Fabella, Virginia and Sugirtharajah, R. S. (eds) *Dictionary of Third World Theologies*, Maryknoll, NY: Orbis, 66–7.

Segundo, J. L. (1976), *The Liberation of Theology*, trans. J. Drury, Maryknoll, NY: Orbis Books.

de Silva, D. A. (2004), *Introduction to the New Testament: Contexts, Methods and Ministry Formation*, Downers Grove, IL: IVP Academic.

Slemmons, T, M. (2012), *Year D: A Quadrennial Supplement to The Revised Common Lectionary*, Eugene, OR: Cascade.

Smit, P.-B. (2017), *Masculinity and The Bible – Survey, Models, and Perspectives*, Leiden: Brill.

Smith, M. J. (2017), Insights From African American Interpretation. Insights: Reading the Bible in the 21st Century, Minneapolis, MN: Fortress Press.

Song, C. S. (1981), *The Tears of Lady Meng: A Parable of People's Political Theology*, Geneva: World Council of Churches.

Soulen, R. N. (2009), *Sacred Scripture. A Short History of Interpretation*, Louisville, KY: Westminster John Knox Press.

Soulen, R. N. and Soulen, R. K. (2011), *Handbook of Biblical Criticism. 4th Edition*, Louisville, KY: Westminster John Knox Press.

Spencer, F. S. (2003), *What Did Jesus Do? Gospel Profiles of Jesus' Personal Conduct*, Harrisburg PA: Trinity Press International.

Stackhouse Jr., J.G. (2004), 'Evangelicals and the Bible Yesterday, Today and Tomorrow', in R. M. Fowler, E. Blumhofer and F. F. Segovia (eds) *New Paradigms for Bible Study: The Bible in the Third Millennium*, New York: T & T Clark, 185–206.

Starr, R. (2018), *Reimagining Theologies of Marriage in Contexts of Domestic Violence: When Salvation Is Survival. Explorations in Practical, Pastoral and Empirical Theology*, London: Routledge.

Stewart, D. T. (2017a), 'Leviticus-Deuteronomy', in S. J. Melcher, M. C. Parsons and A. Yong (eds), *The Bible and Disability: A Commentary. Studies in Religion, Theology, and Disability*, Waco, TX: Baylor University Press, 57–91.

Stewart, D. T. (2017b), 'LGBT/Queer Hermeneutics and The Hebrew Bible', *Currents in Biblical Research* 15(3) (June), 289–314.

Stone, K. (2002), 'What Happens When 'Gays Read the Bible'?' in *The Many Voices of the Bible* Concilium 2002/1, London: SCM, 77–85.

Stone, K. (2006), 'Job', in D. Guest (ed.). *The Queer Bible Commentary*, London: SCM Press, 287–303.

Stone, T. J. (2013), 'Following The Church Fathers: An Intertextual Path from Psalm 107 to Isaiah, Jonah and Matthew 8:23–27', *Journal of Theological Interpretation* 7.1, 37–55.

Sugirtharajah, R. S. (1995), 'Afterword. Culture Texts and Margins: A Hermeneutical Odyssey', in R. S. Sugirtharajah (ed.) *Voices from the Margins: Interpreting the Bible in the Third World*, London: SPCK, 457–75.

Sugirtharajah, R. S. (2002), *Postcolonial Criticism and Biblical Interpretation*, Oxford: Oxford University Press.

Sugirtharajah, R. S. (2003), *Postcolonial Reconfigurations*, London: SCM Press.

Sugirtharajah, R. S. (2013), *The Bible and Asia : From The Pre-Christian Era to The Postcolonial Age*, Cambridge, MA: Harvard University Press.

Sugirtharajah, R. S. (ed.) (1999), *Vernacular Hermeneutics*, Sheffield: Sheffield Academic Press.

Tamez, E. (2002), 'Reading the Bible under a Sky without Stars', in W. Dietrich and U. Luz (eds) *The Bible in a World Context: An Experiment in Cultural Hermeneutics*, Grand Rapids, MI and Cambridge: Eerdmans, 3–15.

REFERENCES AND FURTHER READING

Taussig, H. (2013) *A New New Testament: A Bible for the 21st Century Combining Traditional and Newly Discovered Texts*, Wilmington, MA: Mariner Books.

The Methodist Church (2004), *What is a Deacon?* London: The Methodist Church.

The Pontifical Biblical Commission (1993), *The Interpretation of the Bible in the Church*, The Vatican: Libreria Editrice Vaticana.

The Pontifical Biblical Commission (2014), 'The Inspiration and Truth of Sacred Scripture: The Word that Comes from God and Speaks of God for the Salvation of the World' (22 February 2014).

Theissen, G. (1987), *Psychological Aspects of Pauline Theology*, Edinburgh: T & T Clark.

Thomas, O. (2008), 'A Resistant Biblical Hermeneutic Within The Caribbean', *Black Theology* 6(3), 330–42.

Thomas, O. A. W. (2010), *Biblical Resistance Hermeneutics Within A Caribbean Context*, London: Equinox.

Thompson, J. M. (2012), 'From Judah to Jamaica: The Psalms in Rastafari Reggae', *Religion and The Arts* 16(4), 328–56.

Thurman, H. (1949), *Jesus and the Disinherited*, Nashville, TN: Abingdon Press.

Tiffany, F. C. and Ringe, S. H. (1996), *Biblical Interpretation: A Road Map*, Nashville, TN: Abingdon Press.

Tisdale, L. T. (1997), *Preaching as Local Theology and Folk Art. Fortress Resources for Preaching*, Minneapolis, MN: Fortress Press.

Tolbert, M. A. (1999), 'Reading The Bible With Authority: Feminist Interrogation of the Canon', in H. C. Washington, S. L. Graham, and P. Thimmes (eds), *Escaping Eden: New Feminist Perspectives On The Bible*, New York: New York University Press, 141–62.

Tombs, D. (1999), 'Crucifixion, State Terror, and Sexual Abuse', *Union Seminary Quarterly Review* 53 (Autumn), 89–109.

Toop, D. (1984, 1991, 2000), *Rap Attack African Rap to Global Hip Hop*, London: Serpent's Tail.

Trible, P. (1984), *Texts of Terror: Literary-Feminist Readings of Biblical Narratives*, Philadelphia, PA: Fortress Press.

Trustees for Methodist Church Purposes (1998), Methodist Conference Report 'A Lamp to My Feet and A Light to My Path. The Nature of Authority and The Place of The Bible in The Methodist Church', Peterborough: Methodist Publishing House.

Trustees for Methodist Church Purposes (1999), *The Methodist Worship Book*, Peterborough: Methodist Publishing House.

Turner, M. (2017), *Ecclesiastes: An Earth Bible Commentary: Qoheleth's Eternal Earth. The Earth Bible Commentary*, London: Bloomsbury, T&T Clark.

Tutu, D. (1994), *The Rainbow People of God*, London: Doubleday.

Vander Stichele, C. and Pyper, H. S. (2012), *Text, Image, and Otherness in Children's Bibles: What is in the Picture?*, Atlanta, GA: Society of Biblical Literature.

Vincent, J. J. (2012), *Acts in Practice*, Blandford Forum: Deo Publishing.

Wainwright, E. M. (2012) 'Images, Words and Stories: Exploring their Transformative Power in Reading Biblical Texts Ecologically', *Biblical Interpretation* 20, 280–304.

Walden, W. (2007), 'Luther: The One Who Shaped The Canon', *Restoration Quarterly* 49, No. 1, 1–10.

Walker, A. (1983, 2001), *The Color Purple*, London: The Women's Press.

Warrior, R. A. (1989), 'Canaanites, Cowboys, and Indians: Deliverance, Conquest, and Liberation Theology Today', *Christianity and Crisis* 49(12) (September 11), 261–5.

Warrior, R. A. (1995), 'A Native American Perspective: Canaanites, Cowboys and Indians', in *Voices from the Margins* ed. R. S. Sugirtharajah, 2nd ed., Maryknoll, NY: Orbis, 287–95.

Weber, H-R. (1995), *The Book that Reads Me*, Geneva: WCC.

Weber, H-R. (2002), *Walking On The Way: Biblical Signposts*, Geneva: WCC.

Weems, R. J. (1995), *Battered Love: Marriage, Sex and Violence in The Hebrew Prophets. Overtures to Biblical Theology*, Minneapolis, MN: Fortress.

Weems, R. J. (2003), 'Re-reading for Liberation: African-American Women and the Bible', in S. Schroer and S. Bietenhard (eds) *Feminist Interpretation of the Bible and the Hermeneutic of Liberation*, London: Sheffield Academic Press, 19–32.

West, G. and Dube, M. (eds) (2001), *The Bible in Africa. Transactions, Trajectories and Trends*, Boston, MA: Brill Academic Publishers.

West, G. O. (1999), 'Local is Lekker, but Ubuntu is Best: Indigenous Reading Resources from a South African Perspective', in Sugirtharajah, R. S. (ed.) *Vernacular Hermeneutics*, Sheffield: Sheffield Academic Press, 37–51.

West, G. O. (2003), 'Reading the Bible in the Light of HIV/AIDS in South Africa', *The Ecumenical Review*, 55(4), 335–44.

Westermann, C, and Gaiser, F. J. (1993), 'The Bible and The Life of Faith: A Personal Reflection', *Word & World* 13(4) (September 1), 337–44.

Westermann, C. (1990), 'Experience in The Church and The Work of Theology: A Perspective On "Theology For Christian Ministry"', *Word & World* 10(1) (December 1), 7–13.

Wheeler, S. E. (1995), *Wealth as Peril and Obligation: The New Testament on Possessions*, Grand Rapids, MI: William B. Eerdmans Publishing Company.

Williams, D. S. (1993), *Sisters in The Wilderness: The Challenge of Womanist God-Talk*, Maryknoll, NY: Orbis Books.

Williams, Rowan (2017), *Holy Living. The Christian Tradition for Today*, London: Bloomsbury.

Wimbush, V. L. (ed.) (2000), *African Americans and The Bible: Sacred Texts and Social Textures*, New York: Continuum.

Wink, W. (1992), *Engaging the Powers: Discernment and Resistance in a World of Domination*, Minneapolis, MN: Fortress Press.

Winn, A. (ed.) (2016), *An Introduction to Empire in the New Testament*. Resources For Biblical Study, No. 84, Atlanta, GA: SBL Press.

Winter, M. T. (1990), *Womanword: A Feminist Lectionary and Psalter: Women of The New Testament*, New York: Crossroads.

Winter, M. T. (1991), *Womanwisdom: A Feminist Lectionary and Psalter, Women of The Hebrew Scriptures, Part 1*, New York: Crossroads.

Winter, M. T. (1997), *Womanwitness: A Feminist Lectionary and Psalter, Women of The Hebrew Scriptures, Part 2*, New York: Crossroads.

Wonneberger, R. (1990), *Understanding the BHS: A Manual for Users of Biblica Hebraica Stuttgartensia*, 2nd ed. Subsidia Biblica 8. Rome: Biblical Institute Press.

World Council of Churches Faith and Order (1998), *A Treasure in Earthen Vessels: An instrument for an ecumenical reflection on hermeneutics*, Geneva: WCC.

Wright, A. M. (2011), 'The Oberammergau Passion Play 2010', *Ecumenica* 4(1) (Spring), 107–8.

Wurthwein, E. (1994), *The Text of the Old Testament: An Introduction to the Biblia Hebraica*, rev. ed., Grand Rapids, MI: Eerdmans.

Yamauchi, E. M. (2004), *Africa and The Bible*, Grand Rapids, MI: Baker Academic.

Yancy, G. (ed.) (2012), *Christology and Whiteness: What Would Jesus Do?*, London and New York: Routledge.

Yee, G. A. (2006), 'An Autobiographical Approach to Feminist Biblical Scholarship', *Encounter* 67(4) (Autumn), 375–90.

Yorke, G. (2004), 'Bible Translation in Anglophone Africa and her Diaspora: A Postcolonial Agenda', *Black Theology: An International Journal* 2(2), 153–66.

Index of Biblical References

Genesis	37–8, 56, 158	Exodus	30, 36, 94–5, 160–1, 165
1	118, 140		
1—2	21, 68, 165	1	92
1—3	140	3	70
2.10–14	17	20	129
4	14, 168	20.13	123
4.1–16	193	20.1–17	182
6.20	68		
7.3	68	Leviticus	9, 101–2, 166
9.20–27	95	19.14	101
11.1–9	49–53, 56, 64–5		
16, 21.1–21	30	Numbers	37, 102
19–21	89	6.24–6	124
27	101	23.46	91
29–30	30	35	167–9
32	189		
32.31	102	Deuteronomy	102, 137
35.8	119	26	67
37—50	134		
38	14	Joshua	27
41.39–45	29	2	132
46.28–30	101		

Judges	53	Job	13–14, 40, 100, 138
3.15–25	41		
4	120	Psalms	38, 142–3, 145. 171
4.1–7	41	1	61
4.17–22	41	23	16, 48, 129, 155
6.11–24	41	24.1	94
11	183	58	145
		59	145
Ruth	26, 37, 87, 89, 93–4, 131	69	145
		83	145
4.7–12	132	107	164
		139	23
1 Samuel	53		
1–3	70	Proverbs	40, 105
1–15	70	8.22–31	165
3–4	69–70	8.30–31	100
7–15	11	9.9–10	9
9	70	31.10–31	14
16	3–4, 101		
17	3–4, 100	Ecclesiastes or Qoheleth	139
2 Samuel	53	3.1–13	40
4.4	102		
		Song of Songs	27
1 Kings	53	1.5	95
3.16–28	30		
		Isaiah	27
2 Kings	53, 56	7.10–16	40
5	100	51.9–11	165
6.24–33	30	52.13–53.12	102
		61.1–3	172–3
Nehemiah		65.21	104
1.11	89	66.6–14	92
Esther	26, 27, 41	Jeremiah	99
4.1–17	179	32.1–15	162

INDEX OF BIBLICAL REFERENCES

Lamentations	184	15.21–28	131–2
		16.17–19	108
Ezekiel	171	18.15–17	8
43	156	18.21–35	104
		19.12	89
Daniel	26, 56	19.19	68
3.24–26	160	21.12–17	137
6.6–28	29–30	22.1–14	104–5
Hosea	116, 140	Mark	15, 40, 55, 68, 70 73
		3.1–6	101
Joel	171	5	88
		5.1–20	180–1
Amos	140, 165, 167	5.24–43	178
8.1–2	60	6	72–3
		7	94
Obadiah	42	7.24–30	94, 131–2
		10.11–12	68
Jonah	13, 100, 164	10.17–22	105
		14.22–25	70–1
Habakkuk	37, 49		
		Luke	38, 40, 53, 64, 68–9,
Zechariah			71, 147, 153
8.5	100	2	101, 129
		2.25–40	158
Malachi	26	2.40–52	100, 180
		4.16–21	172
Matthew	14, 28, 37, 39, 64,	9	72–3
	68–9, 71, 78, 80	11.2–4	64
1	93	13.10–17	103
1.18–25	40	15.1–7	156
5	129	16.18	68–9
5.31–32	68	19.1–10	48
5.38–42	159	22.63–5	102
6.9–13	6, 64	23.39–43	185
6.25–27	104	24	169
8	164	24.44	28

John	17, 28, 39, 40, 94	6.1	8
1	129		
2.1–11	22, 179	**Ephesians**	41
8.1–11	119	5.21–3	128
10.1–9	157	5.22–6.9	41, 88
10.14–15	155–6		
14.1–7	99	**Philippians**	48
14.6	62	2.5	158
		2.5ff	174
Acts	53, 63, 165	2.6–11	67
1.26	9		
2	108	**Colossians**	
2.5–11	94	3.18–4.1	88
2.42–27	109		
8	94	**1 Thessalonians**	74
10	94	5.12–28	194
12	97		
27	57–8, 74	**2 Thessalonians**	74
		1 Timothy	
Romans	37, 39, 108, 165	2. 11–15	144
1.14	65		
5.14	171	**Titus**	37
6.3–12	77		
7 and 8	75	**Hebrews**	26, 27, 53
8.18–27	140	11.8–12	158
1 Corinthians	53, 70, 174	**James**	37, 165
1–3	174		
6.9–11	77	**1 Peter**	
11.23–26	70–1	2.13–3.7	88
12.14–31	84		
15.26	15	**2 Peter**	56
		3.15–6	28
2 Corinthians	53		
		Jude	37, 42
Galatians	88, 97, 175		
3.1	75	**Revelation**	26, 37, 47, 53, 74, 130, 165
3.26–9	77, 94		

Index of Names

Abraham, W. J. 35–6, 189
Adamo, D. T. 96
Aharoni, Y. 57
Allen, R. J. 16, 173
Anderson, J. C. 90
Archer, K. J. 107
Athanasius of Alexandria 29
Augustine 141
Aune, D. 74
Aymer, M. 97

Bailey, R. C. 87, 90, 93, 95
Barrett, A. 97
Barth, K. 17
Barton, J. 73, 126
Barton, M. 95
Barton, S. C. 74, 76
Bauckham, R. 56, 122, 178–9, 191
Bauer, D. R. 73, 153
Bechdel, A. 89
Beckford, R. 15, 86
Bedford, N. E. 175
Behar, R. 97
Berger, K. 66
Berlin, A. 36, 184
Berry, L. 34

Betcher, S. V. 102
Betsworth, S. 100
Birch, B. C. 25
Block, J. W. 102–3
Blount, B. K. 194
Boase, E. 99
Bockmuehl, M. 78
Boer, R. 130
Boff, C. 161–2
Bonhoeffer, D. 180–1
Bowe, B. 41
Bradshaw, R. 107
Brenner, A. 91
Brettler, M. Z. 36, 173
Brotzman, E. R. 63
Brown, W. P. 21–2
Brueggemann, W. 11, 17, 43, 108, 155, 172
Bultmann, R. 192
Bunge, M. J. 100
Byron, G. L. 97

Callaway, M. C. 27, 164
Camera, H. 194
Cameron, H. 113
Cannon, K. 34–5

Carroll R. M. D. 130
Carson, D. A. 153
Cave, N. 15
Chan, M. J. 9
Childs, B. 43, 164, 172
Cimperman, M. 115
Clines, D. J. A. 90, 182
Coggins, R. J. 67, 129
Collins, M. A. 15
Cooper, A. 166
Corner, M. 161
Creanga, O. 90
Crenshaw, K. 87

Dalton, R. W. 100
Davies, A. 107
Davies, P. 73
Davis, C. W. 48
Dawes, S. B. 36, 165
Defranza, M. K. 89
Derrida, J. 136
Dietrich, W. 129
Dube, M. W. 34–5, 97, 101, 117–8, 132, 178
Dunbar, E. S. 179
Dyer, R. 96

Elliott, N. 98
Elvey, A. 139
Eusebius 29

Fan, Pu 176
Farmer, K. 145
Farmer, W. R. 128
Ferguson, E. 73
Fishbane, M. 164
Foster, R. J. 109

Fowl, S. E. 180
Francis of Assisi 158
Frechette, C. G. 99
Freire, P. 11

Gafney, W. C. 91–2
Gillingham, S. E. 83
Gnuse, R. 36, 69
Goldingay, J. 153
Gooder, P. 164
Gorman, M. 126, 130, 145
Gorringe, T. 173–4
Goss, R. E. 89–90
Grabbe, L. L. 73
Green, D. 117, 201
Greggs, T. 107–8
Guest, D. 137
Gunn, D. M. 54
Gutierrez, G. 110

Habel, N. C. 139
Haney, E. H. 86–7
von Harnack, A. 37–8
Harvey, J. 98
Hayes, J. H. 128–9
Heidegger, M. 192
Henriot, S. J., P. 110, 115
Hens-Piazza, G. 30, 83, 136, 184
Hoekema, A. G. 176
Holgate, D. A. 58, 146
Holland, J. 110, 115
Horrell, D. G. 97
Horsley, R. A. 98, 181
Houlden, J. L. 67, 129, 190
Howard-Brook W. 146
Hull, J. M. 102

INDEX OF NAMES

Ignatius of Loyola 141
Irenaeus 28

James, L. 12
James, R. 20–1, 23
Jansson, T. 111
Jennings, W. J. 96
John Paul II 12
Johns, C. B. 107–8
Jones, L. G. 180
Justin Martyr 28

Kahl, B. 168–9
Keener, C. S. 130
Kille, D. A. 75
Killerman, S. 88
Kovacs, J. 78
Kwok Pui-lan 131–2, 176–7

Lamb, W. 24
Levine, A. 153, 173
Levison, J. R. 129
Lewis, N. D. 19
Liew, T. B. 87, 98
Litchfield, R. G. 85, 122–3, 187
Longman III, T. 153
Lovelace, V. 97
Luther, M. 37, 108
Luz, U. 78, 80–1, 129, 159, 189

MacDonald, M. Y. 75
Malherbe, A. J. 74
Mann, T. 14
Marcion, 165
Marley, B. 160
Marx, S. 14
Mbata, A. 134

McDonald, L. M. 27–9, 39
McGowan, A. T. B. 24
Mead, J. 92
Melamed, C. 117
Mesters, C. 194
Metzger, B. 62–3
Míguez, N. O. 165–6, 189
Moore, S. D. 90, 96, 135
Moorman, J. R. H. 158
Morley, J. 194
Mosala, I. 12–3
Moschella, M. C. 113
Muddiman, J. 67
Murrell, N. S. 160
Myers, C. 98, 181

Najman, H. 27–8
Neyrey, J. 75
Norris, K. 143
Nouwen, H. J. M. 13–4

O'Connor, K. 184
O'Donnell O.P., G. 142–3
Oakley, M. 34
Oduyoye, M. A. 93
Økland, J. 32
Orevillo-Montenegro, M. 189

Patte, D. 124, 128
Perdue, L. G. 98, 133
Pereira, N. C. 34
Perkins, N. R. 32
Perry, I. 174
Pope-Levison, P. 129
Porter, J. R. 32
Powell, M. A. 54, 56
Pyper, H. S. 100

Raheb, M. 133
Raphael, R. 102
Rasmussen, L. L. 25
Raymer, V. 41
Reaves, J. R. 97
Reddie, A. G. 97
Rhoads, D. 124
Richard, P. 12
Riches, J. 128
Ringe, S. H. 84, 101–2, 146
Rogerson, J. W. 73
Rohr, R. 101
Rollins, W. G. 75
Rowland, C. 78, 161
Rowling, J. K. 15
Ruether, R. R. 166–7

de Sales, F. 143
Saunders, J. A. 164
Sawyer, D. F. 90
Schell, E. L. 103
Schipper, J. 102
Schleiermacher, F. 192
Schneiders, S. 121
Scholz, S. 166
Schottroff, L. 33
Schroer, S. 9
Schüssler Fiorenza, E. 33, 42, 175–6
Segovia, F. F. 87, 130, 136
Segundo, J. L. 193
Sheldon, C. 159
Sherwood, Y. 135
de Silva, D. A. 77
Slemmons, T, M. 40
Smit, P-B. 90
Smith, M. J. 97
Smith, S. 12

Song, C. S. 176
Soulen, R. K. 1, 19, 54, 57, 72, 76, 84, 86, 135, 153, 172, 192
Soulen, R. N. 1, 19, 27–8, 54, 57, 72, 76, 84, 86, 135, 153, 172, 192
Spencer, F. S. 159
Stackhouse Jr., J.G. 23, 108
Starr, R. 116–7
Steinbeck, J. 14
Stewart, D. T. 101–2, 137–8
Stone, K. 82, 138
Stone, T. J. 164
Sugirtharajah, R. S. 9–10, 17, 131, 133–4, 136, 177

Tamez, E. 104, 129–30
Taussig, H. 32
Telford, W. 126
Theissen, G. 75
Thomas, O. A. W. 96, 174–5
Thompson, J. M. 160
Thurman, H. 185
Tiffany, F. C. 84, 101–2,
Tisdale, L. T. 113
Tolbert, M. A. 33
Tombs, D. 90
Toop, D. 174
Trible, P. 183
Turner, M. 139
Tutu, D. 12

Vander Stichele, C. 100
Velazquez, D. 169
Vincent, J. J. 146

de Waal, K. 9
Wacker, M. 33

INDEX OF NAMES

Walden, W. 31, 37
Walker, A. 34
Wallinger, M. 15
Warrior, R. A. 94
Weber, H-R. 47–8, 142, 147, 171
Weems, R. J. 11, 116, 181–2
West, G. O. 96–7, 118–9, 134
West, M. 89–90,
Westermann, C. 38–9
Wheeler, S. E. 105–6
Williams, D. S. 89, 97
Williams, R. 23, 25
Williamson, C. M. 173

Wimbush, V. L. 97
Wink, W. 159
Winn, A. 133
Winter, M. T. 41
Witherington, B. 153
Wonneberger, R. 63
Wright, A. M. 95

Yamauchi, E. M. 96
Yancy, G. 97
Yee, G. A. 87
Yorke, G. 17

Index of Subjects

Acts of Andrew 32
Acts of Paul 32–3
Acts of Thecla 32–3
African interpretation 12–13, 17, 26, 34, 49, 62, 93–7, 111, 118, 124, 127–9, 132, 134, 175, 178
African American interpretation 13, 24, 34–5, 87, 89, 91–3, 95–7, 179, 185
African Caribbean interpretation 15, 97, 129, 160, 175
age, aging 8, 86, 90, 99–103
androcentric interpretation 139–140
Anglicanism, Church of England, 23–4, 31, 39, 96, 124, 163
anthropological criticism 75
anti-Semitism 37, 94–5, 132, 171, 173, 190
Apocrypha 26–7, 31, 40, 56, 171
Apocryphal New Testament 32
Apostolic Fathers 28
Aramaic language 10, 46, 59–63, 148
Asian interpretation, Asian American interpretation 17, 34, 86, 87, 95–6, 129, 131–2, 176–7, 189

Biblia Hebraica Stuttgartensia 62
biblical authority 19–25, 164, 176, 178–9, 183
black interpretation 12, 15, 34, 86, 91, 95–8, 107, 129
Buddhism 17

canon, canons 25–44, 163–8, 176, 189
canonical approach 43, 172
canonical criticism 164–5
Chaereas and Callirhoe 74
children and the Bible 3, 100–1, 176, 182
Christological interpretation 170–4
colonial, colonialism 11–12, 131–3, 180–1
Community of St Anselm 9
Council of Trent 24, 31
cultural interpretation 127–35, 174–7

deconstruction 136–8
denominational interpretations 106–9
deuterocanonical writings 31

INDEX OF SUBJECTS

diachronic criticism 59–81
disability and interpretation 99–103
discipleship, Christian 145–7, 187
discourse analysis 49–53, 78

ecological interpretation 118, 139–40
evangelical interpretation 23–4, 104
exegesis 11, 45–81

feminist interpretation 33, 41–2, 86–9, 91–2, 131–2, 165–7, 175–6
form criticism 65–7
fundamentalism 20–1, 23

gender 88–92
genre 47, 65–7
globalisation 117–120, 124
global readings 117, 123, 128–30
Gospel of Mary 32
Gospel of Thomas 32
Greek, *Koine* 59–65, 152

Hebrew, biblical 10, 59–62, 64–5, 152
hermeneutical circle 192–3
historical background 73–4
historical critical perspectives 59–74
HIV/ AIDS 101, 118–9, 138

ideological criticism 104, 116, 131–3, 135–40
impact history (*Wirkungsgeschichte*) 15, 77–81
implied readers 57–8
biblical inspiration 20–2
intersectionality 87
intertextuality 56, 164

Di Jamaikan Nyuu Testament 15
Jewish interpretation 10, 36, 153, 172–3, and throughout

Latin American interpretation 9, 12, 18, 34, 110–11, 113, 141, 161–2, 165–6, 175, 192–4
Lectio Divina 142–3
lectionaries 34–41
LGBTQI+ interpretation 89–90, 137–8
linguistics 42, 49
literary criticism 46–7, 53, 56, 78, 136–7
Lord's Prayer 6, 64

Methodist Church 22–4, 107–9, 122
masculinities and biblical interpretation 90–1, 116
migration 119–20
Moravian interpretation 8–9
Muslim interpretation 10, 147–8

narrative criticism 54–8
New, New Testament 32–3
Novum Testamentum Graece 62

oral tradition 65–9
Orthodox Christian interpretations 26, 31, 170

Pentecostal interpretations 24, 207–8, 163
political interpretation 103–6, 173–4
Pontifical Biblical Commission 21, 24, 173, 190
postcolonial criticism 131–3

postmodern interpretations 136–7
practice criticism 145–7
prayer 141–3
proof-texting 23
Protevangelium of James 32
Pseudepigrapha 31–3, 56
psychological interpretation 75

Q, *Quelle* source 68
queer criticism 89–90, 137–8
Qur'an 10, 147

Rastafarian interpretation 160
reader-response criticism 83–4
redaction criticism 69, 71–3
Reformed Christian
 interpretation 107–8
Roman Catholic interpretation 21,
 24, 26, 31, 41, 107, 111, 172

Shepherd of Hermas 28
Scriptural Reasoning 147–9
Septuagint 26, 31, 134
sexuality 88–92
social analysis 109–17, 103–6

social scientific criticism 74–7
source criticism 67–9
spiritual approaches 154–7
storytelling 178–9
synchronic approaches 46–58

textual criticism 62–4, 67
tradition criticism 69–71
Thirty-Nine Articles of Religion 31
translation(s) 60–2
typology 171

vernacular interpretation 133–5
violence 4, 6, 15, 30, 90–1, 94, 116–7,
 128, 159, 167–9, 179, 181–5

white identity and critical biblical
 interpretation 86, 93, 96–8
Windsor Report 23
womanist criticism 11, 34–5, 89, 91,
 97
World Council of Churches 121, 123,
 191–2
worship 144–5